EVERYDAY
Slow Cooker
& ONE-DISH RECIPES

TASTE OF HOME BOOKS • RDA ENTHUSIAST BRANDS, LLC • MILWAUKEE, WI

© 2021 RDA Enthusiast Brands, LLC.
1610 N. 2nd St., Suite 102, Milwaukee WI 53212-3906

Visit us at **tasteofhome.com** for other
Taste of Home books and products.

ISBN:
D 978-1-62145-752-7
U 978-1-62145-753-4

Component Number:
D119400104H
U 119400106H

ISSN: 1944-6382

Executive Editor: Mark Hagen
Senior Art Director: Raeann Thompson
Editor: Christine Rukavena
Senior Designer: Jazmin Delgado
Deputy Editor, Copy Desk: Dulcie Shoener
Copy Editor: Sara Strauss
Food Editor: Rashanda Cobbins

Cover
Photographer: Mark Derse
Set Stylist: Stephanie Marchese
Food Stylist: Josh Rink

Pictured on front cover:
Flavorful Chicken Fajitas, p. 122

Pictured on title page:
Tacos Deluxe, p. 170

Pictured on back cover:
Sweet-Sour Beef, p. 24
Jambalaya Rice Salad, p. 152
Rotisserie-Style Chicken, p. 198

Printed in USA
1 3 5 7 9 10 8 6 4 2

STIR-FRIED SCALLOPS &
ASPARAGUS, PAGE 153

Contents

More ways to connect with us:

SHOP.TASTEOFHOME.COM

Dish up a new dinnertime favorite.

Serving comforting meals is a snap with these 334 recipes—each easy to prepare with everyday ingredients.

For decades, family cooks have relied on their slow cookers for hearty, healthy, home-cooked fare without a lot of work. In this new cookbook, you'll find nearly 10 dozen delightful new dishes to try in your slow cooker, from chicken wings and party drinks to meaty entrees and irresistible sweets. Hundreds of easy meals for stovetop and oven, plus bonus 5-ingredient mains for your busiest nights, mean you'll always have tasty options come mealtime. Discover a fresh favorite today!

HANDY ICONS IN THIS BOOK

Recipes are lower in calories, fat and/or sodium, as determined by a registered dietitian nutritionist.

✳ These fix-ahead dishes include directions for freezing and reheating.

SLOW-COOKER
BARBECUE PULLED PORK
SANDWICHES, PAGE 70

35

27

Slow-Cook with Confidence

Follow these tips for slow-cooking success every time.

PLAN AHEAD TO PREP AND GO.
In most cases, you can prepare and load ingredients into the slow-cooker insert beforehand and store it in the refrigerator overnight. But an insert can crack if exposed to rapid temperature changes. Let the insert sit out just long enough to reach room temperature before placing it in the slow cooker.

USE THAWED INGREDIENTS.
Although throwing frozen chicken breasts into the slow cooker may seem easy, it's not a smart shortcut. Thawing foods in a slow cooker can create the ideal environment for bacteria to grow, so thaw frozen meat and veggies ahead of time. The exception: If using a prepackaged slow-cooker meal kit, follow instructions as written.

LINE THE SLOW COOKER FOR EASE OF USE.
Some recipes in this book call for a **foil collar** or **sling.** Here's why:

▶ A **foil collar** prevents scorching of rich, saucy dishes near the slow cooker's heating element. To make a collar, fold two 18-in.-long pieces of foil into strips 4 in. wide. Line the slow cooker's perimeter with the strips; coat with cooking spray.

▶ A **sling** helps you lift layered foods out of the slow cooker without much fuss. To make, fold one or more pieces of heavy-duty foil into strips. Place on bottom and up sides of the slow cooker; coat with cooking spray.

TAKE THE TIME TO BROWN.
Give yourself a few extra minutes to brown your meat in a skillet before placing it in the slow cooker. Doing so will add rich color and more flavor to the finished dish.

KEEP THE LID CLOSED.
Don't peek! While it's tempting to lift the lid and check on your meal's progress, resist the urge. Every time you open the lid, you'll have to add about 30 minutes to the total cooking time.

ADJUST COOK TIME AS NEEDED.
Live at a high altitude? Slow-cooking will take longer. Add about 30 minutes for each hour of cooking the recipe calls for; legumes will take about twice as long.

Want your food done sooner? Cooking one hour on high is roughly equal to two hours on low, so adjust the recipe to suit your schedule.

Stovetop Suppers Are Super Convenient

Stovetop cooking is quick and easy. In fact, many of the stovetop meals in this book need just one pot, making cleanup a breeze. Haul out your favorite skillet and let's get cooking!

CHOOSE THE RIGHT PAN FOR THE JOB.

The right cookware can simplify meal preparation when cooking on the stovetop. The basic skillets every kitchen needs include a 10- or 12-in. skillet with lid and an 8- or 9-in. saute/omelet pan.

104

Good quality cookware conducts heat quickly and cooks food evenly. The type of metal and thickness of the pan affect performance. Consider these pros and cons for each of the most common cookware metals:

Copper does conduct heat the best, but it is expensive, tarnishes (usually requiring periodic polishing) and reacts with acidic ingredients, which is why the interior of a copper pan is usually lined with tin or stainless steel.

Aluminum is a good conductor of heat and is less expensive than copper. However, aluminum reacts with acidic ingredients.

Anodized aluminum has the same positive qualities as aluminum, but the surface is electrochemically treated so it will not react to acidic ingredients. The surface is resistant to scratches and is nonstick.

146

Cast iron conducts heat very well. It is usually heavy. Cast iron also needs regular seasoning to prevent sticking and rusting.

Nonstick is especially preferred for cooking delicate foods such as eggs, pancakes or thin fish fillets. It won't scorch foods if you're cooking batches. It can be scratched easily and has maximum temperature limitations.

122

Stainless steel is durable and retains its new look for years. It isn't a good conductor of heat, which is why its core or bottom is often made with aluminum or copper.

MASTER THESE COMMON STOVETOP COOKING TECHNIQUES.

Sauteing Add a small amount of oil to a hot skillet and heat over medium-high heat. For best results, cut food into uniform pieces before adding. Don't overcrowd in pan. Stir frequently while cooking.

Frying Pour ¼-½ in. oil into a skillet. Heat over medium-high heat until hot. The oil is ready when it shimmers (gives off visible waves of heat). Never leave the pan unattended, and don't overheat the oil or it will smoke. Pat food dry before frying and, if desired, dip in batter or coat with crumbs. Fry, uncovered, until food is golden brown and cooked through.

Braising Season meat; coat with flour if recipe directs. In Dutch oven, brown meat in oil in batches. To ensure nice browning, do not crowd. Set meat aside; cook vegetables, adding flour if recipe directs. Add broth gradually, stirring to deglaze pan and to keep lumps from forming. Return meat to pan and stir until mixture comes to a boil.

Steaming Place a steamer basket or bamboo steamer in a pan with water. Bring water to a boil (boiling water shouldn't touch the steamer) and place food in the basket; cover and steam. Add more boiling water to pan as necessary, making sure pan does not run dry.

229

Oven Entrees Bake Hands-Free

You can't beat a meal-in-one specialty for convenience and comfort. Review these hints while the oven preheats.

CHOOSE THE RIGHT BAKEWARE.
Metal baking pans Excellent conductors of heat, these create nice browning on rolls, coffee cakes and other baked goods. Metal is a safe, smart choice for under the broiler. It may react with acidic foods such as tomato sauce or cranberries and create a metallic taste or discoloration.

Glass baking dishes Glass provides slower, more even baking for egg dishes, custards and casseroles. It takes longer to heat than metal, but once heated, the dish holds the heat longer. This is undesirable for many desserts, as sugary batters may overbrown in glass. If you wish to bake in a glass dish even though the recipe calls for a metal pan, decrease the oven temperature by 25º.

Other baking dishes Ceramic or stoneware baking dishes generally perform much like glass but are more attractive. They may be safer than glass for higher temperatures; refer to the manufacturer's instructions.

CONFIRM THE OVEN'S TEMPERATURE.
Use an oven thermometer to check. Preheat oven to the desired temperature; place an oven thermometer on the center rack. Close the oven door and leave the oven on at the set temperature. Keep thermometer in the oven for 15 minutes before reading. Adjust the oven temperature accordingly to ensure best baking results.

NEGATE HOT OR COOL SPOTS.
To test your oven for uneven temperatures, try the bread test. Heat the oven to 350° while arranging six to nine slices of white bread on a large cookie sheet. Place in oven for 5-10 minutes; check if the slices are starting to brown or burn. If some slices are noticeably darker or lighter than others, the oven may have hot or cool spots. To negate this, rotate pans while baking.

ELIMINATE SPILLS—THE SMART WAY.
Line a rimmed baking sheet with foil and place it on the bottom oven rack directly below the baking dish. Any drips or spills from the recipe will fall onto the foil-lined pan instead of the oven bottom.

We don't recommend lining the bottom of your oven with aluminum foil or other liners, as there's a chance that they could melt and stick to the oven, causing damage.

Want to clean up a drip while it's still hot? Grab your oven mitt, a pair of tongs and a damp dishcloth. Use the tongs to move the cloth and help prevent burns.

195

FAMILY-PLEASING
TURKEY CHILI, PAGE 67

82

57

72

93

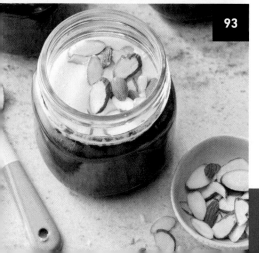

Slow Cooker

From cozy and healthful soups to easy party apps, homey suppers, and even desserts, sides and breads, we can't get enough slow-cooked recipes. Explore these for their convenience, and treasure them for their good taste. What to try first?

Beef & Ground Beef

SLOW-COOKER
BEEF TENDERLOIN

SLOW-COOKER BEEF TENDERLOIN

My local store had beef tenderloin on sale, so I created this recipe when I was having guests over. It's perfect to start in the slow cooker in the morning, and then everything is ready to go when you get home! It tastes incredible with little effort, and your guests will be amazed.
—*Amanda Wentz, Virginia Beach, VA*

- -

PREP: 15 min. • **COOK:** 6 hours
MAKES: 16 servings

- 2 cans (14½ oz. each) diced tomatoes with mild green chiles
- 1½ cups dry red wine
- 1 can (10½ oz.) condensed tomato soup, undiluted
- 1 can (10½ oz.) condensed cream of mushroom soup, undiluted
- 1 can (15 oz.) tomato sauce
- 3 garlic cloves, minced
- 1 Tbsp. Worcestershire sauce
- 2 tsp. ground mustard
- ½ tsp. pepper
- 1 beef tenderloin (6 lbs.)
  Chopped fresh parsley, optional

Stir together tomatoes, wine, soups, tomato sauce, garlic, Worcestershire sauce, mustard and pepper in bottom of 6- or 7-qt. slow cooker. Cut beef tenderloin in half; add to slow cooker, making sure to cover with sauce mixture. Cover and cook on low until meat is tender, 6-8 hours. If desired, top with chopped fresh parsley.

5 oz. cooked beef with ¾ cup sauce:
319 cal., 11g fat (4g sat. fat), 75mg chol., 470mg sod., 10g carb. (4g sugars, 2g fiber), 38g pro.

**SLOPPY JOE
TATER TOT CASSEROLE**

SLOPPY JOE TATER TOT CASSEROLE

This simple casserole is an easy dinner for both you and the kids. Serve with carrot and celery sticks for a fuss-free feast. You can also stir in some spicy brown mustard if the adults want more zing.
—*Laura Wilhelm, West Hollywood, CA*

- -

PREP: 20 min. • **COOK:** 4 hours + standing
MAKES: 10 servings

- 1 bag (32 oz.) frozen Tater Tots, divided
- 2 lbs. ground beef or turkey
- 1 can (15 oz.) tomato sauce
- 1 bottle (8 oz.) sweet chili sauce
- 2 Tbsp. packed brown sugar
- 1 Tbsp. Worcestershire sauce
- 1 Tbsp. dried minced garlic
- 1 Tbsp. dried minced onion
- ½ tsp. salt
- ½ tsp. pepper
- 1¼ cups shredded Colby-Monterey Jack cheese
- ¼ tsp. paprika

1. Place half the Tater Tots in bottom of 5-qt. slow cooker.
2. In a large skillet, cook the beef over medium-high heat until no longer pink, 5-6 minutes, breaking into crumbles. Drain. Stir in the next 8 ingredients; reduce heat and simmer 2-3 minutes. Place beef mixture in slow cooker; top with remaining Taster Tots. Cook, covered, on low 4 hours.
3. Top with the cheese and sprinkle with paprika. Let stand, uncovered, 15 minutes before serving.
1 cup: 466 cal., 24g fat (9g sat. fat), 69mg chol., 1332mg sod., 41g carb. (18g sugars, 4g fiber), 22g pro.

CONFETTI CASSEROLE

To create this comforting casserole, I used a recipe from the cookbook that came with my first slow cooker but added more of the ingredients we love. I like to serve it with fresh bread from my bread maker.
—*Joy Vincent, Newport, NC*

- -

PREP: 20 min. • **COOK:** 8 hours
MAKES: 6 servings

- 1 lb. ground beef
- 1 medium onion, finely chopped
- 1 tsp. garlic powder
- 4 medium potatoes, peeled and quartered
- 3 medium carrots, cut into 1-in. chunks
- 1 pkg. (9 oz.) frozen cut green beans
- 1 pkg. (10 oz.) frozen corn
- 1 can (14½ oz.) Italian diced tomatoes, undrained

1. In a large skillet, cook the beef, onion and garlic powder over medium heat until meat is no longer pink and onion is tender, 5-7 minutes, breaking beef into crumbles; drain.
2. In a 3-qt. slow cooker, layer potatoes, carrots, beans and corn. Top with beef mixture. Pour tomatoes over the top. Cover and cook on low until potatoes are tender, 8-10 hours.
1½ cups: 320 cal., 9g fat (3g sat. fat), 47mg chol., 287mg sod., 43g carb. (10g sugars, 5g fiber), 18g pro. **Diabetic exchanges:** 3 starch, 2 medium-fat meat.

TEST KITCHEN TIP

Potatoes and other dense foods can take a long time to cook in the slow cooker. They are often layered in the bottom of the slow cooker, where they can be closer to the heat than an item that is layered on top. For best results, always follow any layering instructions that a recipe provides.

SLOW-COOKED
FLANK STEAK

SLOW-COOKED FLANK STEAK

My slow cooker gets lots of use, especially during the hectic summer months. I can fix this flank steak in the morning and forget about it until dinner. Serve with noodles and a tossed salad.
—*Michelle Armistead, Keyport, NJ*

- -

PREP: 15 min. • **COOK:** 4 hours
MAKES: 6 servings

- 1 beef flank steak (1½ lbs.)
- 1 Tbsp. canola oil
- 1 large onion, sliced
- ⅓ cup water
- 1 can (4 oz.) chopped green chiles
- 2 Tbsp. vinegar
- 1¼ tsp. chili powder
- 1 tsp. garlic powder
- ½ tsp. sugar
- ½ tsp. salt
- ⅛ tsp. pepper

1. In a skillet, brown steak in oil; transfer to a 5-qt. slow cooker. In the same skillet, saute onion for 1 minute. Gradually add water, stirring to loosen browned bits from pan. Add remaining ingredients; bring to a boil. Pour over flank steak.
2. Cover and cook on low until meat is tender, 4-5 hours. Slice the meat; serve with onion and pan juices.

3 oz. cooked beef: 199 cal., 11g fat (4g sat. fat), 48mg chol., 327mg sod., 4g carb. (2g sugars, 1g fiber), 20g pro.
Diabetic exchanges: 3 lean meat, ½ fat.

"We all love this! We can't always find flank steak, but then we use chuck roast instead. It is now one of our favorite meals."
—PIANOPLAYER500, TASTEOFHOME.COM

BEEF & BARLEY

BEEF & BARLEY

I'm not sure where the recipe originated for this country-style dish, but I have had it for years and rely on it when I'm hosting a meal for several people.
—*Linda Ronk, Melbourne, FL*

- -

PREP: 15 min. • **COOK:** 4 hours
MAKES: 8 servings

- 2 lbs. ground beef
- 2 Tbsp. butter
- 1 cup quick-cooking barley
- 1 can (15 oz.) diced carrots, undrained
- 1 can (14½ oz.) diced tomatoes, undrained
- 1 can (10¾ oz.) condensed tomato soup, undiluted
- 2 celery ribs, finely chopped
- ½ cup water
- 1½ to 2 tsp. salt
- ½ tsp. pepper
- ½ tsp. chili powder
- 1 tsp. Worcestershire sauce
- 1 bay leaf
- 1 cup soft bread crumbs
- 1 cup shredded cheddar cheese
   Minced fresh parsley, optional

1. In a large skillet, cook beef over medium heat until no longer pink, 10-12 minutes, breaking it into crumbles; drain. Add to a 3-qt. slow cooker. In same skillet, melt butter over medium-high heat. Add the barley; cook and stir until lightly browned, 3-5 minutes. Add to slow cooker. Stir in the next 10 ingredients. Sprinkle with bread crumbs and cheese.
2. Cover and cook on high until heated through and barley is tender, 4 hours. Discard bay leaf before serving. Garnish with fresh parsley, if desired.

1 cup: 409 cal., 18g fat (9g sat. fat), 78mg chol., 990mg sod., 34g carb. (9g sugars, 7g fiber), 28g pro.

HEARTY NEW ENGLAND DINNER

This favorite slow-cooker recipe came from a friend. At first my husband was a bit skeptical about a roast that is not made in the oven, but he loves the old-fashioned goodness of this version. The horseradish in the gravy adds zip.
—*Claire McCombs, San Diego, CA*

PREP: 20 min. • **COOK:** 7½ hours
MAKES: 8 servings

- 2   medium carrots, sliced
- 1   medium onion, sliced
- 1   celery rib, sliced
- 1   boneless beef chuck roast (about 3 lbs.)
- 1   tsp. salt, divided
- ¼   tsp. pepper
- 1   envelope onion soup mix
- 2   cups water
- 1   Tbsp. white vinegar
- 1   bay leaf
- ½   small head cabbage, cut into wedges
- 3   Tbsp. butter
- 2   Tbsp. all-purpose flour
- 1   Tbsp. dried minced onion
- 2   Tbsp. prepared horseradish

1. Place the carrots, onion and celery in a 5-qt. slow cooker. Cut roast in half. Place roast over vegetables; sprinkle with ½ tsp. salt and the pepper. Add soup mix, water, vinegar and bay leaf. Cover and cook on low until beef is tender, 7-9 hours.

2. Remove beef and keep warm; discard bay leaf. Add cabbage. Cover and cook on high until the cabbage is tender, 30-40 minutes.

3. Meanwhile, melt butter in a small saucepan; stir in flour and onion. Skim fat from cooking liquid in slow cooker. Add 1½ cups cooking liquid to saucepan. Stir in horseradish and the remaining salt; bring to a boil. Cook and stir until thickened and bubbly, 2 minutes. Serve with roast and vegetables.

1 serving: 371 cal., 21g fat (9g sat. fat), 122mg chol., 747mg sod., 10g carb. (4g sugars, 2g fiber), 35g pro.

SLOW-COOKER BEEF BURGUNDY

Tender cubes of beef are braised in a burgundy wine sauce with savory vegetables. I made this often when I worked full time. It's good over noodles or mashed potatoes.
—*Sherri Mott, New Carlisle, IN*

PREP: 15 min. • **COOK:** 7½ hours
MAKES: 8 servings

- 6   bacon strips, diced
- 1   boneless beef chuck roast (3 lbs.), cut into 1½-in. cubes
- 1   can (10½ oz.) condensed beef broth, undiluted
- 1   small onion, halved and sliced
- 1   medium carrot, sliced
- 2   Tbsp. butter
- 1   Tbsp. tomato paste
- 2   garlic cloves, minced
- ¾   tsp. dried thyme
- ½   tsp. salt
- ½   tsp. pepper
- 1   bay leaf
- ½   lb. fresh mushrooms, sliced
- ½   cup burgundy wine or beef broth
- 5   Tbsp. all-purpose flour
- ⅔   cup cold water
     Optional: Hot cooked noodles and minced fresh parsley

1. In a large skillet, cook bacon over medium heat until crisp. Use a slotted spoon to remove to paper towels. In the drippings, brown the beef; drain.

2. Place beef and bacon in a 5-qt. slow cooker, Add the broth, onion, carrot, butter, tomato paste, garlic, thyme, salt, pepper and bay leaf. Cover and cook on low until meat is tender, 7-8 hours.

3. Add mushrooms and wine. Combine flour and water until smooth; gradually stir into slow cooker. Cover and cook on high until thickened, 30-45 minutes. Discard bay leaf. If desired, serve with noodles and parsley.

¾ cup: 460 cal., 29g fat (12g sat. fat), 130mg chol., 663mg sod., 8g carb. (2g sugars, 1g fiber), 37g pro.

SLOW-COOKER
BEEF BURGUNDY

COMFORTING BARLEY & PUMPKIN BEEF STEW

There's nothing more comforting than a bowl of beef stew—unless, of course, it's a bowl of steaming hot beef stew loaded with lots and lots of barley. Now this is comfort food at its best—a bowl of stew robust enough to be a meal on its own. Rinsing the barley will help remove any dust, dirt or debris.

—*Colleen Delawder, Herndon, VA*

PREP: 30 min. • **COOK:** 6 hours
MAKES: 9 servings (3½ qt.)

- ¼ cup all-purpose flour
- 3 Tbsp. cornstarch
- 1½ tsp. salt, divided
- 1½ tsp. pepper, divided
- 1½ lbs. beef stew meat
- 3 Tbsp. olive oil
- 1 large sweet onion, finely chopped
- 2 cartons (32 oz. each) beef broth
- 1 can (15 oz.) pumpkin
- 1 cup medium pearl barley
- 1 tsp. dried thyme
- ¼ tsp. garlic powder
- ¼ tsp. crushed red pepper flakes
  Optional: Additional red pepper flakes and minced fresh parsley

1. In a shallow dish, mix flour, cornstarch, 1 tsp. salt and 1 tsp. pepper. Add beef, a few pieces at a time, and toss to coat. In a large skillet, heat oil over medium-high heat; brown meat in batches. Transfer meat to a 5- or 6-qt. slow cooker. In the same skillet, cook and stir onion in drippings until tender, 6-8 minutes; add to slow cooker. Stir in broth, pumpkin, barley, thyme, garlic powder and red pepper flakes.
2. Cook, covered, on low until meat is tender, 6-8 hours. If desired, serve with additional red pepper flakes and parsley.
1½ cups: 211 cal., 8g fat (2g sat. fat), 35mg chol., 819mg sod., 20g carb. (3g sugars, 4g fiber), 15g pro. **Diabetic exchanges:** 2 lean meat, 1 starch, 1 fat.

COMFORTING BARLEY &
PUMPKIN BEEF STEW

**DEVILED
SWISS STEAK**

SLOW-COOKED STEAK FAJITAS

We enjoy the flavors of Mexican food, so I was glad when I spotted a recipe that's loaded with vegetables. The beef always comes out nice and tender.
—*Twila Burkholder, Middleburg, PA*

PREP: 10 min. • **COOK:** 8 hours
MAKES: 6 servings

- 1 beef flank steak (1½ lbs.)
- 1 can (14½ oz.) diced tomatoes with garlic and onion, undrained
- 1 jalapeno pepper, seeded and chopped
- 2 garlic cloves, minced
- 1 tsp. ground coriander
- 1 tsp. ground cumin
- 1 tsp. chili powder
- ½ tsp. salt
- 1 medium onion, sliced
- 1 medium green pepper, julienned
- 1 medium sweet red pepper, julienned
- 1 Tbsp. minced fresh cilantro
- 12 flour tortillas (6 in.), warmed
  Optional: Sour cream, salsa, fresh cilantro leaves and lime wedges

1. Thinly slice steak across the grain into strips; place in a 5-qt. slow cooker. Add the tomatoes, jalapeno, garlic, coriander, cumin, chili powder and salt. Cover and cook on low for 7 hours.
2. Add the onion, peppers and cilantro. Cover and cook until meat is tender, 1-2 hours.
3. Using a slotted spoon, spoon about ½ cup meat mixture down the center of each tortilla. Fold bottom of tortilla over filling and roll up. If desired, serve with sour cream, salsa, cilantro and lime wedges.
Freeze option: Freeze cooled meat mixture and juices in freezer containers. To use, partially thaw in refrigerator overnight. Heat through in a saucepan, stirring occasionally; add a little water if necessary.
Note: Wear disposable gloves when cutting hot peppers; the oils can burn skin. Avoid touching your face.
2 fajitas: 435 cal., 15g fat (6g sat. fat), 54mg chol., 897mg sod., 42g carb. (5g sugars, 6g fiber), 28g pro.

🍎
DEVILED SWISS STEAK

This main dish is satisfying all by itself, but you can also serve the Swiss steak over hot mashed potatoes.
—*Melissa Gerken, Zumbrota, MN*

PREP: 20 min. • **COOK:** 6 hours
MAKES: 8 servings

- ½ cup all-purpose flour
- 1 Tbsp. ground mustard
- ½ tsp. salt
- ⅛ tsp. pepper
- 2 beef flank steaks (1 lb. each), halved
- 2 Tbsp. butter
- 1 cup thinly sliced onion
- 1 can (28 oz.) stewed tomatoes
- 2 Tbsp. Worcestershire sauce
- 1 Tbsp. brown sugar

1. In a bowl or shallow dish, combine the flour, mustard, salt and pepper. Add steaks and turn to coat. In a large nonstick skillet, brown steaks on both sides in butter. Transfer to a 5-qt. slow cooker. Top with onion.
2. In a bowl, combine the tomatoes, Worcestershire sauce and brown sugar; pour over meat and onion. Cover and cook on low until beef is tender, 6-8 hours.
1½ cups: 177 cal., 5g fat (2g sat. fat), 35mg chol., 675mg sod., 19g carb. (8g sugars, 5g fiber), 15g pro. **Diabetic exchanges:** 2 meat, 1 starch.

SLOW-COOKED
STEAK FAJITAS

❄ FRENCH ONION PORTOBELLO BRISKET

I use this recipe when I go to winter potlucks and want something everyone will love. Though I have seen kids who scrape away the mushrooms and onion, they still rave about how the meat tastes and gobble it right up.
—Aysha Schurman, Ammon, ID

PREP: 20 min. • **COOK:** 8 hours
MAKES: 9 servings

- 1 fresh beef brisket (4 lbs.)
- 1¾ cups sliced baby portobello mushrooms
- 1 small red onion, sliced
- 2 garlic cloves, minced
- 2 Tbsp. butter
- 1 can (10½ oz.) condensed French onion soup
- ¼ cup dry white wine or beef broth
- ½ tsp. coarsely ground pepper
  Fresh sage, optional

1. Place brisket in a 5-qt. slow cooker.
2. In a large saucepan, cook mushrooms, onion and garlic in butter until onion is crisp-tender, 3-5 minutes. Add the soup, wine and pepper; mix well.
3. Pour mushroom mixture over beef. Cover and cook on low until meat is tender, 8-10 hours. If desired, garnish with sage.
Freeze option: Place individual portions of brisket in freezer containers; top with cooking sauce. Cool and freeze. To use, partially thaw in refrigerator overnight. Heat through in a covered saucepan, stirring occasionally; add a little water if necessary.
5 oz. cooked beef: 301 cal., 12g fat (5g sat. fat), 94mg chol., 324mg sod., 3g carb. (2g sugars, 1g fiber), 42g pro.
Diabetic exchanges: 6 lean meat, ½ fat.

CINCINNATI CHILI DOGS

My in-laws are from Ohio, so we have Cincinnati chili at many of our family gatherings. I spiced up this family classic with cinnamon and cocoa powder and then ladled it over hot dogs. It's perfect for game day, tailgates and potlucks.
—Jennifer Gilbert, Brighton, MI

PREP: 20 min. • **COOK:** 4 hours
MAKES: 10 servings

- 1½ lbs. ground beef
- 2 small onions, chopped, divided
- 2 cans (15 oz. each) tomato sauce
- 1½ tsp. baking cocoa
- ½ tsp. ground cinnamon
- ¼ tsp. chili powder
- ¼ tsp. paprika
- ¼ tsp. garlic powder
- 2 Tbsp. Worcestershire sauce
- 1 Tbsp. cider vinegar
- 10 hot dogs
- 10 hot dog buns, split
  Shredded cheddar cheese

1. In a large skillet over medium heat, cook and stir ground beef until no longer pink, breaking it into crumbles; drain.
2. In a 3-qt. slow cooker, combine beef with 1 chopped onion; add the next 8 ingredients. Cook, covered, on low about 2 hours; add hot dogs. Continue cooking, covered, on low until heated through, about 2 hours longer.
3. Serve on buns; top with shredded cheese and remaining chopped onion.
1 chili dog: 419 cal., 24g fat (9g sat. fat), 67mg chol., 1135mg sod., 29g carb. (6g sugars, 3g fiber), 23g pro.

CINCINNATI CHILI DOGS

SLOW-COOKER
SHORT RIB RAGU
OVER PAPPARDELLE

NORTH WOODS BEEF STEW

I live in northern Wisconsin, where we appreciate hot and hearty meals during our cold winters. Conveniently prepared in a slow cooker, this stew is superb for company.

—Janice Christofferson, Eagle River, WI

- -

PREP: 30 min. • **COOK:** 8 hours
MAKES: 11 servings (2¾ qt.)

- 3 large carrots, cut into 1-in. pieces
- 3 celery ribs, cut into 1-in. pieces
- 1 large onion, cut into wedges
- ¼ cup all-purpose flour
- ½ tsp. salt
- ¼ tsp. pepper
- 3½ lbs. beef stew meat
- 1 can (10¾ oz.) condensed tomato soup, undiluted
- ½ cup dry red wine or beef broth
- 2 Tbsp. quick-cooking tapioca
- 1 Tbsp. Italian seasoning
- 1 Tbsp. paprika
- 1 Tbsp. brown sugar
- 1 Tbsp. beef bouillon granules
- 1 Tbsp. Worcestershire sauce
- ½ lb. sliced baby portobello mushrooms
   Hot cooked egg noodles

1. Place carrots, celery and onion in a 5-qt. slow cooker. In a bowl or shallow dish, combine the flour, salt and pepper. Add beef, a few pieces at a time, and turn to coat. Place beef over vegetables.
2. In a small bowl, combine the soup, wine, tapioca, Italian seasoning, paprika, brown sugar, bouillon and Worcestershire sauce. Pour over the top.
3. Cover and cook on low until meat and vegetables are tender, 8-10 hours, adding mushrooms during the last hour. Serve with noodles.
Freeze option: Freeze cooled stew in freezer containers. To use, partially thaw in refrigerator overnight. Heat through in a saucepan, stirring occasionally; add water if necessary.
1 cup: 285 cal., 10g fat (4g sat. fat), 90mg chol., 582mg sod., 15g carb. (6g sugars, 2g fiber), 30g pro. **Diabetic exchanges:** 4 lean meat, 1 starch, 1 vegetable.

SLOW-COOKER SHORT RIB RAGU OVER PAPPARDELLE

An irresistible sauce gives this beef another dimension of flavor. Nearly any starchy side, such as potatoes or polenta, will work in place of the pasta. Short ribs are my crowd-pleaser weekend meal for all occasions.

—Missy Raho, Morristown, NJ

- -

PREP: 30 min. • **COOK:** 7 hours
MAKES: 12 servings

- 1 Tbsp. olive oil
- 2 lbs. boneless beef short ribs, cut into 2-in. pieces
- 8 oz. sliced mushrooms
- 1 small onion, chopped
- 2 small carrots, peeled and chopped
- 2 bay leaves
- 1 can (12 oz.) tomato paste
- ½ cup dry red wine
- 3 garlic cloves, minced
- 1 Tbsp. Italian seasoning
- 1 tsp. crushed red pepper flakes
- ½ tsp. salt
- ½ tsp. pepper
- 1 can (28 oz.) diced tomatoes, undrained
- 1 lb. pappardelle
   Parmesan cheese, grated or shaved, optional

1. In a large skillet, heat the oil over medium-high heat; brown meat in batches. Transfer meat to a 5- or 6-qt. slow cooker. Add mushrooms, onion, carrots and bay leaves.
2. In the same skillet, add tomato paste, wine, garlic and seasonings. Cook and stir over medium heat until fragrant and slightly darkened, 2-4 minutes. Stir in diced tomatoes until blended. Transfer mixture to slow cooker; cover. Cook on low until beef is tender, 7-9 hours. Discard bay leaves.
3. Cook pasta according to package directions for al dente. Serve ragu over pasta. If desired, serve with Parmesan.
¾ cup ragu over ¾ cup pasta: 302 cal., 8g fat (3g sat. fat), 31mg chol., 328mg sod., 39g carb. (7g sugars, 4g fiber), 18g pro.

ROSEMARY BEEF ROAST
OVER CHEESY POLENTA

ROSEMARY BEEF ROAST OVER CHEESY POLENTA

I love beef roast in the slow cooker, and it's fun to pair it with something a little different than potatoes! This is true comfort food.
—*Elisabeth Larsen, Pleasant Grove, UT*

- -

PREP: 20 min. • **COOK:** 7 hours
MAKES: 8 servings

- ¼ cup minced fresh rosemary
- 3 garlic cloves, minced
- 3 tsp. salt, divided
- 1 tsp. pepper
- 1 boneless beef chuck roast (3 lbs.)
- 1 Tbsp. canola oil
- 1 cup beef broth
- 2 cups water
- 2 cups 2% milk
- 1 cup cornmeal
- ½ cup shredded Parmesan cheese
- 3 Tbsp. butter, cubed
  Optional: Additional rosemary and Parmesan cheese

1. Mix rosemary, garlic, 2 tsp. salt and pepper; rub over meat. In a large skillet, heat oil over medium-high heat; brown meat. Transfer meat a 5- or 6-qt. slow cooker. Add broth to skillet; cook 1 minute, stirring to loosen browned bits from pan. Pour over meat. Cook, covered, on low until meat is tender, 7-9 hours.
2. For polenta, in a large heavy saucepan, bring water, milk and remaining 1 tsp. salt to a boil. Reduce heat to a gentle boil; slowly whisk in cornmeal. Cook and stir with a wooden spoon until polenta is thickened and pulls away cleanly from sides of pan, 15-20 minutes. (Mixture will be very thick.) Remove from heat; stir in Parmesan cheese and butter. Serve with roast. If desired, serve with additional rosemary and Parmesan cheese.
1 serving: 471 cal., 25g fat (11g sat. fat), 130mg chol., 1216mg sod., 19g carb. (3g sugars, 1g fiber), 39g pro.

GINGERED SHORT RIBS WITH GREEN RICE

GINGERED SHORT RIBS WITH GREEN RICE

I love Korean cooking and converted this recipe to give it slow-cooker convenience.
—*Lily Julow, Lawrenceville, GA*

- -

PREP: 35 min. • **COOK:** 8 hours
MAKES: 6 servings

- ½ cup reduced-sodium beef broth
- ⅓ cup sherry or additional reduced-sodium beef broth
- ¼ cup reduced-sodium soy sauce
- 3 Tbsp. honey
- 1 Tbsp. rice vinegar
- 1 Tbsp. minced fresh gingerroot
- 3 garlic cloves, minced
- 4 medium carrots, chopped
- 2 medium onions, chopped
- 3 lbs. bone-in beef short ribs
- ½ tsp. salt
- ½ tsp. pepper
- 3 cups uncooked instant brown rice
- 3 green onions, thinly sliced
- 3 Tbsp. minced fresh cilantro
- 2 Tbsp. chopped pickled jalapenos
- ¾ tsp. grated lime zest
- 1 Tbsp. cornstarch
- 1 Tbsp. cold water

1. In small bowl, whisk first 7 ingredients until blended. Place carrots and onions in a 5-qt. slow cooker. Sprinkle ribs with salt and pepper; place over vegetables. Pour broth mixture over top.
2. Cook, covered, on low 8-10 hours or until meat is tender.
3. Just before serving, prepare rice according to package directions. Stir in green onions, cilantro, jalapenos and lime zest.
4. Remove ribs to a serving plate; keep warm. Transfer cooking juices to a small saucepan; skim fat. Bring juices to a boil. In a small bowl, mix cornstarch and water until smooth; stir into the cooking juices. Return to a boil; cook and stir 2 minutes or until thickened. Serve with ribs and rice.
1 serving: 444 cal., 12g fat (5g sat. fat), 55mg chol., 714mg sod., 56g carb. (14g sugars, 5g fiber), 24g pro.

HAMBURGER SUPPER

My mother-in-law shared this recipe with me when my husband and I were first married. Over the past 50 years, I've relied on this meal more times than I can count.
—*Dolores Hickenbottom, Greensburg, PA*

PREP: 20 min. • **COOK:** 4 hours
MAKES: 4 servings

- 1   lb. ground beef
- ¼   cup hot water
- 3   small potatoes, peeled and diced
- 1   medium onion, chopped
- 1   can (15 oz.) peas and carrots, drained
- 1   can (14½ oz.) diced tomatoes, undrained
- 1   Tbsp. sugar
- ½   tsp. salt
- ¼   tsp. pepper

1. Shape beef into 4 patties. In a large skillet, cook patties over medium heat until no longer pink. Transfer to a 3-qt. slow cooker. Add water to skillet; stir to loosen browned bits from pan. Pour into slow cooker. Add remaining ingredients.
2. Cover and cook on low until potatoes are tender, 4-6 hours.
1 patty with 1⅓ cups vegetables: 380 cal., 13g fat (5g sat. fat), 70mg chol., 778mg sod., 39g carb. (13g sugars, 7g fiber), 27g pro.

TEST KITCHEN TIP

If you prefer, use 1½ cups frozen mixed vegetables instead of the canned peas and carrots in this recipe.

SPECIAL SAUERBRATEN

After simmering in the slow cooker for hours, this rump roast is fork tender and has taken on some of the flavors of the sauce. My family looks forward to having it for dinner. I serve the beef with mashed potatoes and corn.
—*Laura Ehlers, Lafayette, IN*

PREP: 25 min. • **COOK:** 6 hours
MAKES: 6 servings

- 1   Tbsp. olive oil
- 1   beef rump roast or bottom round roast (3 to 4 lbs.), cut in half
- 1½ cups cider vinegar
- 1   medium onion, chopped
- ⅔   cup packed brown sugar
- 1   envelope onion soup mix
- ⅓   cup shredded carrot
- 2   Tbsp. beef bouillon granules
- 1   Tbsp. Worcestershire sauce
- 1   bay leaf
- 1   garlic clove, minced
- 1   tsp. salt
- 1   tsp. celery seed
- 1   tsp. ground ginger
- ½   tsp. mixed pickling spices
- ¼   tsp. ground allspice
- ¼   tsp. pepper
- ¼   cup cornstarch
- ½   cup water

1. In large skillet, heat oil over medium-high heat; brown meat on all sides. Transfer meat and drippings to a 5-qt. slow cooker. In a large bowl, combine vinegar, onion, sugar, soup mix, carrot, bouillon, Worcestershire sauce and seasonings; pour over roast. Cover; cook on low until tender, 6-8 hours.
2. Remove meat to a serving platter; keep warm. Strain cooking juices, discarding vegetables and seasonings.
3. Skim fat from cooking juices; transfer juices to a large saucepan. Bring to a boil. Combine cornstarch and water until smooth; gradually stir into the pan. Bring to a boil; cook and stir until thickened, 2 minutes. Serve with beef.
6 oz. cooked beef with ⅔ cup gravy: 470 cal., 13g fat (4g sat. fat), 136mg chol., 1706mg sod., 37g carb. (27g sugars, 1g fiber), 46g pro.

SPECIAL
SAUERBRATEN

MOM'S
CELERY SEED
BRISKET

🍎 ❄️
GREEN CHILE BEEF BURRITOS

Recipes that are leaner in fat and calories—like this one for these burritos—helped me lose 30 pounds! The meat is so tender and delicious.
—Shirley Davidson, Thornton, CO

- -

PREP: 20 min. • **COOK:** 8 hours
MAKES: 2 dozen

- 2   beef sirloin tip roasts (3 lbs. each)
- 4   cans (4 oz. each) chopped green chiles
- 1   medium onion, chopped
- 3   medium jalapeno peppers, seeded and chopped
- 3   garlic cloves, sliced
- 3   tsp. chili powder
- 1½ tsp. ground cumin
- 1   tsp. salt-free seasoning blend, optional
- 1   cup reduced-sodium beef broth
- 24 fat-free flour tortillas (8 in.), warmed
     Optional: Chopped tomatoes, shredded lettuce and shredded reduced-fat cheddar cheese

1. Trim fat from roasts; cut meat into large chunks. Place in a 5- to 6-qt. slow cooker. Top with chiles, onion, jalapenos, garlic, chili powder, cumin and, if desired, seasoning blend. Pour broth over all. Cover and cook on low for 8-9 hours or until meat is tender.
2. Remove beef; cool slightly. Shred with 2 forks. Cool cooking liquid slightly; skim fat. In a blender, cover and process cooking liquid in batches until smooth.
3. Return liquid and beef to slow cooker; heat through. Place ⅓ cup beef mixture on each tortilla. Top with the tomatoes, lettuce and cheese as desired. Fold in ends and sides of tortilla.
Freeze option: Place cooled meat in freezer containers; cover and freeze. To use, partially thaw in refrigerator overnight. Heat through in a covered saucepan, stirring occasionally; add a little water if necessary.
Note: Wear disposable gloves when cutting hot peppers; the oils can burn skin. Avoid touching your face.
1 burrito: 262 cal., 5g fat (2g sat. fat), 72mg chol., 376mg sod., 26g carb. (0 sugars, 2g fiber), 26g pro. **Diabetic exchanges:** 3 lean meat, 2 starch.

🍎 ❄️
MOM'S CELERY SEED BRISKET

Warning: Keep a close eye on this tangy pot of goodness. Because it's been fine-tuned to perfection, it tends to vanish at gatherings.
—Aysha Schurman, Ammon, ID

- -

PREP: 20 min. • **COOK:** 8 hours
MAKES: 8 servings

- 1   fresh beef brisket (3 to 4 lbs.)
- 1   can (28 oz.) Italian crushed tomatoes
- 1   large red onion, chopped
- 2   Tbsp. red wine vinegar
- 2   Tbsp. Worcestershire sauce
- 4   garlic cloves, minced
- 1   Tbsp. brown sugar
- 1   tsp. celery seed
- 1   tsp. pepper
- ½   tsp. salt
- ½   tsp. ground cumin
- ½   tsp. liquid smoke
- 4   tsp. cornstarch
- 3   Tbsp. cold water

1. Place brisket in a 5-qt. slow cooker. In a large bowl, combine the tomatoes, onion, vinegar, Worcestershire sauce, garlic, brown sugar, celery seed, pepper, salt, cumin and liquid smoke. Pour over the beef. Cover and cook on low until meat is tender, 8-10 hours.
2. Remove meat to a serving platter and keep warm. In a large saucepan, combine cornstarch and water until smooth. Gradually stir in 4 cups cooking liquid. Bring to a boil; cook and stir until thickened, 2 minutes. Slice brisket across the grain; serve with gravy.
Freeze option: Place individual portions of sliced brisket in freezer containers; top with gravy. Cool and freeze. To use, partially thaw in refrigerator overnight. Heat through in a covered saucepan, stirring occasionally; add a little water if necessary.
5 oz. cooked meat with ½ cup gravy: 262 cal., 7g fat (3g sat. fat), 72mg chol., 425mg sod., 10g carb. (5g sugars, 1g fiber), 36g pro. **Diabetic exchanges:** 5 lean meat, 1 vegetable.

SLOW-COOKER MUSHROOM
BEEF STROGANOFF

SWEET-SOUR BEEF

I like to serve this sweet and sour dish over pasta shells and then garnish each serving with fresh chives. Chock-full of tender beef, sliced carrots, green pepper and onion, it is so hearty and delicious.
—*Beth Husband, Billings, MT*

PREP: 15 min. • **COOK:** 7 hours
MAKES: 8 servings

2   lbs. beef top round steak or boneless
    beef chuck roast, cut into 1-in. cubes
2   Tbsp. canola oil
2   cans (8 oz. each) tomato sauce
2   cups sliced carrots
2   cups pearl onions or 2 small onions,
    cut into wedges
1   large green pepper,
    cut into 1-in. pieces
½   cup molasses
⅓   cup cider vinegar
¼   cup sugar
2   tsp. chili powder
2   tsp. paprika
1   tsp. salt
    Hot cooked pasta or egg noodles
    Thinly sliced green onion, optional

1. In a large skillet, brown the steak in oil over medium-high heat; transfer to a 5-qt. slow cooker. Add the next 10 ingredients; stir well.
2. Cover and cook on low until meat is tender, 7-8 hours. If desired, thicken cooking liquid. Serve with pasta. If desired, top with green onions.
1 serving: 302 cal., 8g fat (2g sat. fat), 63mg chol., 641mg sod., 31g carb. (26g sugars, 3g fiber), 27g pro.

"Made this last night. It turned out better than expected. I'm feeding 2 men and myself, and we had barely any leftovers. Double the recipe and serve it on top of brown rice with steamed broccoli. I may add a little less of the molasses next go around, just because it was a hint too sweet. But, overall, this is a very tasty and gluten-free dish!"
—JENCOOKS4FAMILY, TASTEOFHOME.COM

SLOW-COOKER MUSHROOM BEEF STROGANOFF

I love to make this for my husband and myself on a cold night. It warms us right up! Greek yogurt can be substituted for the sour cream.
—*Meg Hilton, Atlanta, GA*

PREP: 15 min. • **COOK:** 6¼ hours
MAKES: 8 servings

2   lbs. boneless beef chuck steak
1   lb. sliced fresh mushrooms
2   medium onions, chopped
1   can (10¾ oz.) condensed
    golden mushroom soup, undiluted
2   Tbsp. reduced-sodium soy sauce
2   Tbsp. Dijon mustard
1   Tbsp. Worcestershire sauce
3   garlic cloves, minced
¾   tsp. salt
½   tsp. pepper
2   Tbsp. cornstarch
2   Tbsp. water
1   cup sour cream
    Hot cooked egg noodles
    Minced fresh parsley, optional

1. Cut steak into 3x½-in. strips. In a 5- or 6-qt. slow cooker, combine the next 9 ingredients. Stir in steak strips. Cook, covered, on low until meat is tender, 6-8 hours.
2. Transfer steak to a serving dish; keep warm. Skim fat from cooking juices. Mix cornstarch and water until smooth; stir into cooking juices. Cook, covered, on high until thickened, 10-15 minutes. Stir in sour cream; pour over beef. Serve with noodles and, if desired, minced parsley.
¾ cup: 317cal., 18g fat (8g sat. fat), 81mg chol., 736mg sod., 11g carb. (4g sugars, 1g fiber), 26g pro.

SWEET-SOUR
BEEF

SLOW-COOKER SPAGHETTI & MEATBALLS

I've been cooking for 50 years, and this dish is still one that guests request frequently. It is my No. 1 standby recipe and also makes amazing meatball sandwiches. The sauce works for any pasta.

—*Jane Whittaker, Pensacola, FL*

PREP: 50 min. • **COOK:** 5 hours
MAKES: 12 servings (about 3½ qt. sauce)

- 1 cup seasoned bread crumbs
- 2 Tbsp. grated Parmesan and Romano cheese blend
- 1 tsp. pepper
- ½ tsp. salt
- 2 large eggs, lightly beaten
- 2 lbs. ground beef

SAUCE

- 1 large onion, finely chopped
- 1 medium green pepper, finely chopped
- 3 cans (15 oz. each) tomato sauce
- 2 cans (14½ oz. each) diced tomatoes, undrained
- 1 can (6 oz.) tomato paste
- 6 garlic cloves, minced
- 2 bay leaves
- 1 tsp. each dried basil, oregano and parsley flakes
- 1 tsp. salt
- ½ tsp. pepper
- ¼ tsp. crushed red pepper flakes
   Hot cooked spaghetti

1. In a large bowl, mix bread crumbs, cheese, pepper and salt; stir in eggs. Add beef; mix lightly but thoroughly. Shape into 1½-in. balls. In a large skillet, brown the meatballs in batches over medium heat; drain.
2. Place the first 5 sauce ingredients in a 6-qt. slow cooker; stir in garlic and seasonings. Add meatballs, stirring gently to coat. Cook, covered, on low 5-6 hours or until meatballs are cooked through.
3. Remove bay leaves. Serve sauce with spaghetti.
1 cup: 254 cal., 11g fat (4g sat. fat), 79mg chol., 1133mg sod., 20g carb. (7g sugars, 3g fiber), 20g pro.

SLOW-COOKER PEPPER STEAK

SLOW-COOKER PEPPER STEAK

Pepper steak is one of my favorite dishes, but sometimes the beef can be tough. This recipe solves that problem! The slow cooker keeps things simple and makes the meat very tender. I've stored leftovers in one big container and also in individual portions for quick lunches.

—*Julie Rhine, Zelienople, PA*

PREP: 30 min. • **COOK:** 6¼ hours
MAKES: 12 servings

- 1 beef top round roast (3 lbs.)
- 1 large onion, halved and sliced
- 1 large green pepper, cut into ½-in. strips
- 1 large sweet red pepper, cut into ½-in. strips
- 1 cup water
- 4 garlic cloves, minced
- ⅓ cup cornstarch
- ½ cup reduced-sodium soy sauce
- 2 tsp. sugar
- 2 tsp. ground ginger
- 8 cups hot cooked brown rice

1. Place roast, onion and peppers in a 5-qt. slow cooker. Add water and garlic. Cook, covered, on low until meat is tender, 6-8 hours.
2. Remove the beef to a cutting board. Transfer vegetables and cooking juices to a large saucepan. Bring to a boil. In a small bowl, mix cornstarch, soy sauce, sugar and ginger until smooth; stir into vegetable mixture. Return to a boil, stirring constantly; cook and stir until thickened, 1-2 minutes.
3. Cut the beef into slices. Stir gently into sauce; heat through. Serve with rice.
Freeze option: Freeze cooled beef mixture in freezer containers. To use, partially thaw in refrigerator overnight. Heat through in a saucepan, stirring occasionally; add a little water if necessary.
1 serving: 322 cal., 5g fat (1g sat. fat), 64mg chol., 444mg sod., 38g carb. (3g sugars, 3g fiber), 30g pro. **Diabetic exchanges:** 3 lean meat, 2 starch.

MELT-IN-YOUR-MOUTH MEAT LOAF

When my husband and I were first married, he refused to eat meat loaf because he said it was bland and dry. Then I prepared this version, and it became his favorite meal.
—*Suzanne Codner, Starbuck, MN*

PREP: 15 min. • **COOK:** 5¼ hours + standing
MAKES: 6 servings

- 2 large eggs
- ¾ cup 2% milk
- ⅔ cup seasoned bread crumbs
- 2 tsp. dried minced onion
- 1 tsp. salt
- ½ tsp. rubbed sage
- 1½ lbs. ground beef
- ¼ cup ketchup
- 2 Tbsp. brown sugar
- 1 tsp. ground mustard
- ½ tsp. Worcestershire sauce

1. Cut two 25x3-in. strips of heavy-duty foil; crisscross so they resemble an X. Place strips on bottom and up sides of a 5-qt. slow cooker. Coat strips with cooking spray.
2. Combine the first 6 ingredients. Crumble beef over mixture; mix lightly but thoroughly. Shape into a round loaf; place in center of strips in slow cooker. Cook, covered, on low 5-6 hours or until a thermometer reads at least 160°.
3. In a small bowl, whisk ketchup, brown sugar, mustard and Worcestershire sauce. Spoon over meat loaf. Cook until heated through, about 15 minutes longer. Using foil strips as handles, remove meat loaf to a platter. Let stand for 10-15 minutes before slicing.
1 piece: 346 cal., 17g fat (7g sat. fat), 150mg chol., 800mg sod., 18g carb. (8g sugars, 1g fiber), 28g pro.

NO-FUSS SWISS STEAK

I make this dish regularly because my kids love the savory steak, tangy gravy and fork-tender veggies.
—*Sharon Morrell, Parker, SD*

PREP: 15 min. • **COOK:** 6 hours
MAKES: 10 servings

- 3 lbs. beef top round steak, cut into serving-size pieces
- 2 Tbsp. canola oil
- 2 medium carrots, sliced
- 2 celery ribs, sliced
- 1¾ cups water
- 1 can (11 oz.) condensed tomato rice soup, undiluted
- 1 can (10½ oz.) condensed French onion soup, undiluted
- ½ tsp. pepper
- 1 bay leaf

1. In a large skillet, brown beef in oil over medium-high heat; drain. Transfer to a 5-qt. slow cooker. Add carrots and celery. Combine the remaining ingredients; pour over meat and vegetables.
2. Cover and cook on low until meat is tender, 6-8 hours. Discard bay leaf. If desired, thicken cooking juices.
1 serving: 246 cal., 8g fat (2g sat. fat), 79mg chol., 477mg sod., 10g carb. (5g sugars, 1g fiber), 32g pro.

MELT-IN-YOUR-MOUTH
MEAT LOAF

Poultry

MOIST DRUMSTICKS

MOIST DRUMSTICKS

I found this in my mom's recipe box years ago. It is very quick to prepare and makes the house smell wonderful while it is cooking. My daughter Molly just loves it!
—*Lianne Felton, Riverside, CA*

PREP: 10 min. • **COOK:** 5 hours 10 min.
MAKES: 6 servings

- 3 lbs. chicken drumsticks, skin removed
- 1 can (8 oz.) tomato sauce
- ½ cup soy sauce
- ¼ cup packed brown sugar
- 1 tsp. minced garlic
- 3 Tbsp. cornstarch
- ¼ cup cold water
  Thinly sliced green onions, optional

1. Place drumsticks in a 5-qt. slow cooker. In a small bowl, combine the tomato sauce, soy sauce, brown sugar and garlic; pour over chicken. Cover and cook on low until a thermometer reads 170°-175°, 5-6 hours.
2. To serve, remove the drumsticks to a 15x10x1-in. pan; arrange in a single layer. Preheat broiler.
3. Skim fat from cooking juices; transfer juices to a small saucepan. Bring liquid to a boil. Combine cornstarch and water until smooth. Gradually stir into the pan. Bring to a boil; cook and stir until thickened, 2 minutes.
4. Meanwhile, broil chicken 3-4 in. from heat until lightly browned, 2-3 minutes. Brush with sauce before serving. If desired, sprinkle with green onions.
1 serving: 304 cal., 12g fat (3g sat. fat), 94mg chol., 1490mg sod., 15g carb. (10g sugars, 0 fiber), 32g pro.

EASY SLOW-COOKER CHICKEN ROPA VIEJA

ORANGE CHICKEN WITH SWEET POTATOES

Orange peel and pineapple juice lend fruity flavor to this super chicken and sweet potato combo. Served over rice, this appealing entree is bound to win you compliments.
—*Vicki Smith, Okeechobee, FL*

PREP: 25 min. • **COOK:** 3 hours
MAKES: 4 servings

- 3 medium sweet potatoes, peeled and sliced
- ⅔ cup plus 3 Tbsp. all-purpose flour, divided
- 1 tsp. salt
- 1 tsp. onion powder
- 1 tsp. ground nutmeg
- 1 tsp. ground cinnamon
- 1 tsp. pepper
- 4 boneless skinless chicken breast halves (5 oz. each)
- 2 Tbsp. butter
- 1 can (10¾ oz.) condensed cream of chicken soup, undiluted
- ¾ cup unsweetened pineapple juice
- 2 tsp. brown sugar
- 1 tsp. grated orange zest
- ½ lb. sliced fresh mushrooms
  Hot cooked rice

1. Layer sweet potatoes in a 3-qt. slow cooker. In a large bowl, combine ⅔ cup flour and seasonings; add the chicken, 1 piece at a time, and shake to coat.
2. In a large skillet over medium heat, cook the chicken in butter until lightly browned, 3 minutes on each side. Arrange chicken over sweet potatoes.
3. Place remaining flour in a small bowl. Stir in the soup, pineapple juice, brown sugar and orange zest until blended. Add mushrooms; pour over chicken. Cover and cook on low until chicken and potatoes are tender, 3-4 hours. Serve with rice.
1 serving: 575 cal., 15g fat (6g sat. fat), 100mg chol.,1276mg sod.,73g carb. (23g sugars, 8g fiber), 37g pro.

EASY SLOW-COOKER CHICKEN ROPA VIEJA

When discussing various methods of cooking ropas, a friend of mine told me her sister adds apple juice. I thought a Granny Smith apple might give the dish an extra kick—and it does. The ropas may also be served with hominy or tortillas, but I think the plantains add a special touch.
—*Arlene Erlbach, Morton Grove, IL*

PREP: 20 min. • **COOK:** 5 hours
MAKES: 6 Servings

- 2 medium sweet red peppers, sliced
- 1 medium Granny Smith apple, peeled and chopped
- 1 cup fresh cilantro leaves
- 1 cup chunky salsa
- 2 Tbsp. tomato paste
- 1 garlic clove, minced
- 1 tsp. ground cumin
- 5 tsp. adobo seasoning, divided
- 1½ lbs. boneless skinless chicken thighs
- 3 to 6 tsp. lime juice
- ¼ cup butter
- 3 ripe plantains, peeled and thinly sliced into thin rounds
  Optional: Hot cooked rice, lime wedges and additional fresh cilantro leaves

1. Place the first 7 ingredients and 1 tsp. adobo in a 5- or 6-qt. slow cooker. Rub remaining adobo seasoning over chicken; add to slow cooker. Cook, covered, on low until chicken is tender, 5-6 hours. Using 2 forks, shred chicken. Stir in lime juice to taste; heat through.
2. Meanwhile, heat the butter in a large skillet over medium heat. Cook the plantains in batches until tender and golden brown, about 3 minutes per side. Drain on paper towels.
3. Serve chicken with plantains using a slotted spoon. If desired, serve with rice, lime wedges and cilantro.
1 serving: 387 cal., 16g fat (7g sat. fat), 96mg chol., 1428mg sod., 39g carb. (20g sugars, 4g fiber), 23g pro.

**BBQ CHICKEN
BAKED POTATOES**

SLOW-COOKER DUCK BREASTS

My husband and son are duck hunters, and I am always trying to find new ways to cook the meat. I created this dish a couple of years ago, and it instantly became a family favorite.
—*Sherri Melotik, Oak Creek, WI*

PREP: 40 min. • **COOK:** 3½ hours
MAKES: 6 servings

6	duck breast halves with skin (5 oz. each)
1	can (10½ oz.) condensed cream of mushroom soup, undiluted
½	cup white wine
½	cup chopped onion
¼	cup chopped celery
¼	tsp. dried marjoram
¼	tsp. dried rosemary, crushed
¼	tsp. pepper
¼	cup cold water
3	tsp. cornstarch
	Hot cooked rice

1. Pat duck breasts dry with paper towel; using a sharp knife, score fat to create a tight diamond pattern. Working in batches, place duck breasts, fat sides down, into a cold skillet. Heat the pan over medium-low. Cook until browned, 15-20 minutes, pouring drippings from pan as needed. Save duck fat for another use.
2. In a bowl, mix mushroom soup, wine, onion, celery and seasonings; pour into a 6-qt. slow cooker. Place duck breasts, fat sides up, on top of the soup mixture. Cook, covered, on low until meat is tender and thermometer reads 170°, 3½-4½ hours. Remove duck breasts and keep warm; skim fat from the slow cooker. Combine the cold water and cornstarch; add to slow cooker. Cook until thickened, 10-15 minutes. Return duck to slow cooker; heat through. Serve over rice.
1 serving: 365 cal., 27g fat (9g sat. fat), 76mg chol., 417mg sod., 7g carb. (1g sugars, 1g fiber), 17g pro.

BBQ CHICKEN BAKED POTATOES

These baked potatoes are meals in themselves, with a smoky barbecue flavor that will make your mouth water. You can top them with your favorite cheese and garnishes.
—*Amber Massey, Argyle, TX*

PREP: 15 min. • **COOK:** 6 hours
MAKES: 10 servings

4½	lbs. bone-in chicken breast halves, skin removed
2	Tbsp. garlic powder
1	large red onion, sliced into thick rings
1	bottle (18 oz.) honey barbecue sauce
1	cup Italian salad dressing
½	cup packed brown sugar
½	cup cider vinegar
¼	cup Worcestershire sauce
2	Tbsp. liquid smoke, optional
10	medium potatoes, baked
	Optional: Crumbled blue cheese and chopped green onions

1. Place chicken in a greased 5- or 6-qt. slow cooker; sprinkle with garlic powder and top with onion. Combine barbecue sauce, salad dressing, brown sugar, vinegar, Worcestershire sauce and, if desired, liquid smoke; pour over chicken.
2. Cover and cook on low for 6-8 hours or until chicken is tender.
3. When cool enough to handle, remove chicken from bones; discard bones and onion. Skim fat from cooking juices.
4. Shred meat with 2 forks and return to slow cooker; heat through. Serve with potatoes, ¾ cup in each. Top with blue cheese and green onions if desired.
1 stuffed potato: 572 cal., 13g fat (2g sat. fat), 91mg chol., 1050mg sod., 72g carb. (32g sugars, 4g fiber), 38g pro.

TEST KITCHEN TIP
Duck fat is a delicacy. Keep it covered in the fridge, and use a small amount to fry potatoes.

**SLOW-COOKER
DUCK BREASTS**

SLOW-COOKER CRANBERRY & ORANGE CHICKEN

My family loves this delicious recipe that I dreamed up. Also try shredding the flavorful chicken and serving it on buns.
—*Frances D. Roberts, Silver Spring, MD*

PREP: 15 min. • **COOK:** 5 hours 10 min.
MAKES: 6 servings

- 1 tsp. garlic powder
- 1 tsp. poultry seasoning
- ½ tsp. salt
- ⅛ to ¼ tsp. pepper
- 3½ lbs. bone-in chicken breast halves, skin removed
- 1 can (14 oz.) jellied cranberry sauce
- ½ cup chili sauce
- ¼ cup Thai chili sauce
- ⅓ cup orange marmalade
- 4 tsp. cornstarch
- 2 Tbsp. cold water

1. Combine the garlic powder, poultry seasoning, salt and pepper; rub over the chicken. Transfer to a 5- to 6-qt. slow cooker.
2. In a small bowl, combine the cranberry sauce, chili sauces and marmalade; pour over chicken. Cover and cook on low until a thermometer reads 170°, 5-6 hours.
3. Remove chicken to a serving platter; keep warm. Skim fat from cooking juices; transfer juices to a small saucepan. Bring to a boil. Combine cornstarch and water until smooth; gradually stir into cooking juices. Return to a boil; cook and stir until thickened, 2 minutes. Serve with chicken.
5 oz. cooked chicken with ⅓ cup sauce: 417 cal., 5g fat (1g sat. fat), 118mg chol., 758mg sod., 48g carb. (34g sugars, 1g fiber), 44g pro.

INDONESIAN PEANUT CHICKEN

INDONESIAN PEANUT CHICKEN

Here's a marvelous make-ahead recipe! I cut up fresh chicken, put it in a bag with the remaining slow-cooker ingredients and freeze it. To cook, just remove the bag a day ahead to thaw in the fridge, then pour all the contents into the slow cooker.
—*Sarah Newman, Mahtomedi, MN*

PREP: 15 min. • **COOK:** 4 hours
MAKES: 6 servings

- 1½ lbs. boneless skinless chicken breasts, cut into 1-in. cubes
- ⅓ cup chopped onion
- ⅓ cup water
- ¼ cup reduced-fat creamy peanut butter
- 3 Tbsp. chili sauce
- ¼ tsp. salt
- ¼ tsp. cayenne pepper
- ¼ tsp. pepper
- 3 cups hot cooked brown rice
- 6 Tbsp. chopped salted peanuts
- 6 Tbsp. chopped sweet red pepper
  Julienned green onions, optional

Place chicken in a 4-qt. slow cooker. In a small bowl, combine the onion, water, peanut butter, chili sauce, salt, cayenne and pepper; pour over chicken. Cook, covered, on low until the meat is tender, 4-5 hours. Serve with the rice. Sprinkle with peanuts, red pepper and, if desired, julienned green onions.
1 serving: 353 cal., 12g fat (2g sat. fat), 63mg chol., 370mg sod., 31g carb. (4g sugars, 3g fiber), 31g pro. **Diabetic exchanges:** 3 lean meat, 2 starch, 2 fat.
Spicy Indonesian Peanut Chicken with Rice Noodles: Use ¼ cup creamy peanut butter and 2 Tbsp. chili garlic sauce. Serve with rice noodles, and garnish with thinly sliced green onions and lime wedges.

MOROCCAN APRICOT CHICKEN

Chili sauce, apricots and Moroccan seasoning create an incredible sauce for slow-cooked chicken thighs. Traditional Moroccan apricot chicken typically includes chili pepper paste, but I use chili sauce in my version. Serve it alone or with couscous for a heartier meal.
—Arlene Erlbach, Morton Grove, IL

- -

PREP: 25 min. • **COOK:** 4¼ hours
MAKES: 6 servings

- 1   tsp. olive oil
- ½   cup slivered almonds
- 6   bone-in chicken thighs
      (about 2¼ lbs.)
- ¾   cup chili sauce
- ½   cup apricot preserves
- ½   cup dried apricots, quartered
- 4   tsp. Moroccan seasoning
      (ras el hanout)
- 1   Tbsp. vanilla extract
- 1½ tsp. garlic powder
- 1   can (15 oz.) garbanzo beans or
      chickpeas, rinsed and drained
- ¼   cup orange juice
      Chopped fresh parsley, optional

1. In a large skillet, heat oil over medium heat. Add the almonds; cook and stir until lightly browned, 2-3 minutes. Remove with a slotted spoon; drain on paper towels. In the same skillet, brown chicken on both sides. Remove from heat. Transfer chicken to a 4- or 5-qt. slow cooker. Stir chili sauce, preserves, apricots, Moroccan seasoning, vanilla and garlic powder into drippings. Pour over chicken.
2. Cook, covered, on low 4-4½ hours or until a thermometer inserted in the chicken reads 170°-175°. Stir in the garbanzo beans and orange juice. Cook, covered, on low until heated through, 15-30 minutes longer.
3. Serve with almonds. If desired, sprinkle with parsley.

1 chicken thigh with ¾ cup chickpea mixture: 482 cal., 21g fat (4g sat. fat), 81mg chol., 633mg sod., 47g carb. (27g sugars, 5g fiber), 28g pro.

SLOW-COOKED COCONUT CHICKEN

One of my favorite things about this recipe is how fabulous it makes my home smell. Everyone who comes by asks, "What are you cooking?" And anyone who tastes it goes home with the recipe.
—Ann Smart, North Logan, UT

- -

PREP: 10 min. • **COOK:** 4 hours
MAKES: 6 servings

- ½   cup light coconut milk
- 2   Tbsp. brown sugar
- 2   Tbsp. reduced-sodium soy sauce
- 2   garlic cloves, minced
- ⅛   tsp. ground cloves
- 6   boneless skinless chicken thighs
      (about 1½ lbs.)
- 6   Tbsp. sweetened shredded coconut,
      toasted
      Minced fresh cilantro

In a large bowl, combine the first 5 ingredients. Place chicken in a 3-qt. slow cooker. Pour coconut milk mixture over top. Cook, covered, on low until chicken is tender, 4-5 hours. Serve with coconut and cilantro.
1 serving: 201 cal., 10g fat (3g sat. fat), 76mg chol., 267mg sod., 6g carb. (5g sugars, 0 fiber), 21g pro. **Diabetic exchanges:** 3 lean meat, ½ starch, ½ fat.

MOROCCAN APRICOT CHICKEN

SHREDDED CHICKEN
TOSTADAS

SHREDDED CHICKEN TOSTADAS

These flavorful tostadas are super easy and family-friendly. You won't believe how tender and juicy the chicken comes out. Just load the tostadas with your favorite fresh toppings, and you'll have one simple, sensational meal.
—Lisa Kenny, Houston, TX

- -

PREP: 10 min. • **COOK:** 3 hours
MAKES: 8 servings

2½ lbs. boneless skinless chicken breasts
1 envelope reduced-sodium taco seasoning
1 can (10 oz.) diced tomatoes and green chiles, undrained
½ tsp. salt
16 tostada shells
2 cups shredded Mexican cheese blend
Optional: Shredded lettuce, chopped tomatoes, sliced avocado, sour cream, sliced jalapenos and fresh cilantro

1. Place chicken in a 3- or 4-qt. slow cooker. Sprinkle with taco seasoning; top with diced tomatoes and green chiles. Cook, covered, on low until a thermometer inserted into the chicken reads 165°, 3-4 hours.
2. Shred meat with 2 forks. Return to slow cooker and add salt; heat through. Serve on tostada shells with cheese and optional ingredients as desired.
Freeze option: Freeze cooled meat mixture and juices in freezer containers. To use, partially thaw in refrigerator overnight. Heat through in a saucepan, stirring occasionally; add a little water if necessary.
2 tostadas: 378 cal., 17g fat (7g sat. fat), 103mg chol., 858mg sod., 18g carb. (1g sugars, 1g fiber), 36g pro.

CARIBBEAN CURRIED CHICKEN

Having grown up in the Virgin Islands, I've eaten my fair share of authentic curried chicken. This recipe hits the mark with big, bold flavors. It's delicious served over rice.
—Sharon Gibson, Hendersonville, NC

- -

PREP: 20 min. • **COOK:** 4 hours
MAKES: 8 servings

1 Tbsp. Madras curry powder
1 tsp. garlic powder
1 tsp. pepper
8 boneless skinless chicken thighs (about 4 oz. each)
1 medium onion, thinly sliced
1½ cups Goya mojo criollo marinade, well shaken
2 Tbsp. canola oil
2 Tbsp. all-purpose flour
Optional: Hot cooked rice, green onions and fresh cilantro leaves

1. Combine curry, garlic and pepper; sprinkle over chicken, pressing to help mixture adhere. Place chicken in a 3-qt. slow cooker. Sprinkle with onion. Carefully pour mojo criollo marinade along sides of slow cooker, avoiding chicken to keep coating intact. Cook, covered, on low until a thermometer reads 170°, 4-6 hours.
2. Remove chicken; keep warm. Pour cooking juices from slow cooker into a measuring cup; skim fat. In a large saucepan, heat oil over medium; whisk in flour until smooth. Gradually whisk in cooking juices. Bring to a boil, stirring constantly; cook and stir until thickened, 1-2 minutes. Reduce heat; add chicken. Simmer about 5 minutes. If desired, serve with rice, onions and cilantro.
Note: Madras curry powder is spicier than regular curry powder. As a substitute, add ¼ tsp. ground cayenne and a few dashes ground mustard to 2¾ tsp. curry powder.
1 chicken thigh with 6 Tbsp. sauce: 249 cal., 13g fat (3g sat. fat), 76mg chol., 514mg sod., 11g carb. (5g sugars, 1g fiber), 22g pro. **Diabetic exchanges:** 3 lean meat, 1 fat.

CARIBBEAN CURRIED CHICKEN

SAUCY BBQ CHICKEN THIGHS

Barbecued chicken gets a makeover in this recipe. The combination of ingredients makes for a mellow flavor that tastes more grown up than the original. It's fantastic over rice, pasta or potatoes.
—*Sharon Fritz, Morristown, TN*

PREP: 15 min. • **COOK:** 5 hours
MAKES: 6 servings

- 6 boneless skinless chicken thighs (about 1½ lbs.)
- ½ tsp. poultry seasoning
- 1 medium onion, chopped
- 1 can (14½ oz.) diced tomatoes, undrained
- 1 can (8 oz.) tomato sauce
- ½ cup barbecue sauce
- ¼ cup orange juice
- 1 tsp. garlic powder
- ¾ tsp. dried oregano
- ½ tsp. hot pepper sauce
- ¼ tsp. pepper
    Hot cooked brown rice, optional

Place the chicken in a 3-qt. slow cooker; sprinkle with the poultry seasoning. Top with onion and tomatoes. In a small bowl, mix the next 7 ingredients; pour over top. Cook, covered, on low 5-6 hours or until chicken is tender. If desired, serve with rice.

Freeze option: Place the cooked chicken mixture in freezer containers. Cool and freeze. To use, partially thaw in refrigerator overnight. Microwave, covered, on high in a microwave-safe dish until heated through, stirring occasionally; add a little water if necessary.

1 serving: 221 cal., 9g fat (2g sat. fat), 76mg chol., 517mg sod., 12g carb. (8g sugars, 2g fiber), 23g pro. **Diabetic exchanges:** 3 lean meat, 1 starch.

"Yum! I literally threw the ingredients in my slow cooker in about 15 minutes. My son made the rice while I was on my way home from work. I paired the dish with pinot grigio and bourbon baked beans on the side. I am one happy camper right now."
—MARSHA HOWARD, TASTEOFHOME.COM

SLOW-COOKER PUMPKIN
CHICKEN TAGINE

SLOW-COOKER PUMPKIN CHICKEN TAGINE

I first discovered tagines—Moroccan stews—when my oldest son was a baby, and I've loved them ever since. The first version I made was in a slow cooker, and since I'm a mom with two active boys, that has stayed my preferred method. The pumpkin mixture is supposed to be thick, but if you like a thinner consistency, stir in chicken broth before serving.
—*Necia Blundy, Bothell, WA*

PREP: 35 min. • **COOK:** 5 hours
MAKES: 4 servings

- 1 lb. boneless skinless chicken thighs, cut into ½-in. pieces
- 1 can (15 oz.) garbanzo beans or chickpeas, rinsed and drained
- 1 can (14½ oz.) diced tomatoes, undrained
- 1 medium green pepper, chopped
- 1 cup canned pumpkin
- ¼ cup golden raisins
- 1 Tbsp. maple syrup
- 2 tsp. ground cumin
- 1 tsp. ground cinnamon
- ½ tsp. salt
- ½ tsp. ground coriander
- ¼ tsp. cayenne pepper
- ¼ tsp. ground cloves
- ¼ tsp. ground allspice
- 1 Tbsp. olive oil
- 1 medium onion, chopped
- 2 garlic cloves, minced
- 1 tsp. minced fresh gingerroot
    Hot cooked couscous and chopped fresh cilantro

1. In a 3- or 4-qt. slow cooker, combine the first 14 ingredients. In a small skillet, heat oil over medium heat. Add onion; cook and stir until tender, 5-7 minutes. Add garlic and ginger; cook 1 minute longer. Stir into slow cooker.

2. Cook, covered, on low until chicken is cooked through and vegetables are tender, 5-6 hours. Serve with couscous; sprinkle with cilantro.

1 serving: 400 cal., 14g fat (3g sat. fat), 76mg chol., 668mg sod., 42g carb. (18g sugars, 10g fiber), 28g pro.

TURKEY IN A POT

I use this recipe often for an easy Sunday dinner. The turkey breast has a holiday feel when served with the cranberry gravy seasoned with cinnamon, cloves and allspice.
—*Lois Woodward, Okeechobee, FL*

PREP: 25 min. • **COOK:** 3½ hours
MAKES: 8 servings

- 1 boneless skinless turkey breast half (3 lbs.)
- 1 can (14 oz.) whole-berry cranberry sauce
- ½ cup sugar
- ½ cup apple juice
- 1 Tbsp. cider vinegar
- 2 garlic cloves, minced
- 1 tsp. ground mustard
- ½ tsp. ground cinnamon
- ¼ tsp. ground cloves
- ¼ tsp. ground allspice
- 2 Tbsp. all-purpose flour
- ¼ cup cold water
- ¼ tsp. browning sauce, optional

1. Place the turkey skin side up in a 5-qt. slow cooker. Combine the cranberry sauce, sugar, apple juice, vinegar, garlic, mustard, cinnamon, cloves and allspice; pour over the turkey. Cover and cook on low until a thermometer reads 170°, 3½-4½ hours.
2. Remove the turkey to a cutting board; keep warm. Strain the cooking juices. In a small saucepan, combine flour and water until smooth; gradually stir in strained juices. Bring to a boil; cook and stir until thickened, 2 minutes. If desired, stir in browning sauce. Serve with sliced turkey.
4 oz. cooked turkey with sauce: 332 cal., 3g fat (1g sat. fat), 97mg chol., 218mg sod., 35g carb. (26g sugars, 1g fiber), 41g pro.

GINGER CHICKEN & QUINOA STEW

This Asian-inspired one-pot chicken dinner is healthy and tasty. You can serve it hot, cold or at room temperature.
—*Doris Kwon, Newport Coast, CA*

PREP: 25 min. • **COOK:** 3½ hours
MAKES: 8 servings

- 2 lbs. boneless skinless chicken thighs, cut into 1-in. pieces
- 1 cup quinoa, rinsed
- 1 medium onion, cut into 1-in. pieces
- 1 medium sweet yellow pepper, cut into 1-in. pieces
- 1 medium sweet red pepper, cut into 1-in. pieces
- 2 cups chicken broth
- ½ cup honey
- ⅓ cup reduced-sodium soy sauce
- ¼ cup mirin (sweet rice wine) or sherry
- 1 Tbsp. minced fresh gingerroot
- 2 garlic cloves, minced
- ¼ to 1 tsp. crushed red pepper flakes
- 1 can (8 oz.) unsweetened pineapple chunks, drained
- 3 green onions, thinly sliced
- 2 tsp. sesame seeds

1. Place the chicken in a 4- or 5-qt. slow cooker. Top with the quinoa, onion and peppers. In a small bowl, whisk the broth, honey, soy sauce, mirin, ginger, garlic and red pepper flakes; pour into slow cooker.
2. Cook, covered, on low until chicken is tender, 3½-4 hours. Serve with the pineapple, onions and sesame seeds.
1 cup: 373 cal., 10g fat (3g sat. fat), 77mg chol., 696mg sod., 43g carb. (26g sugars, 3g fiber), 26g pro.

TURKEY IN A POT

SLOW-COOKER
THAI PEANUT CHICKEN
WITH NOODLES

SPICED LIME & CILANTRO CHICKEN

As a working mom and home cook, I strive to have fabulous, flavor-packed dinners that make my family smile. Nothing is more awesome than an easy slow-cooker recipe that makes it seem as though you've been cooking in the kitchen all day!
—*Mari Smith, Ashburn, VA*

PREP: 15 min. • **COOK:** 3 hours
MAKES: 6 servings

- 2 tsp. chili powder
- 1 tsp. sea salt
- 1 tsp. ground cumin
- 1 tsp. pepper
- ¼ tsp. cayenne pepper
- 6 bone-in chicken thighs (about 2¼ lbs.)
- ⅓ cup lime juice (about 3 limes)
- 1 Tbsp. olive oil
- ½ cup fresh cilantro leaves
- 5 garlic cloves, halved

1. Combine the first 5 ingredients; rub over chicken. Place in a 4- or 5-qt. slow cooker. Combine remaining ingredients in a blender; cover and process pureed. Pour over chicken.
2. Cook, covered, on low until a thermometer inserted in chicken reads 170°-175°, 3-4 hours.

1 chicken thigh: 253 cal., 17g fat (4g sat. fat), 81mg chol., 390mg sod., 2g carb. (0 sugars, 0 fiber), 23g pro.

SLOW-COOKER THAI PEANUT CHICKEN WITH NOODLES

I serve this Thai favorite with noodles mixed into the sauce, but it's also terrific served over rice. Garnish with green onion or cilantro for pops of color and fresh flavor.
—*Catherine Cebula, Littleton, MA*

PREP: 35 min. • **COOK:** 2½ hours
MAKES: 6 servings

- 1½ lbs. boneless skinless chicken breasts, cut into ¾ in. cubes
- 1 medium onion, chopped
- ¾ cup salsa
- ¼ cup creamy peanut butter
- 2 Tbsp. black bean sauce
- 1 Tbsp. reduced-sodium soy sauce
- 8 oz. uncooked linguine
- 1 Tbsp. canola oil
- ½ lb. sliced baby portobello mushrooms
- Thinly sliced green onions, optional

1. Place the chicken and onion in a 4-qt. slow cooker. Combine salsa, peanut butter, bean sauce and soy sauce; add to slow cooker. Cook, covered, on low until the chicken is tender, 2½-3½ hours.
2. Meanwhile, prepare pasta according to package directions. In a large skillet, heat the oil over medium-high heat. Add the mushrooms; cook and stir until tender, 6-8 minutes. Drain pasta; stir into slow cooker. Stir in mushrooms. If desired, sprinkle with green onions.

1⅓ cups: 378 cal., 11g fat (2g sat. fat), 63mg chol., 436mg sod., 37g carb. (5g sugars, 2g fiber), 32g pro.

DID YOU KNOW?

Chili powder is a seasoning blend made primarily from dried chili peppers. Its other ingredients commonly include garlic, onion, salt, oregano, cumin, coriander, cloves, cinnamon and even cocoa powder.

SPICED LIME &
CILANTRO CHICKEN

LEMON CHICKEN WITH GRAVY

Chicken tenders are nicely seasoned with tantalizing lemon and thyme flavors in this recipe. It's especially tasty with brown rice.
—Shona Germino, Casa Grande, AZ

PREP: 25 min. • **COOK:** 3 hours
MAKES: 4 servings

1 lb. chicken tenderloins
¼ cup chicken broth
3 Tbsp. lemon juice
3 Tbsp. butter, cubed
1 Tbsp. grated lemon zest
2 large garlic cloves, peeled and sliced
½ tsp. salt
½ tsp. white pepper
2 Tbsp. minced fresh parsley or
  2 tsp. dried parsley flakes
2 Tbsp. minced fresh thyme or
  2 tsp. dried thyme
2 tsp. cornstarch
2 tsp. cold water
  Hot cooked rice, optional

1. In a 1½-qt. slow cooker, combine the first 8 ingredients. Cover and cook on low for 2½ hours. Add parsley and thyme; cover and cook until chicken is no longer pink, 30 minutes longer.
2. Remove chicken to a serving
3. plate and keep warm. Transfer the juices to a small saucepan. Combine cornstarch and water until smooth; add to juices. Bring to a boil; cook and stir until thickened, 2 minutes.
If desired, serve chicken with rice.

3 oz. cooked chicken: 195 cal., 9g fat (5g sat. fat), 90mg chol., 466mg sod., 4g carb. (0 sugars, 1g fiber), 26g pro. **Diabetic exchanges:** 3 lean meat, 2 fat.

FILIPINO ADOBO AROMATIC CHICKEN

This saucy chicken packs a wallop of flavors—salty, sweet, sour, slightly spicy and even a little umami. It can be made on the stove, too. Any way you make it, I think it tastes even better the next day served over warm rice.
—Loanne Chiu, Fort Worth, TX

PREP: 30 min. • **COOK:** 3 hours 20 min.
MAKES: 6 servings

8 bacon strips, chopped
3 lbs. boneless skinless chicken thighs
1 large onion, chopped
4 garlic cloves, minced
2 medium limes
¼ cup dry sherry
3 Tbsp. soy sauce
3 Tbsp. molasses
2 Tbsp. minced fresh gingerroot
3 bay leaves
1 tsp. pepper
½ tsp. chili garlic sauce
  Minced fresh cilantro and
  toasted sesame seeds
  Hot cooked rice
  Lime wedges, optional

1. In a large skillet, cook the bacon over medium heat until crisp, stirring occasionally. Remove with a slotted spoon; drain on paper towels. Discard drippings, reserving 1 Tbsp. in pan. Brown chicken in bacon drippings in batches. Transfer chicken to a 4- or 5-qt. slow cooker.
2. Add onion to the same pan; cook and stir until tender, 3-5 minutes. Add garlic; cook and stir 1 minute longer. Finely grate enough zest from limes to measure 2 tsp. Cut limes crosswise in half; squeeze juice from limes.
3. Add the lime juice and zest, sherry, soy sauce, molasses, ginger, bay leaves, pepper and chili sauce to pan; cook and stir to loosen browned bits. Pour over chicken. Cook, covered, on high until a thermometer reads 170°, 3-4 hours.
4. Remove chicken; shred meat with 2 forks, keep warm. If desired, slightly thicken juices by cooking in a saucepan over medium-high heat about 20 minutes. Remove bay leaves. Stir in bacon. Pour over chicken; sprinkle with cilantro and sesame seeds. Serve with rice and, if desired, lime wedges.

6 oz. cooked chicken with ¼ cup sauce: 474 cal., 23g fat (7g sat. fat), 164mg chol., 865mg sod., 15g carb. (9g sugars, 1g fiber), 47g pro.

FILIPINO ADOBO AROMATIC CHICKEN

SLOW-COOKER BUTTER CHICKEN

I spent several years in Malaysia eating a variety of Middle Eastern and Southeast Asian food. This was one of my favorite dishes! There are many versions of butter chicken, but this is similar to the Middle Eastern version I had.

—*Shannon Copley, Upper Arlington, OH*

PREP: 10 min. • **COOK:** 3 hours
MAKES: 8 servings

- 2 Tbsp. butter
- 1 medium onion, chopped
- 4 garlic cloves, peeled, thinly sliced
- 2 tsp. garam masala
- 2 tsp. red curry powder
- ½ tsp. chili powder
- 1 tsp. ground ginger
- 2 Tbsp. whole wheat flour
- 1 Tbsp. olive oil
- 1 can (14 oz.) coconut milk
- ¼ cup tomato paste
- 1 tsp. salt
- ¼ tsp. pepper
- 3 lbs. boneless skinless chicken breasts, cut into 1-in. pieces
  Hot cooked rice
  Optional: Fresh cilantro leaves and naan bread

1. Heat large saucepan over medium-high heat; add butter and onion. Cook and stir until onions are tender, 2-3 minutes. Add garlic, cook until fragrant, 1 minute. Add the garam marsala, curry powder, chili powder and ginger; cook and stir 1 minute longer. Add flour. Drizzle in olive oil until a paste is formed. Whisk in the coconut milk and tomato paste; cook and stir until combined and slightly thickened, 1-2 minutes. Season with salt and pepper.
2. Using an immersion blender, carefully puree spice mixture. Transfer mixture into a 5-qt. slow cooker. Add the chicken; gently stir to combine.
3. Cover and cook on low until chicken is no longer pink, 3-4 hours. Serve with rice. If desired, sprinkle with cilantro and serve with naan bread.
1 cup: 242 cal., 9g fat (3g sat. fat), 102mg chol., 407mg sod., 4g carb. (1g sugars, 1g fiber), 35g pro. **Diabetic exchanges:** 5 lean meat, 1 fat.

SLOW-COOKER BUTTER CHICKEN

"This was so easy to make and absolutely incredible. Only 2 Tbsp. of butter, yet it tasted so rich with the coconut milk. The only change I had to make was using 2 tsp. of red curry paste because I had no red curry powder. I always modify recipes, but there's no need on this one. It is perfect. I made turmeric rice to go with it, and it's perfect with garlic naan."
—ROBMALGIERI, TASTEOFHOME.COM

Other Entrees

**SESAME
PORK ROAST**

SESAME PORK ROAST

My trick to making a tasty roast that's pull-apart tender is marinating a boneless cut of pork in a tangy sauce overnight before cooking it slowly the next day. It's unbeatable.
—*Sue Brown, San Miguel, CA*

- -

PREP: 10 min. + marinating
COOK: 9 hours • **MAKES:** 8 servings

- 1 boneless pork shoulder butt roast (4 lbs.)
- 2 cups water
- ½ cup soy sauce
- ¼ cup sesame seeds, toasted
- ¼ cup molasses
- ¼ cup cider or white wine vinegar
- 4 green onions, sliced
- 2 tsp. garlic powder
- ¼ tsp. cayenne pepper
- 3 Tbsp. cornstarch
- ¼ cup cold water
   Additional sesame seeds

1. Cut roast in half and place in a bowl. In a separate bowl or shallow dish, combine water, soy sauce, sesame seeds, molasses, vinegar, onions, garlic powder and cayenne. Pour half over the roast. Turn to coat. Cover and refrigerate roast overnight. Cover and refrigerate remaining marinade.
2. Drain roast, discarding marinade. Place roast in a 5-qt. slow cooker; add the reserved marinade. Cover and cook on high for 1 hour. Reduce temperature to low; cook until the meat is tender, 8-9 hours longer.
3. Remove meat to a serving platter; keep warm. Skim fat from cooking juices; transfer to a small saucepan. Bring liquid to a boil. Combine cornstarch and cold water until smooth. Gradually stir into pan. Bring to a boil; cook and stir until thickened, 2 minutes. Serve with meat. If desired, sprinkle roast with additional sesame seeds.
1 serving: 433 cal., 24g fat (8g sat. fat), 135mg chol., 835mg sod., 10g carb. (6g sugars, 1g fiber), 41g pro.

SLOW-COOKER AL PASTOR BOWLS

You'll love this easy version of a traditional Mexican favorite. It's easy to serve as bowls over rice or in tortillas with your favorite toppings.
—Taste of Home *Test Kitchen*

- -

PREP: 10 min. • **COOK:** 6 hours
MAKES: 8 cups

- 2 cans (7 oz. each) whole green chiles
- 1 can (20 oz.) pineapple chunks, drained
- 1 medium onion, chopped
- ½ cup orange juice
- ¼ cup white vinegar
- 3 garlic cloves, peeled
- 2 Tbsp. chili powder
- 2 tsp. salt
- 1½ tsp. smoked paprika
- 1 tsp. dried oregano
- 1 tsp. ground cumin
- ½ tsp. ground coriander
- 4 lbs. boneless pork loin roast
  Hot cooked rice
  Optional toppings: Black beans, chopped avocado, corn, sliced radishes, lime and Mexican crema

1. Puree the first 12 ingredients in a blender. In a 5- or 6-qt. slow cooker, combine pork and pepper mixture. Cook, covered, on low until pork is very tender, 6-8 hours. Stir to break up pork.
2. Serve pork in bowls over rice. Add toppings as desired.
⅔ cup: 232 cal., 7g fat (3g sat. fat), 75mg chol., 512mg sod., 11g carb. (8g sugars, 1g fiber), 30g pro. **Diabetic exchanges:** 4 lean meat, ½ starch.

APPLE PIE STEEL-CUT OATMEAL

I absolutely love this slow-cooker oatmeal. The steel-cut oats have so much flavor and texture. My family loves to sprinkle toasted pecans on top.
—*Angela Lively, Conroe, TX*

- -

PREP: 10 min. • **COOK:** 6 hours
MAKES: 8 servings

- 6 cups water
- 1½ cups steel-cut oats
- 1½ cups unsweetened applesauce
- ¼ cup maple syrup
- 1½ tsp. ground cinnamon
- ½ tsp. ground nutmeg
- ⅛ tsp. salt
- 1 large apple, chopped
  Optional: Sliced apples, toasted pecans and additional maple syrup

In a 4-qt. slow cooker, combine the first 7 ingredients. Cover and cook on low for 6-8 hours or until liquid is absorbed. Stir in chopped apple. If desired, top servings with apple slices, pecans and syrup.
1¼ cups: 171 cal., 2g fat (0 sat. fat), 0 chol., 39mg sod., 36g carb. (13g sugars, 4g fiber), 4g pro.

SLOW-COOKER
AL PASTOR BOWLS

TEST KITCHEN TIP

In this recipe, it's important to use steel-cut oats, which need to cook longer than rolled oats. You might find them labeled as Irish oats.

APPLE MAPLE CHOPS

This recipe is one of my family's favorites—my children just love it. The pork is super tender, and the maple syrup really makes the dish. It is so easy since it's made in the slow cooker!
—*Niki Schiefer, Attica, OH*

PREP: 10 min. • **COOK:** 3 hours
MAKES: 6 servings

- 6   bone-in center-cut pork loin chops (7 oz. each)
- 1   Tbsp. olive oil
- 3   medium apples, peeled and sliced
- 1   cup water
- ½   cup maple syrup
- ¼   cup apple butter
- 2   Tbsp. Dijon mustard
- 1   Tbsp. Worcestershire sauce
- ¼   tsp. garlic salt with parsley
- ¼   tsp. pepper

1. Pat pork chops dry with a paper towel. In a large skillet, heat oil over medium-high heat. Quickly cook the chops until browned, 1-2 minutes per side; remove from pan. Place chops and apples in a 5-qt. slow cooker.
2. In a small bowl, combine the remaining ingredients; pour sauce mixture over the chops and apples. Cover and cook on low until meat is tender, 3-4 hours.

1 pork chop with apples: 407 cal., 16g fat (6g sat. fat), 97mg chol., 269mg sod., 31g carb. (27g sugars, 1g fiber), 32g pro.

DID YOU KNOW?

It takes between 20 and 50 gallons of tree sap to make just one gallon of maple syrup. So savor the sweet stuff!

**SLOW-COOKER
KALUA PORK & CABBAGE**

SLOW-COOKER
KALUA PORK & CABBAGE

My slow-cooker pork has four ingredients and takes less than 10 minutes to prep. The result tastes just like the kalua pork made in Hawaii that's slow-roasted all day in an underground oven.
—*Rholinelle DeTorres, San Jose, CA*

PREP: 10 min. • **COOK:** 9 hours
MAKES: 12 servings

- 7   bacon strips, divided
- 1   boneless pork shoulder butt roast (3 to 4 lbs.), well trimmed
- 1   Tbsp. coarse sea salt
- 1   medium head cabbage (about 2 lbs.), coarsely chopped

1. Line bottom of a 6-qt. slow cooker with 4 bacon strips. Sprinkle all sides of roast with salt; place in slow cooker. Arrange remaining bacon over top of roast.
2. Cook, covered, on low 8-10 hours or until pork is tender. Add cabbage, spreading cabbage around roast. Cook, covered, 1-1¼ hours longer or until cabbage is tender.
3. Remove the pork to a serving bowl; shred pork with 2 forks. Using a slotted spoon, add cabbage to pork and toss to combine. If desired, skim fat from some of the cooking juices; stir juices into pork mixture or serve on the side.

1 cup: 227 cal., 13g fat (5g sat. fat), 72mg chol., 622mg sod., 4g carb. (2g sugars, 2g fiber), 22g pro.

**APPLE
MAPLE CHOPS**

SLOW-COOKED PORK VERDE

Comforting and hearty, this easy entree is perfect winter fare. Serve with French bread and a salad for a well-rounded weeknight dinner.
—Taste of Home *Test Kitchen*

- -

PREP: 15 min. • **COOK:** 6 hours
MAKES: 8 servings

- 3   medium carrots, sliced
- 1   boneless pork shoulder butt roast (3 to 4 lbs.)
- 1   can (15 oz.) black beans, rinsed and drained
- 1   can (10 oz.) green enchilada sauce
- ¼   cup minced fresh cilantro
- 1   Tbsp. cornstarch
- ¼   cup cold water
     Hot cooked rice

1. Place carrots in a 5-qt. slow cooker. Cut roast in half; place in slow cooker. Add beans, enchilada sauce and cilantro. Cover and cook on low until tender, 6-8 hours. Remove roast to a serving platter; keep warm.

2. Skim fat from cooking juices. Transfer cooking liquid, carrots and beans to a small saucepan. Bring to a boil. Combine the cornstarch and water until smooth. Gradually stir into the pan. Bring to a boil; cook and stir until thickened, 2 minutes. Serve with meat and rice.

1 serving: 346 cal., 18g fat (6g sat. fat), 101mg chol., 384mg sod., 13g carb. (2g sugars, 3g fiber), 32g pro. **Diabetic exchanges:** 4 lean meat, 1 starch.

TERIYAKI-PORTOBELLO PORK LOIN

My family loves this teriyaki pork roast, and the slow cooker does most of the work. When I get home from school, the whole house smells wonderful. Since I serve it with instant rice and frozen vegetables, I'm only five minutes from sitting down to a home-cooked meal.
—Lori Harris, Montgomery City, MO

- -

PREP: 25 min. • **COOK:** 6 hours
MAKES: 8 servings

- 1   boneless pork loin roast (3 to 4 lbs.)
- ½   cup all-purpose flour
- 1   tsp. Montreal steak seasoning
- 2   Tbsp. olive oil, divided
- 2   cups sliced baby portobello mushrooms
- 1   medium onion, thinly sliced
- 1   cup water
- 1   cup reduced-sodium teriyaki sauce
- 1   envelope (¾ oz.) mushroom gravy mix
- 2   Tbsp. cornstarch
- 2   Tbsp. cold water
     Hot cooked rice
     Chopped chives, optional

1. Cut roast in half. In a large shallow dish, combine flour and steak seasoning. Add pork, 1 portion at a time, and turn to coat.

2. In a large skillet, brown the roast in 1 Tbsp. oil on all sides. Transfer meat and drippings to a 4-qt slow cooker. In the same skillet, saute mushrooms and onion in remaining oil until tender; add to slow cooker.

3. In a small bowl, combine the water, teriyaki sauce and gravy mix; pour over pork. Cover and cook on low 6-8 hours or until pork is tender.

4. Remove pork to a serving platter and keep warm. Skim fat from cooking juices; transfer to a large saucepan. Bring liquid to a boil. Combine cornstarch and cold water until smooth; gradually stir into the pan. Bring to a boil; cook and stir for 2 minutes or until thickened. Serve with pork and rice. If desired, top with chives.

5 oz. cooked pork with ½ cup gravy: 308 cal., 11g fat (3g sat. fat), 85mg chol., 852mg sod., 14g carb. (8g sugars, 1g fiber), 36g pro.

TERIYAKI-PORTOBELLO PORK LOIN

**ITALIAN PORK CHOP
DINNER**

PORK & PINTO BEANS

I first tasted this dish
at an office potluck, and
now I serve it often when
company comes. I set out
an array of toppings and
let everyone create their own taco salad.
—*Darlene Brenden, Salem, OR*

PREP: 25 min. + soaking • **COOK:** 8 hours
MAKES: 10 servings

- 1 lb. dried pinto beans
- 1 boneless pork loin roast
  (3 to 4 lbs.), halved
- 1 can (14½ oz.) stewed tomatoes
- 5 medium carrots, chopped
- 4 celery ribs, chopped
- 1½ cups water
- 2 cans (4 oz. each) chopped
  green chiles
- 2 Tbsp. chili powder
- 4 garlic cloves, minced
- 2 tsp. ground cumin
- 1 tsp. dried oregano
  Dash pepper
  Tortilla chips or tortillas (10 in.)
  Optional toppings: Chopped green
  onions, sliced ripe olives, chopped
  tomatoes, shredded cheddar cheese,
  sour cream and shredded lettuce

ITALIAN PORK CHOP DINNER

My family loves this meal after church
services. I serve it with spaghetti, salad
and garlic bread.
—*Martina Williams, Grovetown, GA*

PREP: 30 min. • **COOK:** 4 hours
MAKES: 6 servings

- 6 bacon strips, diced
- ½ lb. fresh mushrooms, sliced
- 1 medium onion, finely chopped
- 1 garlic clove, minced
- ¾ cup all-purpose flour
- 4 tsp. Italian seasoning, divided
- ¼ tsp. salt
- ¼ tsp. garlic powder
- ⅛ tsp. pepper
  Dash cayenne pepper
- 6 bone-in pork loin chops (1 in. thick)
- 1 can (14½ oz.) diced tomatoes,
  undrained
- 1 can (14½ oz.) chicken broth
- 1 can (6 oz.) tomato paste
- 1 pkg. (10 oz.) frozen peas, thawed
  Hot cooked pasta

1. In a large skillet, cook the bacon over
medium heat until crisp. Using a slotted
spoon, remove to paper towels. In the
drippings, saute mushrooms, onion and
garlic until tender. Transfer to a 5-qt. slow
cooker with a slotted spoon. In a shallow
bowl, combine the flour, 3 tsp. Italian
seasoning, salt, garlic powder, pepper
and cayenne; coat pork chops with the
flour mixture.
2. In the same skillet, brown the pork
chops; transfer to the slow cooker.
Top with tomatoes and bacon. Combine
the broth, tomato paste and remaining
Italian seasoning; add to slow cooker.
3. Cover and cook on low until pork is
tender, 4-6 hours; add peas during the
last 30 minutes. Serve with pasta.
1 pork chop: 528 cal., 23g fat (8g sat. fat),
124mg chol., 842mg sod., 31g carb. (8g
sugars, 5g fiber), 48g pro.

1. Sort the beans and rinse with cold
water. Soak beans according to the
package directions.
2. Drain and rinse beans, discarding
liquid. Place roast in a 5-qt. slow cooker.
In a bowl, combine the beans, tomatoes,
carrots, celery, water, chiles, chili powder,
garlic, cumin, oregano and pepper. Pour
over roast.
3. Cover and cook on high for 3 hours.
Reduce heat to low; cook until beans
are tender, 5 hours longer.
4. Remove the meat, shred with 2 forks
and return to slow cooker. With a
slotted spoon, serve the meat mixture
over chips or in tortillas with toppings
as desired.
1 serving: 366cal., 7g fat (2g sat. fat), 68mg
chol., 290mg sod., 37g carb. (5g sugars,
10g fiber), 37g pro.

MUSHROOM
PORK TENDERLOIN

MUSHROOM PORK TENDERLOIN

This juicy pork tenderloin in a savory gravy is the best you'll ever taste. Prepared with canned soups, it couldn't be easier to make.
—*Donna Hughes, Rochester, NH*

PREP: 5 min. • **COOK:** 4 hours
MAKES: 6 servings

- 2 pork tenderloins (1 lb. each)
- 1 can (10¾ oz.) condensed cream of mushroom soup, undiluted
- 1 can (10¾ oz.) condensed golden mushroom soup, undiluted
- 1 can (10½ oz.) condensed French onion soup, undiluted
   Hot mashed potatoes, optional

Place pork in a 3-qt. slow cooker. In a small bowl, combine soups; stir until smooth. Pour over pork. Cover and cook on low until pork is tender, 4-5 hours. If desired, serve with mashed potatoes.

4 oz. cooked pork with ⅔ cup sauce: 269 cal., 10g fat (3g sat. fat), 89mg chol., 951mg sod., 10g carb. (2g sugars, 2g fiber), 32g pro.

"This is a winner! Easy and scrumptious, the soups are the perfect combination for tender, tasty pork loin and create a wonderful gravy. I used a large (2.5 lb.) pork loin and it worked perfectly! Will definitely make this again."
—SOONER GAL, TASTEOFHOME.COM

BARBECUE PORK TACOS
WITH APPLE SLAW

BARBECUE PORK TACOS WITH APPLE SLAW

We celebrate taco Tuesdays, so I like to keep things interesting by switching up the varieties. These pork tacos are super simple to prepare.
—*Jenn Tidwell, Fair Oaks, CA*

PREP: 15 min. • **COOK:** 2¼ hours
MAKES: 8 servings

- 2 pork tenderloins (1 lb. each)
- 1 can (12 oz.) root beer

SLAW
- 6 cups shredded red cabbage (about 12 oz.)
- 2 medium Granny Smith apples, julienned
- ⅓ cup cider vinegar
- ¼ cup minced fresh cilantro
- ¼ cup lime juice
- 2 Tbsp. sugar
- ½ tsp. salt
- ½ tsp. pepper

ASSEMBLY
- 1 bottle (18 oz.) barbecue sauce
- 16 taco shells

1. Place pork in a 3-qt. slow cooker. Pour root beer over top. Cook, covered, on low just until tender (a thermometer inserted in pork should read at least 145°), 2-2½ hours.

2. Meanwhile, in a large bowl, toss the slaw ingredients. Refrigerate, covered, until serving.

3. Remove tenderloins to a cutting board; let stand, covered, 5 minutes. Discard cooking juices.

4. Coarsely chop pork; return to slow cooker. Stir in barbecue sauce; heat through. Serve in taco shells; top with some of the slaw. Serve remaining slaw on the side.

2 tacos with 1 cup slaw: 396 cal., 9g fat (2g sat. fat), 64mg chol., 954mg sod., 53g carb. (31g sugars, 3g fiber), 25g pro.

PEACHY PORK STEAKS

My mom has been preparing this pork dish for years. She always found it a surefire way to get picky children to eat meat. No one can refuse these succulent steaks!
—*Sandy McKenzie, Braham, MN*

PREP: 20 min. • **COOK:** 5 hours
MAKES: 4 servings

- 2 Tbsp. canola oil
- 4 pork blade steaks (½ in. thick and 7 oz. each), trimmed
- ¾ tsp. dried basil
- ¼ tsp. salt
  Dash pepper
- 1 can (15¼ oz.) sliced peaches in syrup, undrained
- 2 Tbsp. white vinegar
- 1 Tbsp. beef bouillon granules
- 2 Tbsp. cornstarch
- ¼ cup cold water
  Hot cooked rice

1. In a large skillet, heat oil over medium-high heat. Brown pork; sprinkle with basil, salt and pepper. Drain peaches, reserving syrup. Place peaches in a 5-qt. slow cooker; top with pork. In a small bowl, combine syrup, vinegar and bouillon; pour over pork.

2. Cover and cook on high, 1 hour. Reduce heat to low and cook until pork is tender, 4 hours longer. Remove pork and peaches to a serving platter; keep warm.

3. Skim fat from cooking liquid; place liquid in a small saucepan. Combine cornstarch and cold water until smooth; stir into cooking liquid. Bring to a boil; cook and stir until thickened, 2 minutes. Serve the pork, peaches and sauce with rice.

1 serving: 490 cal., 27g fat (8g sat. fat), 118mg chol., 869mg sod., 25g carb. (20g sugars, 1g fiber), 34g pro.

CHICKEN-FRIED CHOPS

CHICKEN-FRIED CHOPS

It takes only a few minutes to brown the meat before assembling this savory meal. The pork chops simmer all day in a flavorful sauce until they're tender.
—*Connie Slocum, Brunswick, GA*

PREP: 15 min. • **COOK:** 6 hours
MAKES: 6 servings

- ½ cup all-purpose flour
- 2 tsp. salt
- 1½ tsp. ground mustard
- ½ tsp. garlic powder
- 6 pork loin chops (¾ in. thick), trimmed
- 2 Tbsp. canola oil
- 1 can (10¾ oz.) condensed cream of chicken soup, undiluted
- ⅓ cup water

In a shallow bowl, combine flour, salt, mustard and garlic powder; add pork chops and turn to coat. In a large skillet, heat oil over medium-high heat; brown meat on both sides in batches. Place in a 5-qt. slow cooker. Combine soup and water; pour over chops. Cover and cook on low until meat is tender, 6-8 hours. If desired, thicken pan juices and serve with the pork chops.

1 pork chop: 453 cal., 27g fat (9g sat. fat), 115mg chol., 1232mg sod., 13g carb. (0 sugars, 1g fiber), 38g pro.

LAZY MAN'S RIBS

I've made these tender ribs for a lot of my buddies—including my preacher. Some have even suggested that I try bottling my sauce and selling it to the public!
—*Allan Stackhouse Jr., Jennings, LA*

PREP: 20 min. • **COOK:** 5 hours
MAKES: 4 servings

- 2½ lbs. pork baby back ribs, cut into 8 pieces
- 2 tsp. Cajun seasoning
- 1 medium onion, sliced
- 1 cup ketchup
- ½ cup packed brown sugar
- ⅓ cup orange juice
- ⅓ cup cider vinegar
- ¼ cup molasses
- 2 Tbsp. Worcestershire sauce
- 1 Tbsp. barbecue sauce
- 1 tsp. stone-ground mustard
- 1 tsp. paprika
- ½ tsp. garlic powder
- ½ tsp. liquid smoke, optional

Dash salt
- 5 tsp. cornstarch
- 1 Tbsp. cold water

1. Rub ribs with Cajun seasoning. Layer ribs and onion in a 5-qt. slow cooker. In a small bowl, combine the ketchup, brown sugar, orange juice, vinegar, molasses, Worcestershire sauce, barbecue sauce, mustard, paprika, garlic powder, liquid smoke if desired, and salt. Pour over ribs. Cover and cook on low until meat is tender, 5-6 hours.

2. Remove ribs and keep warm. Strain cooking juices and skim fat; transfer to a small saucepan. Combine cornstarch and water until smooth; stir into the juices. Bring to a boil; cook and stir until thickened, 2 minutes. Serve with ribs.

1 serving: 753 cal., 39g fat (14g sat. fat), 153mg chol., 1335mg sod., 70g carb. (52g sugars, 2g fiber), 33g pro.

CANADIAN PORK ROAST WITH GRAVY

My son wanted a recipe he could make in the slow cooker while he took his new girlfriend out for a bike ride on their second date. This is the meal I came up with for him.
—*Marilyn McCrory, Creston, BC*

PREP: 20 min. • **COOK:** 5 hours
MAKES: 10 servings

- 1 boneless pork loin roast (3 lbs.)
- ⅓ cup maple syrup
- 1 Tbsp. lemon juice
- 1 Tbsp. Dijon mustard
- 1 garlic clove, minced
- 2 Tbsp. cornstarch
- ¼ cup cold water

1. Cut roast in half. Transfer to a 5-qt. slow cooker. Combine syrup, lemon juice, mustard and garlic; pour over pork. Cover and cook on low 5-6 hours or until meat is tender.

2. Remove meat to a serving platter; keep warm. Strain cooking juices; transfer 1 cup to a small saucepan. Combine cornstarch and water until smooth; stir into cooking juices. Bring to a boil; cook and stir for 2 minutes or until thickened. Slice roast; serve with gravy.

1 serving: 205 cal., 6g fat (2g sat. fat), 68mg chol., 76mg sod., 9g carb. (6g sugars, 0 fiber), 26g pro. **Diabetic exchanges:** 4 lean meat, ½ starch.

LAZY MAN'S RIBS

HEARTY SLOW-COOKER BREAKFAST HASH

SLOW-COOKER SAUCY PORK CHOPS

I serve these tender chops a couple of times a month because we love them. The rich and zesty sauce is delicious over mashed potatoes, rice or even noodles.
—*Sharon Polk, Lapeer, MI*

PREP: 10 min. • **COOK:** 4 hours
MAKES: 8 servings

- 8 boneless pork loin chops (4 oz. each)
- ¼ tsp. salt
- ⅛ tsp. pepper
- 2 Tbsp. canola oil
- 2 cans (10¾ oz. each) condensed cream of chicken soup, undiluted
- 1 medium onion, chopped
- ½ cup ketchup
- 2 Tbsp. Worcestershire sauce
  Hot cooked mashed potatoes or rice

1. Sprinkle pork chops with salt and pepper. In a large skillet, heat oil over medium heat. Brown pork chops in batches; drain. Transfer to a 3-qt. slow cooker.
2. In a large bowl, combine soup, onion, ketchup and Worcestershire sauce; pour over chops. Cover and cook on high for 4-5 hours or until meat is tender. Serve with potatoes or rice.

1 pork chop with ⅓ cup sauce: 282 cal., 15g fat (4g sat. fat), 61mg chol., 890mg sod., 12g carb. (6g sugars, 2g fiber), 23g pro.

HEARTY SLOW-COOKER BREAKFAST HASH

This sweet and savory hash certainly won't leave you hungry—the sausage, veggies and eggs will fill you up. The hint of maple syrup makes it all feel extra cozy.
—*Colleen Delawder, Herndon, VA*

PREP: 25 min. • **COOK:** 5 hours
MAKES: 4 servings

- 8 to 10 frozen fully cooked breakfast sausage links
- 4 cups diced red potatoes (about 1½ lbs.)
- 4 medium carrots, diced
- 2 green onions, thinly sliced (white and pale green parts only)
- 2 Tbsp. extra virgin olive oil
- 1 Tbsp. red wine vinegar
- 1 Tbsp. plus 2 tsp. snipped fresh dill, divided
- 1 tsp. kosher salt
- ½ tsp. coarsely ground pepper, divided
- ¼ tsp. crushed red pepper flakes
- 2 Tbsp. crumbled feta cheese
- 1 Tbsp. butter
- 4 large eggs
- 2 Tbsp. maple syrup

1. In a large skillet over medium heat, cook sausages, turning occasionally, until heated through, 8-9 minutes. Combine the next 5 ingredients in a 3-qt. slow cooker. Add 1 Tbsp. dill, kosher salt, ¼ tsp. pepper and red pepper flakes. Arrange sausages on top of vegetable mixture. Cook, covered, on low until the vegetables are tender, 5-6 hours. Transfer the vegetables to a serving platter; sprinkle with feta cheese. Top with sausages.
2. Meanwhile, in a large skillet, heat butter over medium heat. Add the eggs; cook to desired doneness. Arrange eggs over vegetables. Sprinkle with remaining dill and pepper; drizzle with maple syrup.
1 serving: 446 cal., 25g fat (8g sat. fat), 212mg chol., 911mg sod., 42g carb. (12g sugars, 5g fiber), 14g pro.

SLOW-COOKER
SAUCY PORK CHOPS

PORK SPARERIBS

Who knew that five ingredients could be so delicious? These ribs are so tender they literally fall off the bone.
—*Shari Sieg, Silver Springs,, FL*

- -

PREP: 5 min. • **COOK:** 6 hours
MAKES: 8 servings

- 4 lbs. pork spareribs
- 2 cans (28 oz. each) diced tomatoes, undrained
- 2 cups barbecue sauce
- ¼ cup packed brown sugar
- ¼ cup white wine vinegar

Place ribs in a 4- or 5-qt. slow cooker. Combine the remaining ingredients; pour over ribs. Cover and cook on low until pork is tender, 6-8 hours. Serve with a slotted spoon.

1 serving: 606 cal., 33g fat (12g sat. fat), 129mg chol., 1114mg sod., 44g carb. (36g sugars, 4g fiber), 33g pro.

CITRUS-HERB PORK ROAST

The genius combination of seasonings and citrus in this tender roast reminds us why we cherish tasty recipes.
—*Laura Brodine, Colorado Springs, CO*

- -

PREP: 25 min. • **COOK:** 4 hours
MAKES: 8 servings

- 1 boneless pork sirloin roast (3 to 4 lbs.)
- 1 tsp. dried oregano
- ½ tsp. ground ginger
- ½ tsp. pepper
- 2 medium onions, cut into thin wedges
- 1 cup plus 3 Tbsp. orange juice, divided
- 1 Tbsp. sugar
- 1 Tbsp. white grapefruit juice
- 1 Tbsp. steak sauce
- 1 Tbsp. reduced-sodium soy sauce
- 1 tsp. grated orange zest
- ½ tsp. salt
- 3 Tbsp. cornstarch
  Hot cooked egg noodles
  Minced fresh oregano, optional

1. Cut the roast in half. In a small bowl, combine the oregano, ginger and pepper; rub over pork. In a large nonstick skillet coated with cooking spray, brown roast on all sides. Transfer to a 4-qt. slow cooker; add onions.

2. In a small bowl, combine 1 cup orange juice, sugar, grapefruit juice, steak sauce and soy sauce; pour over top. Cover and cook on low for 4-5 hours or until meat is tender. Remove meat and onions to a serving platter; keep warm.

3. Skim fat from cooking juices; transfer to a small saucepan. Add orange zest and salt. Bring to a boil. Combine cornstarch and the remaining orange juice until smooth. Gradually stir into the pan. Bring to a boil; cook and stir for 2 minutes or until thickened. Serve with pork and noodles; if desired, sprinkle with oregano.

5 oz. cooked pork with 2 Tbsp. gravy: 289 cal., 10g fat (4g sat. fat), 102mg chol., 326mg sod., 13g carb. (8g sugars, 1g fiber), 35g pro. **Diabetic exchanges:** 5 lean meat, 1 starch.

CITRUS-HERB PORK ROAST

PEAR & POMEGRANATE LAMB TAGINE

Pomegranate, pear and orange go together so well that I decided to use them to prepare a Middle Eastern-themed tagine with lamb. This tastes delicious served over couscous, polenta or cauliflower mashed with some feta cheese.
—*Arlene Erlbach, Morton Grove, IL*

PREP: 20 min. • **COOK:** 6 hours
MAKES: 4 servings

2½ lbs. lamb shanks
2 large pears, finely chopped
3 cups thinly sliced shallots
½ cup orange juice, divided
½ cup pomegranate juice, divided
1 Tbsp. honey
1½ tsp. ground cinnamon
1 tsp. salt
1 tsp. ground allspice
1 tsp. ground cardamom
¼ cup pomegranate seeds
¼ cup minced fresh parsley
Cooked couscous, optional

1. Place lamb in a 5- or 6-qt. oval slow cooker. Add pears and shallots. Combine ¼ cup orange juice, ¼ cup pomegranate juice, honey and seasonings; pour mixture over shallots.
2. Cook, covered, on low for 6-8 hours or until meat is tender. Remove lamb to a rimmed serving platter; keep warm. Stir remaining orange and pomegranate juices into cooking liquid; pour over lamb. Sprinkle with pomegranate seeds and parsley. If desired, serve over couscous.
½ lamb shank with 1 cup vegetables: 438 cal., 13g fat (5g sat. fat), 99mg chol., 680mg sod., 52g carb. (28g sugars, 5g fiber), 31g pro.

TEST KITCHEN TIPS
• D'Anjou pears are a smart choice and are usually available from November through late spring.
• Fresh-squeezed orange juice (with its pulp) adds an extra-special touch to the recipe.

PEAR &
POMEGRANATE
LAMB TAGINE

PORTOBELLO
ROPA VIEJA

PORTOBELLO ROPA VIEJA

I created this version of a Mexican favorite for my family using meaty portobello mushrooms to mimic meat. Serve with rice to round out the meal.
—*Arlene Erlbach, Morton Grove, IL*

PREP: 25 min. • **COOK:** 5 hours
MAKES: 6 servings

- 2 Tbsp. canola oil
- 1 medium onion, halved and thinly sliced
- 1 poblano pepper, thinly sliced
- 1 medium sweet red pepper, thinly sliced
- 1 jar (12 oz.) sofrito tomato cooking base
- 1 cup fire-roasted diced tomatoes
- 3 Tbsp. lime juice, divided
- 2 Tbsp. brown sugar
- ¾ tsp. garlic powder
- 6 large portobello mushrooms, thinly sliced
- 1 Tbsp. adobo seasoning
  Hot cooked rice
  Minced fresh cilantro

1. In a large skillet, heat oil over medium-high heat. Add onion; cook and stir until tender, 5-7 minutes. Add poblano and red peppers; cook and stir until crisp-tender, 3-4 minutes. Transfer to a greased 5- or 6-qt. slow cooker. Stir in sofrito, tomatoes, 2 Tbsp. lime juice, brown sugar and garlic powder.
2. Toss the mushrooms with the adobo seasoning; place on top of pepper mixture. Cook, covered, on low until mushrooms are tender, 5-6 hours. Stir in remaining 1 Tbsp. lime juice. Serve warm with rice and cilantro.
⅔ cup: 253 cal., 15g fat (0 sat. fat), 0 chol., 1449mg sod., 19g carb. (9g sugars, 4g fiber), 10g pro.

GREEK SAUSAGE
& PEPPERS

GREEK SAUSAGE & PEPPERS

This recipe is an old family favorite. My grandmother, mother and I make this every year for Christmas Eve. Just toss all the ingredients in your slow cooker and let the meal cook all day on low. It makes the house smell amazing and is wonderful comfort food for a chilly holiday. You can double the recipe and freeze the other portion for a hot meal in a pinch.
—*Debbie Vair, Wake Forest, NC*

PREP: 30 min. • **COOK:** 5½ hours
MAKES: 12 servings

- 4 lbs. loukaniko or other smoked sausage, cut into ½-in. slices
- 1 each large sweet yellow, orange and red peppers, chopped
- 1 large sweet onion, chopped
- 2 cups beef stock
- 1 whole garlic bulb, minced
- 1 Tbsp. minced fresh oregano or 1 tsp. dried oregano
- 1 tsp. coarse sea salt
- 1 tsp. coarsely ground pepper
- 3-3½ cups cherry tomatoes
  Hot cooked rice, optional

In a 7- or 8-qt. slow cooker, combine sausage, sweet peppers, onion, stock, garlic, oregano, salt and pepper. Cook, covered, on low until vegetables are tender, 5-6 hours. Add tomatoes; cook until wilted, about 30 minutes longer. If desired, serve with rice.
1¼ cups: 504 cal., 41g fat (17g sat. fat), 101mg chol., 1958mg sod., 10g carb. (7g sugars, 2g fiber), 23g pro.

MEXICAN PORK ROAST

Friends who live in Mexico shared this dish with me years ago. They cooked the roast in a clay pot in a slow oven, but I found the recipe works well in a slow cooker. The leftovers make excellent burritos and tacos.

—*Chuck Allen, Dana Point, CA*

- -

PREP: 25 min. • **COOK:** 8 hours
MAKES: 8 servings

- 2 Tbsp. olive oil
- 2 medium onions, sliced
- 2 medium carrots, sliced
- 2 jalapeno peppers, seeded and chopped
- 3 garlic cloves, minced
- ½ cup water
- ½ cup chicken broth
- 1 tsp. ground coriander
- ½ tsp. salt
- ½ tsp. ground cumin
- ½ tsp. dried oregano
- ¼ tsp. pepper
- 1 boneless pork shoulder butt roast (3 lbs.)

1. In a large skillet, heat oil over medium-high heat. Cook the onions, carrots and jalapenos until tender, 2-3 minutes. Add garlic; cook 1 minute longer. Transfer to a 5-qt. slow cooker; add water and broth.
2. In a small bowl, combine coriander, salt, cumin, oregano and pepper; rub over roast. Cut roast in half; place in the slow cooker. Cover and cook on low until meat is tender, 8-9 hours.
3. Transfer the roast and vegetables to a serving platter; keep warm. Strain cooking juices and skim fat. Pour into a small saucepan. Bring to a boil; cook until liquid is reduced to about 1 cup. Serve with roast and vegetables.
Note: Wear disposable gloves when cutting hot peppers; the oils can burn skin. Avoid touching your face.
1 serving: 479 cal., 24g fat (8g sat. fat), 194mg chol., 386mg sod., 6g carb. (3g sugars, 2g fiber), 56g pro.

SATAY-STYLE
PORK STEW

❄ SATAY-STYLE PORK STEW

Thai cuisine features flavors that are hot and sour, salty and sweet. This pork satay balances all of them using ginger and red pepper flakes, rice vinegar, garlic and creamy peanut butter.

—*Nicole Werner, Ann Arbor, MI*

- -

PREP: 25 min. • **COOK:** 8 hours
MAKES: 6 servings

- 1 boneless pork shoulder butt roast (3 to 4 lbs.), cut into 1½-in. cubes
- 2 medium parsnips, peeled and sliced
- 1 small sweet red pepper, thinly sliced
- 1 cup chicken broth
- ¼ cup reduced-sodium teriyaki sauce
- 2 Tbsp. rice vinegar
- 1 Tbsp. minced fresh gingerroot
- 1 Tbsp. honey
- 2 garlic cloves, minced
- ½ tsp. crushed red pepper flakes
- ¼ cup creamy peanut butter
     Hot cooked rice, optional
- 2 green onions, chopped
- 2 Tbsp. chopped dry roasted peanuts

In a 3-qt. slow cooker, combine the first 10 ingredients. Cover and cook on low until pork is tender, 8-10 hours. Skim fat; stir in peanut butter. Serve with rice if desired; top with onions and peanuts.
Freeze option: Before adding toppings, freeze cooled stew in freezer containers. To use, partially thaw in refrigerator overnight. Heat through in a saucepan, stirring occasionally; if necessary, add a little broth or water.
1 cup: 519 cal., 30g fat (10g sat. fat), 135mg chol., 597mg sod., 19g carb. (9g sugars, 3g fiber), 44g pro.

PORK ROAST CUBANO

It takes me just minutes to prepare this recipe, and the slow cooker does the rest of the work! It's a one-dish meal that's real comfort food for my family.
—*Roxanne Chan, Albany, CA*

PREP: 30 min. • **COOK:** 7 hours
MAKES: 8 servings

- 3 lbs. boneless pork shoulder butt roast
- 2 Tbsp. olive oil
- 1 can (15 oz.) black beans, rinsed and drained
- 1 medium sweet potato, cut into ½-in. cubes
- 1 small sweet red pepper, cubed
- 1 can (13.66 oz.) light coconut milk
- ½ cup salsa verde
- 1 tsp. minced fresh gingerroot
- 2 green onions, thinly sliced
  Sliced papaya

1. In a large skillet, brown roast in oil on all sides. Transfer to a 5-qt. slow cooker. Add black beans, sweet potato and red pepper. In a small bowl, mix coconut milk, salsa and ginger; pour over meat.
2. Cook, covered, on low 7-9 hours or until pork is tender. Sprinkle with green onions; serve with papaya.

6 oz. cooked pork with ¾ cup vegetables: 430 cal., 24g fat (9g sat. fat), 101mg chol., 322mg sod., 18g carb. (6g sugars, 5g fiber), 33g pro.

"This is fantastic! I don't usually like pork, but this dish is one of my favorites. I make this alongside some rice and Cuban black beans. Yum!"
—THETALLENTREE, TASTEOFHOME.COM

HERBED SAUSAGE & TOMATO PASTA SAUCE

I believe in the wisdom of using a wine for cooking that you'd be happy to drink, rather than an inferior one. I use a Chianti for this sausage and herb sauce.
—*Jennifer Storment, Belgrade, MT*

PREP: 30 min. • **COOK:** 6½ hours
MAKES: 12 servings (3 qt.)

- 2 lbs. bulk pork sausage
- 1 lb. Italian sausage links, chopped
- 1 small onion, chopped
- 1 Tbsp. olive oil
- 5 garlic cloves, minced
- 2 Tbsp. plus ½ cup dry red wine, divided
- 2 cans (28 oz. each) whole tomatoes, undrained
- 2 cans (15 oz. each) tomato sauce
- 1 can (6 oz.) tomato paste
- 1 Tbsp. chicken bouillon granules
- 3 tsp. each Italian seasoning and dried oregano
- 2 tsp. sugar
- 1 tsp. each dried thyme, marjoram and rosemary, crushed
- 2 bay leaves
- ¼ tsp. pepper
  Hot cooked pasta

1. In a Dutch oven over medium heat, cook pork sausage, Italian sausage and onion in oil until meat is no longer pink, breaking pork into crumbles. Add garlic; cook 1 minute longer. Transfer to a 6-qt. slow cooker.
2. Add 2 Tbsp. wine to Dutch oven, stirring to loosen browned bits from pan. Pour over meat mixture. Stir in tomatoes, tomato sauce and paste, bouillon, Italian seasoning, oregano, sugar, thyme, marjoram, rosemary, bay leaves and pepper.
3. Cover and cook on low, 6-8 hours. Stir in remaining wine; cover and cook 30 minutes longer. Discard bay leaves; serve sauce with pasta.

1 cup: 297 cal., 20g fat (7g sat. fat), 43mg chol., 1274mg sod., 15g carb. (8g sugars, 3g fiber), 13g pro.

PORK ROAST CUBANO

Soups, Sides & Sandwiches

BLACKBERRY SRIRACHA CHICKEN SLIDERS

❄ BLACKBERRY SRIRACHA CHICKEN SLIDERS

Dump everything in a slow cooker and then watch these spicy-sweet sliders become an instant party-time classic.
—*Julie Peterson, Crofton, MD*

- -

PREP: 20 min. • **COOK:** 5 hours
MAKES: 1 dozen

- 1   jar (10 oz.) seedless blackberry spreadable fruit
- ¼   cup ketchup
- ¼   cup balsamic vinegar
- ¼   cup Sriracha chili sauce
- 2   Tbsp. molasses
- 1   Tbsp. Dijon mustard
- ¼   tsp. salt
- 3½   lbs. bone-in chicken thighs
- 1   large onion, thinly sliced
- 4   garlic cloves, minced
- 12   pretzel mini buns, split
      Addtional Sriracha chili sauce
      Leaf lettuce and tomato slices

1. In a 4- or 5-qt. slow cooker, stir together the first 7 ingredients. Add chicken, onion and garlic. Toss to combine.

2. Cook, covered, on low until chicken is tender, 5-6 hours. Remove chicken. When cool enough to handle, remove bones and skin; discard. Shred meat with 2 forks. Reserve 3 cups cooking juices; discard remaining juices. Skim fat from reserved juices. Return chicken and reserved juices to slow cooker; heat through. Using slotted spoon, serve on pretzel buns. Drizzle with additional chili sauce; top with lettuce and tomato.

Freeze option: Freeze cooled chicken mixture in freezer containers. To use, partially thaw in refrigerator overnight. Heat through in a covered saucepan, stirring occasionally; add a little broth if necessary.

1 slider: 352 cal., 14g fat (3g sat. fat), 63mg chol., 413mg sod., 35g carb. (12g sugars, 1g fiber), 21g pro.

SAVORY RICE-STUFFED APPLES

My family loves apples. Since we have several trees, I am challenged to create new recipes every fall. This side dish is wonderful with pork roast and so carefree due to the use of the slow cooker.
—*Roxanne Chan, Albany, CA*

PREP: 15 min. • **COOK:** 1½ hours
MAKES: 6 servings

- 6   medium apples
- ½   cup cooked brown rice
- 1   Tbsp. thinly sliced green onions
- 1   Tbsp. chopped sweet red pepper
- 1   Tbsp. minced fresh parsley
- 1   Tbsp. finely chopped celery
- 1   Tbsp. chopped carrot
- 1   Tbsp. chopped walnuts
- ½   tsp. ground cinnamon
- 2   Tbsp. shredded cheddar cheese
- 1   cup unsweetened apple juice
- 1   Tbsp. chili sauce

Core apples, leaving bottoms intact. In a medium bowl, combine the brown rice and next 8 ingredients; mix well. Fill each apple with about 2 Tbsp. filling, packing it well. Place the stuffed apples in a greased 4-qt. slow cooker. Pour in the apple juice and chili sauce. Cover and cook on high until the apples are soft, 1½-2 hours. Spoon liquid over each apple serving.

1 stuffed apple: 139 cal., 2g fat (1g sat. fat), 2mg chol., 60mg sod., 31g carb. (20g sugars, 4g fiber), 2g pro. **Diabetic exchanges:** 1 starch, 1 fruit.

SAVORY RICE-STUFFED
APPLES

GLAZED CARROTS WITH GREEN GRAPES

SLOW-COOKER MUSHROOM POTATOES

I jazzed up sliced potatoes with mushrooms, onions, canned soup and cheese to create this versatile side. With its comforting flavor, it's an ideal accompaniment to a special meal.
—Linda Bernard, Golden Meadow, LA

PREP: 25 min. • **COOK:** 6 hours
MAKES: 10 servings

- 7 medium potatoes, peeled and thinly sliced
- 1 medium onion, sliced
- 4 garlic cloves, minced
- 2 green onions, chopped
- 1 can (8 oz.) mushroom stems and pieces, drained
- ¼ cup all-purpose flour
- 2 tsp. salt
- ½ tsp. pepper
- ¼ cup butter, cubed
- 1 can (10¾ oz.) condensed cream of mushroom soup, undiluted
- 1 cup shredded Colby-Monterey Jack cheese

In a 3-qt. slow cooker, layer half the potatoes, onion, garlic, green onions, mushrooms, flour, salt, pepper and butter. Repeat layers. Pour soup over the top. Cover and cook on low until potatoes are tender, 6-8 hours; sprinkle with cheese during last 30 minutes of cooking time.
¾ cup: 249 cal., 9g fat (6g sat. fat), 23mg chol., 893mg sod., 35g carb. (4g sugars, 4g fiber), 7g pro.
Smoky Mushroom Potatoes: Sprinkle in 2 tsp. chili powder, smoked paprika or chipotle powder between the layers for a hint of smoky flavor. Proceed as directed.

TEST KITCHEN TIP

Mushroom lover? Layer thinly sliced fresh mushrooms for more mushroom flavor. Try using reconstituted dried mushrooms or a combination of fresh mushrooms (button, baby bella and shiitake) to elevate the recipe.

GLAZED CARROTS WITH GREEN GRAPES

After receiving a slow cooker many years ago and not knowing what to do with the thing, I finally branched out and read up on what it was all about. This is one of the recipes I make that is really enjoyed by all at any time of the year. It is so colorful and a delightful side for any meal.
—Lorraine Caland, Shuniah, ON

PREP: 20 min. • **COOK:** 3½ hours
MAKES: 7 servings

- 8 medium carrots, sliced (14 oz.)
- ⅓ cup orange marmalade
- 2 Tbsp. water
- ¼ tsp. salt
- 1 cup halved green grapes
- 1 Tbsp. butter
  Chopped fresh parsley, optional

In a 3-qt. slow cooker, combine the carrots, marmalade, water and salt. Cook, covered, on low heat until carrots are almost tender, about 2¾ hours. Add the grapes and butter. Cover and cook on low until tender, 45 minutes longer. If desired, sprinkle with parsley.
½ cup: 98 cal., 2g fat (1g sat. fat), 4mg chol., 157mg sod., 21g carb. (16g sugars, 2g fiber), 1g pro.

SLOW-COOKER
MUSHROOM POTATOES

ASIAN SHREDDED PORK
SANDWICHES

❄ ASIAN SHREDDED PORK SANDWICHES

On cool-weather weeknights, the slow cooker is our friend. The plums might surprise in these juicy pork sandwiches, but they add a little sweetness and make the meat extra tender.

—Holly Battiste, Barrington, NJ

PREP: 30 min. • **COOK:** 6 hours
MAKES: 10 servings

- 1 can (15 oz.) plums, drained and pitted
- 1 Tbsp. Sriracha chili sauce
- 1 Tbsp. hoisin sauce
- 1 Tbsp. reduced-sodium soy sauce
- 1 Tbsp. rice vinegar
- 1 Tbsp. honey
- 2 garlic cloves, minced
- 1 tsp. pepper
- 1 tsp. sesame oil
- ½ tsp. ground ginger
- ¼ tsp. salt
- 2 Tbsp. canola oil
- 1 boneless pork shoulder butt roast (3 lbs.)
- 4 medium carrots, finely chopped
- 10 ciabatta rolls, split
  Shredded napa or other cabbage

1. Mix the first 11 ingredients. In a large skillet, heat oil over medium-high heat. Brown roast on all sides.

2. Place carrots in a 4- or 5-qt. slow cooker. Add roast; pour plum mixture over top. Cook, covered, on low until pork is tender, 6-8 hours.

3. Remove pork; shred with 2 forks. Skim fat from carrot mixture; stir in pork and heat through. Serve on rolls with cabbage.

Freeze option: Freeze cooled pork mixture in freezer containers. To use, partially thaw in refrigerator overnight. Heat through in a covered saucepan, stirring occasionally; add a little broth if necessary.

1 sandwich: 637 cal., 21g fat (6g sat. fat), 81mg chol., 864mg sod., 85g carb. (17g sugars, 5g fiber), 34g pro.

64 TASTEOFHOME.COM

❄ PIZZA BEANS

This dish is wonderful for parties or as a main dish. It can even be made the day before and reheated.
—Taste of Home *Test Kitchen*

PREP: 20 min. • **COOK:** 6 hours
MAKES: 20 servings

- 1 lb. bulk Italian sausage
- 2 cups chopped celery
- 2 cups chopped onion
- 1 can (14½ oz.) cut green beans, drained
- 1 can (14½ oz.) cut wax beans, drained
- 1 can (16 oz.) kidney beans, rinsed and drained
- 1 can (16 oz.) butter beans, drained
- 1 can (15 oz.) pork and beans
- 3 cans (8 oz. each) pizza sauce
  Optional toppings: Grated Parmesan cheese, minced fresh oregano and crushed red pepper flakes

1. In large skillet, brown the sausage over medium heat until no longer pink, breaking it into crumbles. Transfer to a 5-qt. slow cooker with a slotted spoon. Add celery and onion to the pan; cook until softened, about 5 minutes. Drain.
2. Add vegetable mixture and the next 6 ingredients to slow cooker; mix well. Cover and cook on low until bubbly, 6-8 hours. If desired, serve with toppings.
Freeze option: Freeze cooled beans in freezer containers. To use, partially thaw in refrigerator overnight. Heat through in a saucepan, stirring occasionally; add a little water or broth if necessary.
¾ cup: 142 cal., 6g fat (2g sat. fat), 12mg chol., 542mg sod., 17g carb. (4g sugars, 5g fiber), 7g pro.

TEST KITCHEN TIP

If you don't have a slow cooker, these can also be made in the oven. Bake at 325° until bubbly, 1½ hours.

SPLIT PEA & SAUSAGE SOUP

A big bowl of satisfying soup is the perfect antidote to cold weather. Whether for a family meal or an informal get-together, I pull out my tried-and-true soup recipe and simply relax.
—Trisha Kruse, Eagle, ID

PREP: 25 min. • **COOK:** 7 hours
MAKES: 6 servings (2¼ qt.)

- 1 lb. smoked sausage, sliced
- 1 medium potato, peeled and cubed
- 2 medium carrots, thinly sliced
- 2 celery ribs, thinly sliced
- 1 medium onion, chopped
- 2 Tbsp. butter
- 3 garlic cloves, minced
- ¼ tsp. dried oregano
- 1 cup dried green split peas
- 2½ tsp. chicken bouillon granules
- 1 bay leaf
- 5 cups water

1. Saute the sausage, potato, carrots, celery and onion in butter in a large skillet until vegetables are crisp-tender. Add garlic and oregano; cook 2 minutes longer.
2. Transfer to a 5-qt. slow cooker. Add the peas, bouillon, bay leaf and water. Cover and cook on low for 7-8 hours or until peas are tender. Discard bay leaf.
1½ cups: 429 cal., 25g fat (11g sat. fat), 61mg chol., 1267mg sod., 33g carb. (7g sugars, 10g fiber), 20g pro.

PIZZA BEANS

FAMILY-PLEASING
TURKEY CHILI

❄ FAMILY-PLEASING TURKEY CHILI

My children really love this recipe, and it's become one of their favorite comfort foods. The ingredients are relatively inexpensive, and the leftovers are wonderful!
—*Sheila Christensen, San Marcos, CA*

PREP: 25 min. • COOK: 4 hours
MAKES: 6 servings (2¼ qt.)

- 1   lb. lean ground turkey
- 1   medium green pepper, finely chopped
- 1   small red onion, finely chopped
- 2   garlic cloves, minced
- 1   can (28 oz.) diced tomatoes, undrained
- 1   can (16 oz.) kidney beans, rinsed and drained
- 1   can (15 oz.) black beans, rinsed and drained
- 1   can (14½ oz.) reduced-sodium chicken broth
- 1¾ cups frozen corn, thawed
- 1   can (6 oz.) tomato paste
- 1   Tbsp. chili powder
- ½   tsp. pepper
- ¼   tsp. ground cumin
- ¼   tsp. garlic powder
     Optional toppings: Reduced-fat sour cream and minced fresh cilantro

1. In a large nonstick skillet, cook the turkey, green pepper and onion over medium heat until meat is no longer pink, breaking it into crumbles. Add garlic; cook 1 minute longer. Drain.
2. Transfer to a 4-qt. slow cooker. Stir in tomatoes, kidney beans, black beans, broth, corn, tomato paste, chili powder, pepper, cumin and garlic powder.
3. Cover and cook on low until heated through, 4-5 hours. If desired, serve with toppings.
Freeze option: Freeze cooled chili in freezer containers. To use, partially thaw in refrigerator overnight. Heat through in a saucepan, stirring occasionally; add a little water if necessary.
1½ cups: 349 cal., 7g fat (2g sat. fat), 60mg chol., 725mg sod., 47g carb. (11g sugars, 12g fiber), 27g pro.
Diabetic exchanges: 3 lean meat, 2 starch, 2 vegetable.

GARDEN GREEN BEANS & POTATOES

🍎 GARDEN GREEN BEANS & POTATOES

Fresh green beans paired with red potatoes make for an easy and satisfying side dish. To make it even better, add crumbled bacon!
—*Kelly Zinn, Cicero, IN*

PREP: 10 min. • COOK: 6 hours
MAKES: 16 servings

- 2   lbs. fresh green beans, trimmed
- 1½ lbs. red potatoes, quartered
- 1   medium onion, chopped
- ½   cup beef broth
- 1½ tsp. salt
- 1   tsp. dried thyme
- ½   tsp. pepper
- ¼   cup butter, softened
- 1   Tbsp. lemon juice

In a 6-qt. slow cooker, combine the first 7 ingredients. Cook, covered, on low until beans are tender, 6-8 hours. Stir in the butter and lemon juice. Remove with a slotted spoon.
¾ cup: 77 cal., 3g fat (2g sat. fat), 8mg chol., 278mg sod., 12g carb. (2g sugars, 3g fiber), 2g pro. **Diabetic exchanges:** 1 vegetable, ½ starch, ½ fat.

TEST KITCHEN TIP
Adding the lemon juice at the end ensures a bright, fresh flavor—and it keeps the green beans vibrant and firm.

SIMPLE ITALIAN BEEF SANDWICHES

It takes very little effort to make these delicious sandwiches—the slow cooker does all the hard work for you.
—Cher Schwartz, Ellisville, MO

PREP: 20 min. • **COOK:** 8 hours
MAKES: 12 servings

- 1 beef rump roast or bottom round roast (3 lbs.)
- 3 cups reduced-sodium beef broth
- 1 envelope Italian salad dressing mix
- 1 tsp. garlic powder
- 1 tsp. onion powder
- 1 tsp. dried parsley flakes
- 1 tsp. dried basil
- 1 tsp. dried oregano
- 1 tsp. pepper
- 1 large onion, julienned
- 1 large green pepper, julienned
- 4½ tsp. olive oil
- 12 hamburger buns, split
- 12 slices reduced-fat provolone cheese

1. Cut roast in half; place in a 4-qt. slow cooker. Combine the broth, dressing mix and seasonings; pour over meat. Cover and cook on low for 8 hours or until tender.

2. Remove roast; cool slightly. Skim fat from cooking juices; reserve 1 cup juices. Shred beef and return to slow cooker. Stir in reserved cooking juices; heat through.

3. Meanwhile, in a large skillet, saute the onion and green pepper in oil until tender.

4. Using a slotted spoon, place beef on bun bottoms; layer with cheese and vegetables. Replace bun tops.

1 serving: 346 cal., 12g fat (5g sat. fat), 79mg chol., 707mg sod., 25g carb. (5g sugars, 2g fiber), 32g pro. **Diabetic exchanges:** 4 lean meat, 1½ starch, 1 fat.

HONEY & ALE PULLED CHICKEN SLIDERS

Score big with your guests with a little bit of sweet heat! This recipe works well for a football party—the extra liquid in the slow cooker keeps the chicken nice and juicy all day long.
—Julie Peterson, Crofton, MD

PREP: 20 min. • **COOK:** 6 hours
MAKES: 12 servings

- ¼ cup honey
- 2 Tbsp. cider vinegar
- 2 Tbsp. Sriracha chili sauce
- 1 Tbsp. chili powder
- 1 tsp. smoked paprika
- 1 tsp. garlic powder
- 1 tsp. onion powder
- ½ tsp. salt
- 2 lbs. boneless skinless chicken thighs (about 8 thighs)
- ¾ cup brown ale
- 3 Tbsp. cornstarch
- 3 Tbsp. water
- 12 slider buns
  Optional: Sweet pickles and additional Sriracha sauce

1. In a 3- or 4-qt. slow cooker, combine the first 8 ingredients. Add chicken and ale; toss to coat. Cook, covered, on low until chicken is tender, 6-8 hours. Remove meat; when cool enough to handle, shred with 2 forks.

2. Strain cooking juices; skim fat. Transfer juices to a small saucepan; bring to a boil. In a small bowl, mix cornstarch and water until smooth; stir into saucepan. Return to a boil, stirring constantly; cook and stir until thickened, about 5 minutes. Add chicken to the sauce; toss to coat. Serve on buns. Add pickles and additional Sriracha sauce if desired.

1 slider: 224 cal., 7g fat (2g sat. fat), 51mg chol., 357mg sod., 22g carb. (8g sugars, 1g fiber), 17g pro.

HONEY & ALE PULLED CHICKEN SLIDERS

SLOW-COOKER CHEESY BROCCOLI SOUP

SLOW-COOKER CHEESY BROCCOLI SOUP

Whenever I order soup at a restaurant, I go for the broccoli-cheese option. I finally put my slow cooker to the test and made my own. It took a few tries, but now the soup is exactly how I like it.
—Kristen Hills, Layton, UT

- -

PREP: 15 min. • **COOK:** 3 hours
MAKES: 4 servings

2 **Tbsp. butter**
1 **small onion, finely chopped**
2 **cups finely chopped fresh broccoli**
3 **cups reduced-sodium chicken broth**
1 **can (12 oz.) evaporated milk**
½ **tsp. pepper**
1 **pkg. (8 oz.) Velveeta, cubed**

1½ **cups shredded extra-sharp cheddar cheese**
1 **cup shredded Parmesan cheese**
   Additional shredded extra-sharp cheddar cheese

1. In a small skillet, heat butter over medium-high heat. Add onion; cook and stir 3-4 minutes or until tender. Transfer to a 3- or 4-qt. slow cooker. Add broccoli, broth, milk and pepper.
2. Cook, covered, on low 3-4 hours or until broccoli is tender. Stir in process cheese until melted. Add shredded cheeses; stir until melted. Just before serving, stir soup to combine. Top each serving with additional cheddar cheese.
1¾ cups: 675 cal., 49g fat (30g sat. fat), 165mg chol., 1964mg sod., 21g carb. (15g sugars, 2g fiber), 39g pro.

"Loved it! I used 2% Velveeta and reduced-fat sharp cheddar cheese, and it turned out perfect!"
—OJC0806, TASTEOFHOME.COM

SLOW-COOKER BARBECUE
PULLED PORK SANDWICHES

SLOW-COOKER SAUERKRAUT

The recipe was made by a special someone in my life. I was never a fan of sauerkraut until I tried this and fell in love. It's terrific as a side dish or on Reuben sandwiches.
—Karen Tringali, Minooka, IL

PREP: 20 min. • **COOK:** 1 hour
MAKES: 10 servings

- ½ lb. bacon strips, chopped
- 1 medium onion, chopped
- ¾ cup white vinegar
- ¾ cup sugar
- 2 cans (14 oz. each) sauerkraut, rinsed and well drained
- ½ tsp. caraway seeds

1. In a large skillet, cook bacon and onions over medium heat until bacon is crisp and onions are just tender, 5-7 minutes. Add vinegar and sugar to skillet; cook and stir 5 minutes. Add sauerkraut and caraway seeds to skillet; stir to combine.
2. Transfer mixture to 4-qt. slow cooker. Cover and cook on low to allow flavors to blend, 1-2 hours.
½ cup: 173 cal., 9g fat (3g sat. fat), 15mg chol., 675mg sod., 20g carb. (17g sugars, 2g fiber), 4g pro.

TEST KITCHEN TIP

The longer this dish sits, the better. It's a fantastic make-ahead option. If the sauerkraut gets too dry, add a little water.

❄️
SLOW-COOKER BARBECUE PULLED PORK SANDWICHES

Foolproof and wonderfully delicious describe my barbecue pork recipe. Just four ingredients and a slow cooker make a fabulous dish with little effort.
—Sarah Johnson, Chicago, IL

PREP: 15 min. • **COOK:** 7 hours
MAKES: 6 servings

- 1 Hormel lemon-garlic pork loin filet (about 1⅓ lbs.)
- 1 can (12 oz.) Dr Pepper
- 1 bottle (18 oz.) barbecue sauce
- 6 hamburger buns, split

1. Place pork in a 3-qt. slow cooker. Pour Dr Pepper over top. Cover and cook on low until meat is tender, 7-9 hours.
2. Remove meat; cool slightly. Discard cooking juices. Shred meat with 2 forks and return to slow cooker. Stir in barbecue sauce; heat through. Serve on buns.
Freeze option: Place individual portions of cooled meat mixture and juice in freezer containers. To use, partially thaw in the refrigerator overnight. Microwave, covered, on high in a microwave-safe dish until heated through, stirring occasionally; add a little water if necessary.
1 sandwich: 348 cal., 8g fat (2g sat. fat), 45mg chol., 1695mg sod., 43g carb. (22g sugars, 2g fiber), 25g pro.

SLOW-COOKER
SAUERKRAUT

ZIPPY BEEF CHILI

Not only is this zesty chili chock-full of ground beef but it's also loaded with veggies. I put everything in the slow cooker, let it cook and then come home to a marvelous, ready-to-eat meal.
—Bonnie Chocallo, Wyoming, PA

PREP: 30 min. • **COOK:** 6 hours
MAKES: 12 servings

- 2 lbs. lean ground beef (90% lean)
- 1 can (16 oz.) kidney beans, rinsed and drained
- 2 cans (14½ oz. each) diced tomatoes
- 1 can (11½ oz.) pork and beans
- 2 large onions, chopped
- 2 medium carrots, shredded
- 1 medium sweet red pepper, chopped
- 1 medium green pepper, chopped
- 2 celery ribs, chopped
- 1 cup water
- ½ cup ketchup
- 1 can (6 oz.) tomato paste
- 2 jalapeno peppers, seeded and chopped
- 3 Tbsp. brown sugar
- 4 garlic cloves, minced
- 1 Tbsp. dried oregano
- 1 Tbsp. chili powder
- 1 tsp. salt
- 1 tsp. crushed red pepper flakes
- 1 tsp. pepper

1. In a large skillet, cook beef over medium heat until no longer pink, breaking it into crumbles; drain.
2. Transfer to a 5-qt. slow cooker. Add the remaining ingredients. Cover and cook on low for 6-8 hours or until heated through.
Freeze option: Freeze cooled chili in freezer containers. To use, partially thaw in refrigerator overnight. Heat through in a saucepan, stirring occasionally; add a little water if necessary.
Note: Wear disposable gloves when cutting hot peppers; the oils can burn skin. Avoid touching your face.
1 cup: 243 cal., 6g fat (2g sat. fat), 37mg chol., 644mg sod., 29g carb. (15g sugars, 7g fiber), 20g pro. **Diabetic exchanges:** 2 starch, 2 lean meat.

HOLY MOLY POTATO SOUP

This is a spiced-up version of cheesy potato soup. We eat this often, especially on cold winter evenings, but it would be lovely for family get-togethers or potlucks during the holidays, too! Crushed red pepper flakes really turn up the heat.
—Angela Sheridan, Opdyke, IL

PREP: 20 min. • **COOK:** 4 hours
MAKES: 10 servings

- 4 cans (14½ oz. each) diced new potatoes, undrained
- 2 cans (10¾ oz. each) condensed cream of mushroom soup, undiluted
- 2½ cups water
- 1 can (11 oz.) whole kernel corn, drained
- 1 can (10 oz.) diced tomatoes and green chiles, undrained
- 6 green onions, chopped
- 1 medium sweet red pepper, chopped
- 1 Tbsp. dried minced onion
- 1 tsp. cayenne pepper
- ¼ tsp. pepper
- 1 lb. bulk spicy pork sausage
- 2 cups (8 oz.) shredded sharp cheddar cheese
- 1 carton (8 oz.) French onion dip
  Tortilla chips

1. In a 6-qt. slow cooker, combine the first 10 ingredients. In a large skillet, cook sausage over medium heat 6-8 minutes or until no longer pink, breaking it into crumbles; drain. Add to slow cooker.
2. Cook, covered, on low to allow flavors to blend, 4-5 hours. Add cheese and onion dip in the last 30 minutes of cooking. Stir before serving. Serve with tortilla chips.
Freeze option: Freeze cooled soup in freezer containers. To use, partially thaw in refrigerator overnight. Heat through in a saucepan, stirring occasionally; add a little water if necessary.
1½ cups: 529 cal., 30g fat (13g sat. fat), 62mg chol., 1981mg sod., 43g carb. (5g sugars, 8g fiber), 18g pro.

HOLY MOLY POTATO SOUP

SLOW-COOKED CHICKEN CAESAR WRAPS

SLOW-COOKED SHREDDED BEEF SANDWICHES

It's easy to feed a crowd with this tender and tasty beef on hamburger buns. The recipe came from my grandchildren's third grade teacher, and it remains one of our favorites.
—*Myra Innes, Auburn, KS*

PREP: 10 min. • **COOK:** 10 hours
MAKES: 12 servings

1	boneless beef roast (3 lbs.)
1	medium onion, chopped
⅓	cup white vinegar
3	bay leaves
½	tsp. salt, optional
¼	tsp. ground cloves
⅛	tsp. garlic powder
12	hamburger buns, split

Cut roast in half; place in a 3-qt. slow cooker. Combine onion, vinegar, bay leaves, salt if desired, cloves and garlic powder; pour over roast. Cover and cook on low for 10-12 hours or until the meat is very tender. Discard bay leaves. Remove meat and shred with a fork. Serve on buns.

Freeze option: Freeze cooled beef mixture in freezer containers. To use, partially thaw in refrigerator overnight. Heat through in a covered saucepan, stirring occasionally; add a little broth if necessary.

1 sandwich: 318 cal., 13g fat (5g sat. fat), 74mg chol., 264mg sod., 23g carb. (4g sugars, 1g fiber), 27g pro.

SLOW-COOKED CHICKEN CAESAR WRAPS

I first made this recipe for our daughter, who loves Caesar salads, then later for our extended family while we were on vacation. It's such an easy meal—perfect for when you'd rather be outside than inside cooking all day.
—*Christine Hadden, Whitman, MA*

PREP: 10 min. • **COOK:** 3 hours
MAKES: 6 servings

1½	lbs. boneless skinless chicken breast halves
2	cups chicken broth
¾	cup creamy Caesar salad dressing
½	cup shredded Parmesan cheese
¼	cup minced fresh parsley
½	tsp. pepper
6	flour tortillas (8 in.)
2	cups shredded lettuce
	Optional: Salad croutons, cooked crumbled bacon and additional shredded Parmesan cheese

1. Place chicken and broth in a 1½- or 3-qt. slow cooker. Cook, covered, on low 3-4 hours or until a thermometer inserted in chicken reads 165°. Remove chicken and discard cooking juices. Shred chicken with 2 forks; return to slow cooker.
2. Stir in dressing, Parmesan, parsley and pepper; heat through. Serve in tortillas with lettuce and, if desired, salad croutons, crumbled bacon and additional shredded Parmesan cheese.

1 wrap: 472 cal., 25g fat (5g sat. fat), 81mg chol., 795mg sod., 29g carb. (1g sugars, 2g fiber), 31g pro.

CREAMY CHEESE
POTATOES

CREAMY CHEESE POTATOES

This easy potato dish is a comfort-food classic. It's popular at gatherings.
—*Greg Christiansen, Parker, KS*

PREP: 10 min. • **COOK:** 3¼ hours
MAKES: 10 servings

- 1 can (10¾ oz.) condensed cream of chicken soup, undiluted
- 1 can (10¾ oz.) condensed cream of mushroom soup, undiluted
- 3 Tbsp. butter, melted
- 1 pkg. (30 oz.) frozen shredded hash brown potatoes, thawed
- 2 cups shredded cheddar cheese
- 1 cup sour cream
  Minced fresh parsley, optional

1. In a 3-qt. slow cooker coated with cooking spray, combine the soups and butter. Stir in potatoes.
2. Cover and cook on low for 3-4 hours or until potatoes are tender. Stir in cheese and sour cream. Cover and cook until heated through, 15-30 minutes longer. If desired, top with additional shredded cheddar cheese and minced fresh parsley.
¾ cup: 278 cal., 17g fat (10g sat. fat), 52mg chol., 614mg sod., 21g carb. (2g sugars, 2g fiber), 9g pro.

"I make this recipe a lot, substituting milk for the cream of mushroom soup. It is wonderful for holidays or church potlucks where it frees up the oven and cooks in 3-4 hours. The ingredients are forgiving, so if you have a little more or less, it still maintains fabulous flavor. It goes well with beef, pork and chicken."
—TKUEHL, TASTEOFHOME.COM

MOM'S MOLASSES
HAM & BEANS

🍎 ❄️
MOM'S MOLASSES HAM & BEANS

This is a recipe my mom made frequently while I was growing up. It's perfect for a cold day when you don't want to bother with lots of cooking. My mother actually used lima beans, but not many people are into those, so I tweaked this dish to make it more enjoyable for my own family.
—*Nancy Heishman, Las Vegas, NV*

PREP: 15 min. • **COOK:** 7 hours
MAKES: 8 servings

- 4 cans (15½ oz. each) navy or cannellini beans, rinsed and drained
- 2 smoked ham hocks (about 1 lb.)
- 1 can (15 oz.) tomato sauce
- 1 large onion, chopped
- ¾ cup packed brown sugar
- ¾ cup molasses
- ¼ cup cider vinegar
- 1 Tbsp. Worcestershire sauce
- 2½ tsp. ground mustard
- 1 tsp. salt
- ½ tsp. pepper
- 12 bacon strips, cooked and crumbled
  Optional: Pickled jalapeno peppers and pickled red onions

1. In a greased 5-qt. slow cooker, combine all ingredients, except the bacon. Cook, covered, on low 7-9 hours.
2. Remove ham hocks. When cool enough to handle, remove meat from bones; discard bones. Cut meat into small cubes; return to slow cooker. Stir in crumbled bacon. If desired, serve with pickled jalapeno peppers and pickled red onions.
Freeze option: Freeze cooled beans in freezer containers. To use, partially thaw in refrigerator overnight. Heat through in a saucepan, stirring occasionally; add a little water or broth if necessary.
¾ cup: 521 cal., 7g fat (2g sat. fat), 19mg chol., 1543mg sod., 93g carb. (45g sugars, 13g fiber), 24g pro.

TEX-MEX CHILI WITH A CINCINNATI TWIST

My husband grew up in Cincinnati, where chili is served over spaghetti, and I grew up in the South. This family pleaser is a mingling of both worlds—and a superb way to make a meal go further.

—Stephanie Rabbitt-Schapp, Cincinnati, OH

PREP: 35 min. • **COOK:** 6 hours
MAKES: 7 servings

- 1 lb. ground beef
- 1 cup chopped sweet onion
- ¼ cup chili powder
- 2 Tbsp. ground cumin
- 2 tsp. baking cocoa
- 1½ tsp. ground cinnamon
- ¾ tsp. cayenne pepper
- ½ tsp. salt
- 1 can (16 oz.) chili beans, undrained
- 1 can (16 oz.) kidney beans, rinsed and drained
- 1 can (14½ oz.) diced tomatoes, undrained
- 1 can (8 oz.) tomato sauce
- 1 medium tomato, chopped
- 1 jalapeno pepper, seeded and chopped
  Hot cooked spaghetti
  Optional toppings: Oyster crackers, hot pepper sauce, chopped sweet onion and shredded cheddar cheese

1. In a large skillet, cook beef and onion over medium heat until meat is no longer pink, breaking it into crumbles; drain. Stir in the chili powder, cumin, cocoa, cinnamon, cayenne and salt.
2. Transfer to a 4- or 5-qt. slow cooker. Stir in the chili beans, kidney beans, diced tomatoes, tomato sauce, tomato and jalapeno.
3. Cover and cook on low for 6-8 hours or until heated through. Serve over spaghetti. Garnish with toppings of your choice.
Note: Wear disposable gloves when cutting hot peppers; the oils can burn skin. Avoid touching your face.
1 cup: 288 cal., 9g fat (3g sat. fat), 40mg chol., 767mg sod., 34g carb. (6g sugars, 11g fiber), 22g pro.

MIXED VEGGIES & RICE

MIXED VEGGIES & RICE

To add variety to side dishes for those who don't care for potatoes, I came up with one of the most colorful and easy slow-cooker sides. Put it on the buffet table and forget it until dinnertime.

—Judy Batson, Tampa, FL

PREP: 5 min. • **COOK:** 3 hours
MAKES: 8 servings

- 4 pkg. (10 oz. each) frozen long grain white rice with mixed vegetables
- 12 oz. frozen mixed vegetables
- ½ cup vegetable broth or light beer
- 1 tsp. onion powder
- 1 tsp. garlic powder
- 1 tsp. seasoned salt
  Butter, optional

In a 5-qt. slow cooker, combine the first 6 ingredients. Cook, covered, on low until heated through, 3-4 hours. If desired, serve with butter.
¾ cup: 120 cal., 0 fat (0 sat. fat), 0 chol., 254mg sod., 26g carb. (3g sugars, 3g fiber), 3g pro. **Diabetic exchanges:** 1½ starch.

SLOW-COOKED SPICY PORTUGUESE CACOILA

You are probably used to pulled pork coated with barbecue sauce and made into sandwiches. Portuguese pulled pork is a spicy dish often served at our large family functions. Each cook generally adds his or her own touches that reflect their taste and Portuguese heritage. A mixture of beef roast and pork can also be used.
—*Michele Merlino, Exeter, RI*

PREP: 20 min. + marinating
COOK: 6 hours • **MAKES:** 12 servings

- 4 lbs. boneless pork shoulder butt roast, cut into 2-in. pieces
- 1½ cups dry red wine or reduced-sodium chicken broth
- 4 garlic cloves, minced
- 4 bay leaves
- 1 Tbsp. salt
- 1 Tbsp. paprika
- 2 to 3 tsp. crushed red pepper flakes
- 1 tsp. ground cinnamon
- 1 large onion, chopped
- ½ cup water
- 12 bolillos or hoagie buns, split, optional

1. Place pork in a large bowl; add wine, garlic and seasonings. Turn to coat; cover and refrigerate overnight.

2. Transfer pork mixture to a 5- or 6-qt. slow cooker; add onion and water. Cook, covered, on low 6-8 hours or until meat is tender.

3. Skim fat. Remove bay leaves. Shred meat with 2 forks. If desired, serve with a slotted spoon on bolillos.

1 sandwich: 489 cal., 20g fat (7g sat. fat), 90mg chol., 1075mg sod., 38g carb. (6g sugars, 2g fiber), 34g pro.

SLOW-COOKED SPICY PORTUGUESE CACOILA

ALL-DAY SOUP

I start this soup in the morning, and by evening, dinner's ready to go! My family loves all of the hearty vegetable and steak pieces in the zesty tomato broth.
—*Cathy Logan, Sparks, NV*

PREP: 25 min. • **COOK:** 8 hours
MAKES: 8 servings

- 1 beef flank steak (1½ lbs.), cut into ½-in. cubes
- 1 medium onion, chopped
- 1 Tbsp. olive oil
- 5 medium carrots, thinly sliced
- 4 cups shredded cabbage
- 4 medium red potatoes, diced
- 2 celery ribs, diced
- 2 cans (14½ oz. each) diced tomatoes, undrained
- 2 cans (14½ oz. each) beef broth
- 1 can (10¾ oz.) condensed tomato soup, undiluted
- 1 Tbsp. sugar
- 2 tsp. Italian seasoning
- 1 tsp. dried parsley flakes

In large skillet, brown steak and onion in oil; drain. Transfer to a 5-qt. slow cooker. Stir in the remaining ingredients. Cover and cook on low for 8-10 hours or until meat is tender.

1¾ cups: 274 cal., 8g fat (3g sat. fat), 41mg chol., 679mg sod., 29g carb. (12g sugars, 5g fiber), 21g pro. **Diabetic exchanges:** 2 starch, 2 lean meat, 1 vegetable.

"We really liked this soup. I was concerned that my kids would complain about the cabbage, but they didn't even notice it! I did all the prep the night before and just put it all in the slow cooker in the morning. I will probably add some corn and green beans next time."
—SMSTILLINGER, TASTEOFHOME.COM

TOMATO BEEF BARLEY SOUP

SOPA DE CAMARONES (SHRIMP SOUP)

My daughter and I came up with this soup recipe when she was younger, and it's been a favorite with family and friends ever since. It may even be tastier as leftovers the next day!
—*Patti Fair, Valdosta, GA*

PREP: 20 min. • **COOK:** 2 hours
MAKES: 6 cups (1½ qt.)

- 3 Tbsp. butter
- 3 celery ribs, sliced
- 1 small onion, chopped
- ⅓ cup lemon juice
- 6 garlic cloves, minced
- 1 to 2 Tbsp. sugar
- 2 cans (14½ oz. each) Mexican petite diced tomatoes, undrained
- 1 lb. peeled and deveined cooked shrimp (61-70 per lb.)
- 1 can (6 oz.) tomato paste
   Hot cooked rice
   Optional: Lime wedges and chopped cilantro

1. In a large skillet, heat the butter over medium heat. Add celery and onion; cook and stir until crisp-tender, 3-4 minutes. Add lemon juice, garlic and sugar; cook 1 minute longer.
2. Transfer to a 3- or 4-qt. slow cooker. Add undrained tomatoes, shrimp and tomato paste. Cook, covered, on low until heated through, 2-3 hours. Serve with rice and, if desired, lime wedges and chopped cilantro.
1½ cups: 313 cal., 11g fat (6g sat. fat), 195mg chol., 712mg sod., 26g carb. (16g sugars, 4g fiber), 28g pro.

TOMATO BEEF BARLEY SOUP

When my children were young, I needed a soup that everyone would eat—something filling but also delicious. My sons really liked barley soup from a can, so I decided to try making it myself. My boys are now adults, and this is one of the first things they ask me to make when they come visit.
—*Karla Johnson, Winter Haven, FL*

PREP: 20 min. • **COOK:** 7 hours
MAKES: 8 servings (2½ qt.)

- 1 lb. ground beef
- 1 medium onion, finely chopped
- ½ medium head cabbage, coarsely shredded (about 5 cups)
- 1 large carrot, chopped
- 1¼ tsp. salt
- 1 tsp. pepper
- 1 carton (32 oz.) beef broth
- 2 cans (8 oz. each) roasted garlic tomato sauce
- 1 can (14½ oz.) diced tomatoes, undrained
- 2 cups fresh or frozen corn (about 10 oz.), thawed
- ½ cup medium pearl barley

1. In a large skillet, cook and crumble beef with onion over medium-high heat until no longer pink, 5-7 minutes. Using a slotted spoon, transfer beef mixture to a 5-qt. slow cooker.
2. Stir in cabbage, carrot, salt, pepper, broth, tomato sauce and tomatoes. Cook, covered, on low 6 hours.
3. Stir in corn and barley; turn up to high and cook until barley is tender, about 1 hour.
1⅓ cups: 239 cal., 8g fat (3g sat. fat), 35mg chol., 1372mg sod., 28g carb. (9g sugars, 6g fiber), 16g pro.

SOPA DE CAMARONES
(SHRIMP SOUP)

Snacks & Sweets

SLOW-COOKER PINA COLADA BANANAS FOSTER

I took bananas Foster one step further and combined it with the flavors of my favorite tropical drink—a pina colada. Make sure your bananas are not super ripe. You will want to choose ones that are still nice and firm, as they'll work best in this recipe.
—*Trisha Kruse, Eagle, ID*

PREP: 10 min. • **COOK:** 2 hours
MAKES: 3 cups

4 medium firm bananas
1 can (8 oz.) pineapple tidbits, drained
¼ cup butter, melted
1 cup packed brown sugar
¼ cup rum
½ tsp. coconut extract
½ cup sweetened shredded coconut, toasted
Optional: Coconut ice cream, vanilla wafers and cream-filled wafer cookies

Cut bananas in half lengthwise, then widthwise. Layer sliced bananas and pineapple in bottom of a 1½-qt. slow cooker. Combine butter, brown sugar, rum and coconut extract in small bowl; pour over fruit. Cover and cook on low until heated through, 2 hours. Sprinkle with toasted coconut. If desired, serve with coconut ice cream, vanilla wafers or cream-filled wafer cookies.

½ cup: 358 cal., 11g fat (7g sat. fat), 20mg chol., 95mg sod., 63g carb. (53g sugars, 3g fiber), 1g pro.

TEST KITCHEN TIP
If you want your bananas to stay somewhat firm, add them to the slow cooker during the last 20 minutes of cooking.

SLOW-COOKER PINA COLADA BANANAS FOSTER

BLUEBERRY ICED TEA

APPLE GRANOLA DESSERT

I would be lost without my slow cooker. Besides using it to prepare our evening meals, I often make desserts in it. We love these tender apples that get a tasty treatment from granola cereal.
—*Janis Lawrence, Childress, TX*

- -

PREP: 15 min. • **COOK:** 3 hours
MAKES: 6 servings

4	medium tart apples, peeled and sliced
2	cups granola cereal with fruit and nuts
¼	cup honey
2	Tbsp. butter, melted
1	tsp. ground cinnamon
½	tsp. ground nutmeg
	Whipped topping, optional

In a 1½-qt. slow cooker, combine apples and cereal. In a small bowl, combine honey, butter, cinnamon and nutmeg; pour over apple mixture and mix well. Cover and cook on low, 3-4 hours. If desired, serve with whipped topping.
1 serving: 372 cal., 15g fat (5g sat. fat), 15mg chol., 117mg sod., 60g carb. (40g sugars, 5g fiber), 5g pro.
Spiced Pear Granola Dessert: Use 4 medium Bosc pears, peeled and sliced, instead of apples. Substitute ½ tsp. ground ginger for the nutmeg. Proceed as directed.

"I made this for a party that I hosted and it was a hit!"
—L2BAKE, TASTEOFHOME.COM

BLUEBERRY ICED TEA

I enjoy coming up with new ways to use my slow cooker in the kitchen. If it's going to take up space, it needs to earn its keep! Serve this refreshing tea over plenty of ice and garnish with blueberries if desired. For fun, freeze blueberries in your ice cubes.
—*Colleen Delawder, Herndon, VA*

- -

PREP: 10 min. • **COOK:** 3 hours + cooling
MAKES: 11 servings

12	cups water
2	cups fresh blueberries
1	cup sugar
¼	tsp. salt
4	family-sized tea bags
	Ice cubes
	Optional: Additional blueberries, lemon slices and fresh mint leaves

1. In a 5-qt. slow cooker, combine water, blueberries, sugar and salt. Cover and cook on low heat 3 hours.
2. Turn off slow cooker; add tea bags. Cover and let stand 5 minutes. Discard tea bags; cool 2 hours. Strain and discard blueberries. Pour into pitcher; serve over ice cubes. If desired, top each serving with additional blueberries, lemon slices and fresh mint leaves.
1 cup: 73 cal., 0 fat (0 sat. fat), 0 chol., 61mg sod., 19g carb. (18g sugars, 0 fiber), 0 pro.

LIP-SMACKING PEACH & WHISKEY WINGS

These sweet, spicy, sticky chicken wings are lip-smacking good! You could use fresh peaches in place of canned. Just add a few tablespoons of brown sugar if doing so.
—*Sue Falk, Sterling Heights, MI*

PREP: 20 min. • COOK: 4¼ hours
MAKES: 2 dozen pieces

- 3 lbs. chicken wings (about 1 dozen)
- 1 tsp. salt
- ½ tsp. pepper
- 1 can (29 oz.) sliced peaches in extra-light syrup, undrained
- ½ cup whiskey
- ¼ cup honey
- 1 Tbsp. lime juice
- 1 Tbsp. Louisiana-style hot sauce
- 3 garlic cloves, minced
- 4 tsp. cornstarch
- 2 Tbsp. cold water
  Minced chives, optional

1. Pat chicken wings dry. Using a sharp knife, cut through 2 wing joints; discard wing tips. Season wings with salt and pepper. Place in a 3- or 4-qt. slow cooker.
2. Pulse peaches with syrup in a food processor until pureed. Add the next 5 ingredients; pulse to combine. Pour over wings; toss to coat. Cook, covered, on low until chicken is tender, 4-6 hours.
3. Combine the cornstarch and water until smooth; stir into slow cooker. Cook, covered, on high until sauce is thickened, about 15 minutes.
4. Preheat broiler. Remove wings to a 15x10x1-in. pan; arrange in a single layer. Broil wings 3-4 in. from heat until lightly browned, 2-3 minutes. Brush with sauce before serving. Serve with remaining sauce and, if desired, chives.
1 piece: 93 cal., 4g fat (1g sat. fat), 18mg chol., 140mg sod., 8g carb. (7g sugars, 0 fiber), 6g pro.

HOT COCOA FOR A CROWD

This is a simple, delicious and comforting hot cocoa with a hint of cinnamon. It has just the right amount of sweetness.
—*Deborah Canaday, Manhattan, KS*

PREP: 10 min. • COOK: 3 hours
MAKES: 12 servings

- 5 cups nonfat dry milk powder
- ¾ cup sugar
- ¾ cup baking cocoa
- 1 tsp. vanilla extract
- ¼ tsp. ground cinnamon
- 11 cups water
  Optional: Miniature marshmallows and peppermint candy sticks

1. In a 5- or 6-qt. slow cooker, combine the milk powder, sugar, cocoa, vanilla and cinnamon; gradually whisk in water until smooth. Cover and cook on low until heated through, 3-4 hours.
2. If desired, top with marshmallows and use peppermint sticks for stirrers.
1 cup: 164 cal., 1g fat (0 sat. fat), 5mg chol., 156mg sod., 31g carb. (28g sugars, 1g fiber), 11g pro.
Mexican Hot Cocoa for a Crowd: Increase cinnamon to 1 tsp. and add ½ tsp. ground ancho chili pepper. Top each serving with whipped cream and chocolate shavings.

LIP-SMACKING PEACH
& WHISKEY WINGS

NEW ENGLAND INDIAN PUDDING

This recipe was inspired by traditional New England Indian pudding. My version is made in the slow cooker instead of being baked for hours in the oven. If the molasses flavor is too strong, cut amount to ⅓ cup.
—Susan Bickta, Kutztown, PA

- -

PREP: 15 min. • **COOK:** 3½ hours
MAKES: 8 servings

- 1 pkg. (8½ oz.) cornbread/muffin mix
- 1 pkg. (3.4 oz.) instant butterscotch pudding mix
- 4 cups whole milk
- 3 large eggs, lightly beaten
- ½ cup molasses
- 1 tsp. ground cinnamon
- ¼ tsp. ground cloves
- ¼ tsp. ground ginger
  Optional: Vanilla ice cream or sweetened whipped cream

1. In a large bowl, whisk cornbread mix, pudding mix and milk until blended. Add eggs, molasses and spices; whisk until combined. Transfer to a greased 4- or 5-qt. slow cooker. Cover and cook on high for 1 hour.

2. Reduce heat to low. Stir pudding, making sure to scrape sides well. Cover and cook until very thick, 2½-3 hours longer, stirring once per hour. Serve warm with ice cream if desired.

⅔ cup: 330 cal., 9g fat (4g sat. fat), 83mg chol., 526mg sod., 51g carb. (36g sugars, 2g fiber), 8g pro.

SLAW-TOPPED BEEF SLIDERS

SLAW-TOPPED BEEF SLIDERS

When I was working full time, I relied on these delicious, fast-to-fix beef sliders for simple meals. To speed prep time and to avoid extra cleanup, I used bagged coleslaw mix and bottled slaw dressing.
—Jane Whittaker, Pensacola, FL

- -

PREP: 20 min. • **COOK:** 6 hours
MAKES: 1 dozen

- 3 cups coleslaw mix
- ½ medium red onion, chopped (about ⅔ cup)
- ⅛ tsp. celery seed
- ¼ tsp. pepper
- ⅓ cup coleslaw salad dressing
- **SANDWICHES**
- 1 boneless beef chuck roast (2 lbs.)
- 1 tsp. salt
- ½ tsp. pepper
- 1 can (6 oz.) tomato paste
- ¼ cup water
- 1 tsp. Worcestershire sauce
- 1 small onion, diced
- 1 cup barbecue sauce
- 12 slider buns or dinner rolls, split

1. Combine coleslaw, onion, celery seed and pepper. Add salad dressing; toss to coat. Refrigerate until serving.

2. Sprinkle roast with salt and pepper; transfer roast to a 5-qt. slow cooker. Mix tomato paste, water and Worcestershire sauce; pour over roast. Top with onion. Cook, covered, on low 6-8 hours or until meat is tender.

3. Shred meat with 2 forks; return to slow cooker. Stir in barbecue sauce; heat through. Serve beef on buns; top with coleslaw. Replace bun tops.

1 slider: 322 cal., 12g fat (4g sat. fat), 67mg chol., 726mg sod., 34g carb. (13g sugars, 3g fiber), 20g pro.

SLOW-COOKER BLUEBERRY COBBLER

I love blueberries, and this easy cake-mix cobbler showcases them wonderfully. Serve the treat warm with a big scoop of French vanilla ice cream or a dollop of whipped cream.
—*Teri Rasey, Cadillac, MI*

PREP: 15 min. • **COOK:** 3 hours
MAKES: 12 servings

- 4 cups fresh or frozen blueberries
- 1 cup sugar
- 1 Tbsp. cornstarch
- 2 tsp. vanilla extract
- 1 pkg. French vanilla cake mix (regular size)
- ½ cup butter, melted
- ⅓ cup chopped pecans
  Vanilla ice cream, optional

In a greased 5-qt. slow cooker, combine blueberries, sugar and cornstarch; stir in vanilla. In a large bowl, combine cake mix and melted butter. Crumble over blueberries. Top with pecans. Cover slow cooker with a double layer of white paper towels; place lid securely over towels. Cook, covered, on low until topping is set, 3-4 hours. If desired, serve with ice cream.
½ cup: 331 cal., 11g fat (6g sat. fat), 20mg chol., 343mg sod., 58g carb. (39g sugars, 2g fiber), 2g pro.

TEST KITCHEN TIPS
- If you can't find French vanilla cake mix, use vanilla or yellow cake mix instead.
- Paper towels under the lid will catch condensation and keep it from dripping onto the cobbler topping.

SLOW-COOKER BLUEBERRY COBBLER

HAWAIIAN KIELBASA

Savory sausage teams up with juicy, tangy pineapple for a winning combination that you can prep in a flash. The sweet barbecue-style sauce is a tasty way to tie them together.
—*Louise Kline, Fort Myers, FL*

PREP: 15 min. • **COOK:** 2½ hours
MAKES: 12 servings

- 2 lbs. smoked kielbasa or Polish sausage, cut into 1-in. pieces
- 1 can (20 oz.) unsweetened pineapple chunks, undrained
- ½ cup ketchup
- 2 Tbsp. brown sugar
- 2 Tbsp. yellow mustard
- 1 Tbsp. cider vinegar
- ¾ cup lemon-lime soda
- 2 Tbsp. cornstarch
- 2 Tbsp. cold water

1. Place sausage in a 3- or 4-qt. slow cooker. Drain pineapple, reserving ¾ cup juice; set pineapple aside. In a small bowl, whisk the ketchup, brown sugar, mustard and vinegar. Stir in soda and reserved pineapple juice. Pour mixture over sausage; stir to coat. Cover and cook on low until heated through, 2-3 hours.
2. Stir in pineapple. In a small bowl, combine cornstarch and water until smooth. Stir into slow cooker. Cover and cook until sauce is thickened, 30 minutes longer. Serve with toothpicks.
½ cup: 289 cal., 21g fat (7g sat. fat), 51mg chol., 975mg sod., 15g carb. (12g sugars, 0 fiber), 10g pro.
Jalapeno Peach Kielbasa: Substitute 1 can (20 oz.) unsweetened peaches for the pineapple. Add 2 thinly sliced fresh jalapenos. Proceed as directed.

SLOW-COOKER
BANANA BREAD

SLOW-COOKER BANANA BREAD

I love to use my slow cooker. I started to experiment with making bread in it so I wouldn't have to heat up my kitchen by turning on my oven. It's so easy and simple. I now make it this way all the time.
—Nicole Gackowski, Antioch, CA

- -

PREP: 10 min. • **COOK:** 2½ hours
MAKES: 16 servings

- 5 medium ripe bananas
- 2½ cups self-rising flour
- 1 can (14 oz.) sweetened condensed milk
- 1 tsp. ground cinnamon
   Cinnamon sugar, optional

1. Place a piece of parchment paper into a 5-qt. slow cooker, letting ends extend up sides. Grease paper with cooking spray. Combine the first 4 ingredients in a large bowl. Pour batter into prepared slow cooker. If desired, sprinkle cinnamon sugar over the top of batter. Cover slow cooker with a double layer of white paper towels; place lid securely over towels.
2. Cook, covered, on high until bread is lightly browned, 2½-3 hours. To avoid scorching, rotate slow cooker insert a half turn midway through cooking, lifting carefully with oven mitts. Remove bread from slow cooker using parchment to lift; cool slightly before slicing.
Note: As a substitute for each cup of self-rising flour, place 1½ tsp. baking powder and ½ tsp. salt in a measuring cup. Add all-purpose flour to measure 1 cup.
1 slice: 210 cal., 3g fat (2g sat. fat), 11mg chol., 276mg sod., 41g carb. (23g sugars, 2g fiber), 5g pro.

SLOW-COOKER
SPICED FRUIT

SLOW-COOKER SPICED FRUIT

My late aunt who lived in Hawaii gave me this cherished recipe. She would prepare a traditional tropical meal for us whenever we visited and always included this fruity delight. I always think of her when I make it, whether it is for the holidays or an everyday meal.
—Joan Hallford, North Richland Hills, TX

- -

PREP: 10 min. • **COOK:** 3 hours
MAKES: 8 servings

- 1 can (20 oz.) pineapple chunks, drained
- 1 can (15¼ oz.) sliced peaches, drained
- 1 can (15¼ oz.) sliced pears, drained
- 1 can (15 oz.) apricot halves, drained
- 1 can (11 oz.) mandarin oranges, drained
- 1 jar (10 oz.) maraschino cherries, drained
- 8 whole cloves
- 2 cinnamon sticks (3 in. each)
- ½ cup packed brown sugar
- ½ tsp. curry powder
- 1 cup white wine or white grape juice
- ½ cup slivered almonds, toasted

1. In a 3- or 4-qt. slow cooker, combine the first 6 ingredients. Place cloves and cinnamon sticks on a double thickness of cheesecloth. Gather corners of cloth to enclose seasonings; tie securely with string. Place bag in slow cooker. In a small bowl, mix brown sugar, curry powder and wine; pour over fruit.
2. Cook, covered, on low until heated through, 3-4 hours. Discard spice bag; sprinkle with almonds. Serve with a slotted spoon.
Note: To toast nuts, bake in a shallow pan in a 350° oven for 5-10 minutes or cook in a skillet over low heat until lightly browned, stirring occasionally.
¾ cup: 323 cal., 4g fat (0 sat. fat), 0 chol., 18mg sod., 72g carb. (65g sugars, 4g fiber), 2g pro.

CHERRY COLA CHOCOLATE CAKE

For a truly different chocolate cake, think outside the box and inside the slow cooker. This easy dessert comes out moist, fudgy and fantastic. It won't heat up the kitchen.
—*Elaine Sweet, Dallas, TX*

- -

PREP: 30 min. + standing
COOK: 2 hours + standing
MAKES: 8 servings

- ½ cup cola
- ½ cup dried tart cherries
- 1½ cups all-purpose flour
- ½ cup sugar
- 2 oz. semisweet chocolate, chopped
- 2½ tsp. baking powder
- ½ tsp. salt
- 1 cup chocolate milk
- ½ cup butter, melted
- 2 tsp. vanilla extract

TOPPING

- 1¼ cups cola
- ½ cup sugar
- ½ cup packed brown sugar
- 2 oz. semisweet chocolate, chopped
- ¼ cup dark rum
  Optional: Vanilla ice cream and maraschino cherries

1. In a small saucepan, bring cola and dried cherries to a boil. Remove from heat; let stand for 30 minutes.
2. In a large bowl, combine flour, sugar, chocolate, baking powder and salt. Combine chocolate milk, butter and vanilla; stir into dry ingredients just until moistened. Fold in cherry mixture. Pour into a 3-qt. slow cooker coated with cooking spray.
3. For topping, in a small saucepan, combine cola, sugar and brown sugar. Cook; stir until sugar is dissolved. Remove from heat; stir in chocolate and rum until smooth. Pour over batter; do not stir.
4. Cover and cook on high 2-2½ hours or until set. Turn off heat; let stand, covered, for 30 minutes. If desired, serve warm with ice cream and maraschino cherries.
1 piece: 500 cal., 17g fat (10g sat. fat), 34mg chol., 380mg sod., 80g carb. (59g sugars, 2g fiber), 5g pro.

Orange Cranberry Chocolate Cake: Use 1¾ cups orange soda, divided, and ½ cup dried cranberries. Add 1 tsp. orange zest. Proceed with recipe as directed.

WARM FETA CHEESE DIP

We're huge fans of appetizers, and this easy dip is a mashup of some of our favorite ingredients. It goes so well with tortilla chips or sliced French bread.
—*Ashley Lecker, Green Bay, WI*

- -

PREP: 5 min. • **COOK:** 2 hours
MAKES: 2 cups

- 1 pkg. (8 oz.) cream cheese, softened
- 1½ cups (6 oz.) crumbled feta cheese
- ½ cup chopped roasted sweet red peppers
- 3 Tbsp. minced fresh basil or 2 tsp. dried basil
  Sliced French bread baguette or tortilla chips

1. In small bowl, beat cream cheese, feta cheese, peppers and basil until blended.
2. Transfer to a greased 1½-qt. slow cooker; cook, covered, on low until heated through, 2-3 hours. Serve with bread or tortilla chips.
¼ cup: 155 cal., 13g fat (8g sat. fat), 42mg chol., 362mg sod., 2g carb. (1g sugars, 1g fiber), 5g pro.

WARM FETA
CHEESE DIP

COCONUT-MANGO MALVA PUDDING

My friend shared this amazing malva pudding recipe with me. Malva pudding is a dense, spongy cake drenched in a rich, sticky butter sauce. My slow-cooked tropical spin incorporates a creamy coconut sauce and juicy mangoes!
—*Carmell Childs, Orangeville, UT*

PREP: 20 min. **COOK:** 2½ hours + standing
MAKES: 12 servings

- 4 large eggs, room temperature
- 1½ cups sugar
- ¼ cup apricot preserves
- 2 Tbsp. butter, melted
- 1 can (13.66 oz.) coconut milk
- 2 tsp. vanilla extract
- 2 tsp. white vinegar
- 2 cups all-purpose flour
- 1¼ tsp. baking soda
- 1 tsp. salt

SAUCE
- 1 cup canned coconut milk
- ½ cup butter, melted
- ½ cup sugar
- 2 Tbsp. apricot preserves
- ½ tsp. coconut extract
- 2 medium mangoes, peeled and chopped
- ¼ cup sweetened shredded coconut, toasted
- 1 container (8 oz.) frozen whipped topping, thawed

1. In large bowl, beat eggs, sugar, apricot preserves and butter until combined. Add coconut milk, vanilla and vinegar; stir to combine (batter will be thin). In another bowl, whisk flour, baking soda and salt. Gradually stir flour mixture into batter just until moistened. Transfer to a greased 5-qt. slow cooker. Cook, covered, on high until a toothpick inserted in cake comes out with moist crumbs, 2½-3 hours.
2. Meanwhile, for sauce, whisk together coconut milk, butter, sugar, apricot preserves and extract until smooth. Poke holes in warm cake with a skewer or chopstick. Pour mixture evenly over pudding; let stand to allow pudding to absorb sauce, 15-20 minutes. Serve with chopped mango, coconut and whipped topping.

1 serving: 518 cal., 24g fat (19g sat. fat), 87mg chol., 452mg sod., 71g carb. (52g sugars, 2g fiber), 6g pro.

COCONUT-MANGO
MALVA PUDDING

PINEAPPLE UPSIDE-DOWN DUMP CAKE

RANCH MUSHROOMS

I got this recipe from my sister-in-law and it has become a favorite at family gatherings and parties. They don't last long once people know I have made them.
—*Jackie McGee, Byron, MN*

PREP: 10 min. • **COOK:** 3 hours
MAKES: 4 cups

- 1½ lbs. whole fresh mushrooms
- 1 cup butter, melted
- 1 envelope ranch salad dressing mix
  Optional: Chopped fresh dill weed or parsley

Place mushrooms in a 4- or 5-qt. slow cooker. In a small bowl, whisk butter and ranch mix; pour over mushrooms. Cook, covered, on low until the mushrooms are tender, about 3 hours. Serve with a slotted spoon. If desired, sprinkle with dill.

Freeze option: Freeze the mushrooms and juices in freezer containers. To use, partially thaw mushrooms in refrigerator overnight. Microwave, covered, on high in a microwave-safe dish until heated through, stirring occasionally; add a little broth or water if necessary.

¼ cup: 21 cal., 1g fat (1g sat. fat), 3mg chol., 47mg sod., 2g carb. (1g sugars, 0 fiber), 1g pro.

PINEAPPLE UPSIDE-DOWN DUMP CAKE

No matter the season, this dump cake recipe is marvelous! It works well with gluten-free and sugar-free cake mixes, too.
—*Karin Gatewood, Dallas, TX*

PREP: 10 min. • **COOK:** 2 hours + standing
MAKES: 10 servings

- ¾ cup butter, divided
- ⅔ cup packed brown sugar
- 1 jar (6 oz.) maraschino cherries, drained
- ½ cup chopped pecans, toasted
- 1 can (20 oz.) unsweetened pineapple tidbits or crushed pineapple, undrained
- 1 pkg. yellow cake mix (regular size)
  Vanilla ice cream, optional

1. In a microwave, melt ½ cup butter; stir in brown sugar. Spread evenly onto bottom of a greased 5-qt. slow cooker. Sprinkle with cherries and pecans; top with pineapple. Sprinkle evenly with dry cake mix. Melt remaining butter; drizzle over top.

2. Cook, covered, on high until the fruit mixture is bubbly, about 2 hours. (To avoid scorching, rotate the slow-cooker insert a half turn midway through cooking, lifting carefully with oven mitts.)

3. Turn off the slow cooker; let stand, uncovered, 30 minutes before serving. If desired, serve with ice cream.

½ cup: 455 cal., 22g fat (10g sat. fat), 37mg chol., 418mg sod., 66g carb. (47g sugars, 1g fiber), 3g pro.

TEST KITCHEN TIP

Sprinkle the cake mix in an even layer over the pineapple. If it's piled high in the center, the middle of the cake may be undercooked. A large slow cooker is used to keep the ingredient layers thin and to promote even cooking.

PINEAPPLE UPSIDE-DOWN DUMP CAKE

RANCH
MUSHROOMS

CINNAMON ORANGE CIDER

This pretty fall beverage is sure to be popular. You just might want to double this recipe and then fill the punch bowl for guests.
—*Mark Morgan, Waterford, WI*

- -

TAKES: 20 min. • **MAKES:** 1½ qt.

- 4 cups apple cider or juice
- 2 cups orange juice
- 3 Tbsp. Red Hots
- 1½ tsp. whole allspice
- 4½ tsp. honey

1. In a large saucepan, combine cider, juice and candies. Place allspice on a double thickness of cheesecloth; bring up corners of cloth and tie with string to form a bag. Add to pan. Bring to a boil. Reduce heat; cover and simmer until flavors are blended, 5 minutes.
2. Discard spice bag; stir in the honey. Transfer to a 3-qt. slow cooker; keep warm over low heat.

1 cup: 161 cal., 0 fat (0 sat. fat), 0 chol., 17mg sod., 40g carb. (34g sugars, 0 fiber), 0 pro.

"We've served this at our church's big fundraiser each Christmas for the past four years, and it's a huge hit! We make enough for 300 people, and we rarely have leftovers."
—BECKYJAYNE17 TASTEOFHOME.COM

INDIAN RICE & CARROT PUDDING

This recipe is rich in flavor and taste, and it is very easy to prepare.
—*Daljeet Singh, Coral Springs, FL*

- -

PREP: 15 min. • **COOK:** 2¾ hours
MAKES: 9 servings

- 3½ cups 1% milk
- 1 cup shredded carrots
- ½ cup uncooked basmati rice, washed and drained
- ¾ tsp. ground cardamom
- ½ tsp. ground cinnamon
- ¼ tsp. ground ginger
- ¼ cup unsalted pistachios, chopped, divided
- ½ cup agave nectar
- ⅓ cup raisins
- ¼ tsp. rose water, optional

Combine milk, carrots, rice, cardamom, cinnamon and ginger in a 4-qt. slow cooker. Stir in half the chopped pistachios. Cook, covered, on high heat for 2½ hours, stirring occasionally. Add agave and raisins; reduce heat to low. Cover and cook until rice is tender, 15 minutes longer. If desired, stir in rose water. Serve warm or refrigerate and serve chilled. Garnish each serving with remaining pistachios.

½ cup: 176 cal., 3g fat (1g sat. fat), 5mg chol., 66mg sod., 35g carb. (23g sugars, 1g fiber), 5g pro.

INDIAN RICE & CARROT PUDDING

FUDGY CHOCOLATE-ALMOND SLOW-COOKER BROWNIES

When the heating element in my oven broke, I knew I would have to think of another way to make the brownies I had promised to take to a potluck that evening. But without an oven, how could I possibly make the promised brownies? The solution equaled these divine slow-cooker brownies.

—*Marion Karlin, Waterloo, IA*

- -

PREP: 30 min. • **COOK:** 2 hours
MAKES: 8 servings

- ½ cup butter, softened
- 1 cup sugar
- 4 large eggs, room temperature
- 2 cups chocolate syrup
- 1 tsp. vanilla extract
- 1 cup all-purpose flour
- ½ tsp. baking powder
- 1 cup chopped almonds
- 8 half-pint jars and lids
- 3 cups hot water

GANACHE

- ½ cup refrigerated nondairy creamer
- 6 oz. white candy coating, chopped
- ⅓ cup sliced almonds

1. In large bowl, cream butter and sugar until light and fluffy, 5-7 minutes. Add eggs, 1 at a time, beating well after each addition. Beat in chocolate syrup and vanilla. Add flour and baking powder, stirring just until moistened. Stir in chopped almonds.

2. Spoon mixture into 8 greased half-pint jars. Center lids on jars and screw on bands until fingertip tight. Add hot water to a 7-qt. oval slow cooker; place jars in slow cooker. Cook, covered, on high until a toothpick inserted in center of brownies comes out clean, 2-3 hours. Remove jars from slow cooker to wire racks to cool completely.

3. Meanwhile, bring creamer to a boil in a small saucepan over high heat. Stir in candy coating until melted. Remove from heat; cool to room temperature. Spread ganache over cooled brownies. Sprinkle with sliced almonds.

1 serving: 743 cal., 32g fat (16g sat. fat), 124mg chol., 198mg sod., 107g carb. (82g sugars, 5g fiber), 11g pro.

FUDGY CHOCOLATE-ALMOND
SLOW-COOKER BROWNIES

SLOW-COOKER
MONKEY BREAD

SLOW-COOKER MONKEY BREAD

I often take this monkey bread to church potlucks—children and adults love it! The rum extract is optional.
—*Lisa Leaper, Worthington, OH*

PREP: 20 min. • **COOK:** 2½ hours
MAKES: 10 servings

- 1 cup sugar
- ¾ cup packed brown sugar
- 2 tsp. ground cinnamon
- ½ tsp. ground allspice
- 4 tubes (6 oz. each) refrigerated buttermilk biscuits, quartered
- ¾ cup butter, melted
- ½ cup apple juice
- 1 tsp. vanilla extract
- 1 tsp. rum extract
  Toasted chopped pecans, optional

1. Line a 5-qt. slow cooker with a piece of aluminum foil, letting ends extend up the sides. Grease foil.
2. Combine the sugars, cinnamon and allspice in a large bowl; sprinkle 3 Tbsp. sugar mixture in bottom of prepared slow cooker. Add biscuit pieces to bowl; toss to coat. Transfer coated biscuits to slow cooker; sprinkle any remaining sugar mixture over biscuits.
3. Stir together butter, apple juice and extracts; pour over biscuits.
4. Cook, covered, on low 2½-3 hours. Remove lid and let stand for 10 minutes. Carefully invert onto serving platter. If desired, sprinkle with pecans.

8 biscuit pieces: 473 cal., 22g fat (12g sat. fat), 37mg chol., 675mg sod., 68g carb. (41g sugars, 0 fiber), 4g pro.

SLOW-COOKER STRAWBERRY PUDDING CAKE

SLOW-COOKER STRAWBERRY PUDDING CAKE

This recipe was created because of my love for strawberry cheesecake. I had these ingredients in my pantry and thought I'd give it a whirl. Wow, the flavors are just like strawberry cheesecake—only in a warm, comforting cake version. It's a whole lot easier than making cheesecake, too!
—*Lisa Renshaw, Kansas City, MO*

PREP: 20 min. • **COOK:** 4 hours + standing
MAKES: 10 servings

- 3 cups cold 2% milk
- 1 pkg. (3.4 oz.) instant cheesecake or vanilla pudding mix
- 1 pkg. strawberry cake mix (regular size)
- 1 cup water
- 3 large eggs, room temperature
- ⅓ cup canola oil
- 2 cups toasted coconut marshmallows, quartered
  Optional: Strawberry ice cream topping and sliced fresh strawberries

1. In a large bowl, whisk milk and pudding mix 2 minutes. Transfer to a greased 4- or 5-qt. slow cooker. Prepare cake mix batter according to package directions with water, eggs and oil; pour over pudding.
2. Cook, covered, on low until edges of cake are golden brown (center will be moist), about 4 hours.
3. Remove slow-cooker insert; sprinkle cake with marshmallows. Let cake stand, uncovered, 10 minutes before serving. If desired, serve with ice cream topping and strawberries.

1 serving: 377 cal., 13g fat (4g sat. fat), 62mg chol., 540mg sod., 56g carb. (37g sugars, 1g fiber), 6g pro.

PINEAPPLE SHRIMP
TACOS, PAGE 148

150

141

99

119

Stovetop Suppers

From tacos and fish sticks to hearty stews and chicken parmigiana, nothing warms the heart like good, simple meals cooked on the stovetop. These are the go-to dishes called for on busy weeknights.

Beef & Ground Beef

SOUTHWEST
FRITO PIE

SOUTHWEST FRITO PIE

I got a rweal culture shock when we moved to New Mexico several years ago, but we grew to love the food. Now back in South Carolina, we still crave New Mexican dishes. This is one of my go-to favorites.
—*Janet Scoggins, North Augusta, SC*

- -

PREP: 20 min. • **COOK:** 25 min.
MAKES: 6 servings

- 2 lbs. lean ground beef (90% lean)
- 3 Tbsp. chili powder
- 2 Tbsp. all-purpose flour
- 1 tsp. salt
- 1 tsp. garlic powder
- 2 cups water
- 1 can (15 oz.) pinto beans, rinsed and drained, optional
- 4½ cups Fritos corn chips
- 2 cups shredded lettuce
- 1½ cups shredded cheddar cheese
- ¾ cup chopped tomatoes
- 6 Tbsp. finely chopped onion
  Optional: Sour cream and minced fresh cilantro

1. In a 6-qt. stockpot, cook the beef over medium heat until no longer pink, breaking into crumbles; drain. Stir in chili powder, flour, salt and garlic powder until blended. Gradually stir in water and, if desired, beans.

2. Bring to a boil. Reduce heat; simmer, uncovered, 12-15 minutes or until thickened, stirring occasionally.

3. To serve, divide chips among 6 serving bowls. Top with beef mixture, lettuce, cheese, tomatoes and onion. If desired, top with sour cream and cilantro.

1 serving: 615 cal., 38g fat (16g sat. fat), 143mg chol., 915mg sod., 25g carb. (2g sugars, 3g fiber), 43g pro.

RED FLANNEL
STEW

STUFFED GREEN PEPPERS

My family always asks me to make this dish for them, especially in the summer when fresh tomatoes and green peppers are readily available. I got the recipe from my mother-in-law.

—*Helen Englehart, Maplewood, MN*

PREP: 25 min. • **COOK:** 55 min.
MAKES: 4 servings

- 6 medium fresh tomatoes, peeled, seeded and chopped
- 1 medium onion, chopped
- 3 celery ribs, diced
- 1 can (8 oz.) tomato sauce
- 1 cup water
- 2 tsp. salt, divided
- ½ tsp. pepper, divided
- 4 medium green peppers
- 1 lb. lean ground beef (90% lean)
- 1 cup instant rice, cooked
- 1 tsp. dried basil

1. In a large saucepan or Dutch oven, combine tomatoes, onion, celery, tomato sauce, water, 1 tsp. salt and ¼ tsp. pepper. Bring to a boil. Reduce heat and simmer, 10-15 minutes.

2. Meanwhile, cut the tops off the green peppers and remove seeds; set aside. In a bowl, combine ground beef, rice, basil and remaining salt and pepper; mix well. Fill peppers with beef mixture. Carefully place peppers in tomato sauce. Spoon some sauce over tops of peppers.

3. Cover and simmer until beef is cooked and peppers are tender, 40-45 minutes.

1 serving: 324 cal., 9g fat (4g sat. fat), 56mg chol., 1565mg sod., 34g carb. (13g sugars, 7g fiber), 27g pro.

❄

RED FLANNEL STEW

When I was a child, every Saturday night was red flannel night. Grandpa and I wore our red flannel long underwear to supper and Grandma, the cook, dressed in a long calico dress and sunbonnet. We'd eat this stew spooned over fluffy southern-style biscuits. Grandma learned to make the stew from earlier generations of our family.

—*Kathy Padgett, Diamond City, AR*

PREP: 25 min. • **COOK:** 1½ hours
MAKES: 5 servings

- 2 whole fresh beets, washed, trimmed and halved
- 6 cups water, divided
- 1 lb. corned beef brisket, trimmed and cut into 1-in. pieces
- 4 small carrots, sliced
- 1 large potato, cubed
- 1 small turnip, peeled and cubed
- 1 small onion, chopped
- 1 tsp. each dried parsley flakes, basil and thyme
- ¼ tsp. salt
- ⅛ tsp. pepper

1. In a large saucepan, bring beets and 4 cups water to a boil. Reduce heat; simmer, uncovered, 20-25 minutes or until tender. Drain, reserving 2 cups cooking liquid. Peel and dice beets; set aside.

2. In the same pan, combine corned beef, carrots, potato, turnip, onion, seasonings, remaining water and reserved cooking liquid. Bring to a boil. Reduce heat; cover and simmer until meat and vegetables are tender, 1¼-1½ hours. Stir in diced beets; heat through.

Freeze option: Freeze cooled stew in freezer containers. To use, partially thaw in refrigerator overnight. Heat through in a saucepan, stirring occasionally; add water if necessary.

1⅓ cups: 209 cal., 9g fat (3g sat. fat), 31mg chol., 881mg sod., 22g carb. (6g sugars, 3g fiber), 11g pro.

TEST KITCHEN TIP

Since instant rice doubles in volume, 1 cup instant rice makes 2 cups cooked. You can substitute 2 cups of your favorite cooked rice in this recipe, or cook ⅔ cup long grain rice.

SPICY BEEF & PEPPER STIR-FRY

Think of this stir-fry as your chance to play with heat and spice. I balance the beef with coconut milk and a spritz of lime.
—*Joy Zacharia, Clearwater, FL*

PREP: 20 min. + standing • **COOK:** 10 min.
MAKES: 4 servings

- 1   lb. beef top sirloin steak, cut into thin strips
- 1   Tbsp. minced fresh gingerroot
- 3   garlic cloves, minced, divided
- ¼   tsp. pepper
- ¾   tsp. salt, divided
- 1   cup light coconut milk
- 2   Tbsp. sugar
- 1   Tbsp. Sriracha chili sauce
- ½   tsp. grated lime zest
- 2   Tbsp. lime juice
- 2   Tbsp. canola oil, divided

- 1   large sweet red pepper, cut into thin strips
- ½   medium red onion, thinly sliced
- 1   jalapeno pepper, seeded and thinly sliced
- 4   cups fresh baby spinach
- 2   green onions, thinly sliced
- 2   Tbsp. chopped fresh cilantro

1. In a large bowl, toss beef with ginger, 2 garlic cloves, pepper and ½ tsp. salt; let stand 15 minutes. In a small bowl, whisk coconut milk, sugar, chili sauce, lime zest, lime juice and remaining salt until blended.
2. In a large skillet, heat 1 Tbsp. oil over medium-high heat. Add beef; stir-fry until no longer pink, 2-3 minutes. Remove from the pan.
3. Stir-fry red pepper, red onion, jalapeno and the remaining garlic in the remaining oil just until the vegetables are crisp-tender, 2-3 minutes. Stir in coconut milk mixture; heat through. Add spinach and beef; cook until spinach is wilted and beef is heated through, stirring occasionally. Sprinkle with green onions and cilantro.
Note: Wear disposable gloves when cutting hot peppers; the oils can burn skin. Avoid touching your face.
¾ cup: 312 cal., 16g fat (5g sat. fat), 46mg chol., 641mg sod., 15g carb. (10g sugars, 2g fiber), 26g pro. **Diabetic exchanges:** 3 lean meat, 2 fat, 1 vegetable, ½ starch.

CHEESEBURGER SOUP WITH RICE

I don't have a lot of extra time to spend in the kitchen, so I appreciate that I can cook this soup's ground beef and rice in advance to speed up my dinner prep on busy days.
—*Jane Rowe, Wichita, KS*

TAKES: 30 min.
MAKES: 10 servings

- 1   cup shredded carrot
- 1   cup chopped onion
- ½   cup chopped celery
- 2   cans (14½ oz. each) chicken broth
- 1   lb. ground beef, cooked, crumbled and drained
- 2   cups cooked long grain rice
- 3   cups 2% milk
- 1   lb. Velveeta, cubed
- 1   cup sour cream

1. In a large saucepan, combine carrot, onion, celery and broth. Bring to a boil. Reduce heat; simmer, uncovered, for 15 minutes or until vegetables are tender.
2. Stir in the beef, rice, milk and cheese; simmer, uncovered, until cheese is melted, stirring occasionally (do not boil). Just before serving, whisk in sour cream; heat through.
1 cup: 368 cal., 22g fat (13g sat. fat), 77mg chol., 790mg sod., 19g carb. (10g sugars, 1g fiber), 22g pro.

SPICY BEEF & PEPPER STIR-FRY

CHEESEBURGER SOUP
WITH RICE

ITALIAN BEEF & SHELLS

I fix this supper when I'm pressed for time. It's as tasty as it is fast. Team it with salad, bread and fresh fruit for a healthy meal that really satisfies.
—*Mike Tchou, Pepper Pike, OH*

TAKES: 30 min. • **MAKES:** 4 servings

1½ cups uncooked medium pasta shells
1 lb. lean ground beef (90% lean)
1 small onion, chopped
1 garlic clove, minced
1 jar (24 oz.) marinara sauce
1 small yellow summer squash, quartered and sliced
1 small zucchini, quartered and sliced
¼ cup dry red wine or reduced-sodium beef broth
½ tsp. salt
½ tsp. Italian seasoning
½ tsp. pepper

1. Cook the pasta according to the package directions.
2. Meanwhile, in a Dutch oven, cook beef, onion and garlic over medium heat until meat is no longer pink, breaking it into crumbles; drain. Stir in marinara sauce, squash, zucchini, wine and seasonings. Bring to a boil. Reduce heat; simmer, uncovered, 10-15 minutes or until thickened. Drain pasta; stir into beef mixture and heat through.

1¾ cups: 396 cal., 10g fat (4g sat. fat), 71mg chol., 644mg sod., 45g carb. (16g sugars, 5g fiber), 29g pro. **Diabetic exchanges:** 3 starch, 3 lean meat.

GARLIC-BUTTER STEAK

This quick and easy skillet entree is restaurant quality. It is sure to be a staple in your house, as it is in mine! It's a cozy dinner for two.

—*Lily Julow, Lawrenceville, GA*

TAKES: 20 min. • **MAKES:** 2 servings

2 Tbsp. butter, softened, divided
1 tsp. minced fresh parsley
½ tsp. minced garlic
¼ tsp. reduced-sodium soy sauce
1 beef flat iron steak or boneless top sirloin steak (¾ lb.)
⅛ tsp. salt
⅛ tsp. pepper

1. Mix 1 Tbsp. butter with the parsley, garlic and soy sauce.
2. Sprinkle steak with salt and pepper. In a large skillet, heat remaining butter over medium heat. Add steak; cook until meat reaches desired doneness (for medium-rare, a thermometer should read 135°; medium, 140°; medium-well, 145°), 4-7 minutes per side. Serve with garlic butter.

4 oz. cooked beef with 2 tsp. garlic butter: 316 cal., 20g fat (10g sat. fat), 124mg chol., 337mg sod., 0 carb. (0 sugars, 0 fiber), 32g pro.

TEST KITCHEN TIPS

• To achieve a perfect sear on your steak, sprinkle it with salt and pepper and then let it stand 10-15 minutes at room temperature. Salt draws moisture to the surface of the steak, which creates a luscious browning when it meets the heat.

• Let the meat stand a few minutes after cooking so the juices can redistribute throughout. This results in a nice and juicy steak.

GARLIC-BUTTER STEAK

BEST VEAL SCALLOPINI

FRIED MUSTARD CUBED STEAKS

This recipe is a cinch to make and so flavorful. Instead of Dijon, you can use regular mustard, hot-and-spicy mustard or your favorite variety.
—*Lori Shepherd, Warsaw, IN*

TAKES: 30 min. • **MAKES:** 6 servings

- 1 jar (10 oz.) Dijon mustard
- 1¼ cups water
- 6 beef cubed steaks (⅓ lb. each)
- 2 cups all-purpose flour
- ½ tsp. salt
- ⅛ tsp. pepper
  Oil for frying

1. In a large resealable bag, combine the mustard and water; add steaks. Seal bag and turn to coat; let stand for 10 minutes. Drain steaks, discarding marinade.
2. In a shallow bowl, combine the flour, salt and pepper. Dip the steaks in flour mixture. In an electric skillet, heat ¼ in. oil to 375°.
3. Fry steaks, in batches, until crisp and lightly browned, 3-4 minutes on each side.
1 serving: 368 cal., 7g fat (2g sat. fat), 85mg chol., 813mg sod., 34g carb. (1g sugars, 1g fiber), 40g pro.

"I used half Dijon and half yellow mustard because that's what I had on hand. This was very easy to put together, and I like stronger flavors than just salt and pepper."
—WORSHIPGUY, TASTEOFHOME.COM

BEST VEAL SCALLOPINI

I found the original version of this dish in a magazine and adjusted it to suit my family's tastes. Delicate, fine-textured veal needs only a short cooking time, which is something that makes this simple entree even more attractive.
—*Ruth Lee, Troy, ON*

TAKES: 25 min. • **MAKES:** 2 servings

- 2 veal cutlets (about 4 oz. each)
- 2 Tbsp. all-purpose flour
- ½ tsp. salt
- ¼ tsp. pepper
- 3 Tbsp. butter, divided
- 1 Tbsp. olive oil
- ¼ lb. fresh mushrooms, thinly sliced
- ⅓ cup chicken broth
- 2 tsp. minced fresh parsley

1. Flatten cutlets to ⅛-in. thickness. In a shallow dish, combine flour, salt and pepper. Add veal; turn to coat. In a skillet, heat 2 Tbsp. butter and oil over medium heat. Add veal; cook until juices run clear, about 1 minute on each side. Remove and keep warm.
2. Add the mushrooms to skillet; cook and stir until tender, 2-3 minutes. Spoon over the veal. Stir broth into skillet, stirring to loosen any browned bits. Add parsley and the remaining butter; cook and stir until slightly thickened, 1-2 minutes longer. Pour over veal and mushrooms.
1 serving: 435 cal., 35g fat (16g sat. fat), 120mg chol., 941mg sod., 8g carb. (0 sugars, 0 fiber), 21g pro.
Wiener Schnitzel: Omit oil, mushrooms, chicken broth and parsley. Coat cutlets with flour mixture, then dip in 1 beaten egg and coat with ⅓ cup dry bread crumbs. Cook veal in the entire amount of butter. Serve with lemon slices.

SKILLET STEAK SUPPER

ALBONDIGAS

My Grandmother Trinidad loved to make this dish. We like to serve the albondigas over tostadas sprinkled with raw cabbage.
—*Wanda Knutson, Waco, TX*

PREP: 15 min. • **COOK:** 20 min.
MAKES: 10 cups

- 1 large onion, finely chopped
- 2 garlic cloves, finely chopped
- 1½ cups tomato sauce
- 8 cups beef broth
- 1½ lbs. lean ground beef (90% lean)
- ⅓ cup uncooked long grain rice
- 1 large egg, lightly beaten
- 1 tsp. salt
- 1 tsp. pepper
- 1 Tbsp. 2% milk
- ⅛ tsp. ground cumin
- ⅛ tsp. saffron threads or
  ½ tsp. ground turmeric
- 10 saltines, crushed
  Optional: Tostadas, shredded cabbage and cilantro

1. In a Dutch oven, cook onion, garlic and ½ cup tomato sauce with olive oil until onion is tender. Add broth and ½ cup tomato sauce; bring to a simmer.
2. Meanwhile, in a bowl, mix beef, rice, egg, salt, pepper, milk, cumin, saffron, crushed crackers and remaining ½ cup tomato sauce until combined. With wet hands, form into 1-in. balls. Gently add meatballs to simmering broth; cook, stirring occasionally, 20-25 minutes. If desired, serve with tostadas, cabbage and cilantro.
1½ cups: 300 cal., 12g fat (4g sat. fat), 102mg chol., 1998mg sod., 19g carb. (2g sugars, 2g fiber), 28g pro.

DID YOU KNOW?

Saffron, the fine stigmas of the tiny purple crocus flower, is the most expensive spice in the world. It grows mainly in a belt that runs from Morocco and Spain in the west to Tajikistan and India in the east. Each flower makes just three stigmas, which must be gathered by hand. A gram of good-quality saffron costs around $13, and that works out to $6,000 a pound! Luckily, a little bit goes a long way.

SKILLET STEAK SUPPER

With all the ingredients cooked in one skillet, this steak dish couldn't be quicker to prepare—or to clean up! The wine and mushroom sauce makes it seem special.
—*Sandra Fisher, Missoula, MT*

TAKES: 20 min. • **MAKES:** 2 servings

- 1 beef top sirloin steak (¾ lb.)
- ½ tsp. salt, divided
- ½ tsp. pepper, divided
- 1 Tbsp. olive oil
- 1 to 2 Tbsp. butter
- ½ lb. sliced fresh mushrooms
- 2 Tbsp. white wine or chicken broth
- 3 Tbsp. chopped green onions
- 1 Tbsp. Worcestershire sauce
- 1 tsp. Dijon mustard

1. Sprinkle steak with ¼ tsp. each salt and pepper. In a skillet, heat oil over medium-high heat; cook steak to desired doneness (for medium-rare, a thermometer should read 135°; medium, 140°), 4-6 minutes per side. Remove from pan; keep warm.
2. In same skillet, heat the butter over medium-high heat; saute mushrooms until tender. Stir in wine; bring to a boil, stirring to loosen browned bits from pan. Stir in green onions, Worcestershire sauce, mustard and the remaining salt and pepper. Cut steak in half; serve with mushroom mixture.
1 serving: 368 cal., 20g fat (7g sat. fat), 85mg chol., 915mg sod., 6g carb. (3g sugars, 2g fiber), 40g pro.

ALBONDIGAS

BEEF SHORT RIBS
IN BURGUNDY SAUCE

BEEF SHORT RIBS IN BURGUNDY SAUCE

My stepdad—a U.S. Army general—got this recipe from his aide, who said it was his mother's best Sunday meal. It's now a mouthwatering favorite in our family, too.
—*Judy Batson, Tampa, FL*

PREP: 35 min. • **COOK:** 2¼ hours
MAKES: 6 servings

- 3 lbs. bone-in beef short ribs
- 3 Tbsp. butter
- 1 large sweet onion, halved and sliced
- 2 celery ribs, thinly sliced
- 1 medium carrot, thinly sliced
- 1 garlic clove, minced
  Dash dried thyme
- 2 Tbsp. all-purpose flour
- 1 cup water
- 1 cup dry red wine or beef broth
- 1 beef bouillon cube or
  1 tsp. beef bouillon granules
- 2 Tbsp. minced fresh parsley
- ½ tsp. Worcestershire sauce
- ¼ tsp. salt
- ¼ tsp. browning sauce, optional
- ⅛ tsp. pepper

1. Preheat oven to 450°. Place the short ribs on a rack in a shallow roasting pan. Roast 30-40 minutes or until browned, turning once.
2. Meanwhile, in a Dutch oven, heat butter over medium heat. Add the onion, celery and carrot; cook and stir until tender, 10-12 minutes. Add garlic and thyme; cook 1 minute longer. Stir in flour until blended; gradually stir in the water and wine. Add bouillon and parsley, stirring to dissolve bouillon.
3. Transfer the ribs to Dutch oven; bring to a boil. Reduce heat; simmer, covered, 2-2½ hours or until meat is tender.
4. Remove short ribs; keep warm. Skim the fat from sauce; stir in the remaining ingredients. Serve with ribs.
1 serving: 264 cal., 17g fat (8g sat. fat), 70mg chol., 355mg sod., 8g carb. (4g sugars, 1g fiber), 19g pro.

STEAK & MUSHROOM STROGANOFF

STEAK & MUSHROOM STROGANOFF

This homey recipe of steak and egg noodles in a creamy sauce is just like what we had at my gran's house when we visited. It's one of my favorite memory meals, as I call them.
—*Janelle Shank, Omaha, NE*

TAKES: 30 min. • **MAKES:** 6 servings

- 6 cups uncooked egg noodles (about 12 oz.)
- 1 beef top sirloin steak (1½ lbs.), cut into 2x½-in. strips
- 1 Tbsp. canola oil
- ½ tsp. salt
- ½ tsp. pepper
- 2 Tbsp. butter
- 1 lb. sliced fresh mushrooms
- 2 shallots, finely chopped
- ½ cup beef broth
- 1 Tbsp. snipped fresh dill
- 1 cup sour cream

1. Cook noodles according to package directions; drain.
2. Meanwhile, toss beef with oil, salt and pepper. Place a large skillet over medium-high heat; saute half the beef until browned, 2-3 minutes. Remove from pan; repeat with remaining beef.
3. In same pan, heat butter over medium-high heat; saute mushrooms until lightly browned, 4-6 minutes. Add shallots; cook and stir until tender, 1-2 minutes. Stir in broth, dill and beef; heat through. Reduce heat to medium; stir in sour cream until blended. Serve with noodles.
1 serving: 455 cal., 19g fat (10g sat. fat), 115mg chol., 379mg sod., 34g carb. (4g sugars, 2g fiber), 34g pro.

TEST KITCHEN TIP

A simple switch to reduced-fat sour cream will save 40 calories and 5g fat per serving.

STOUT & SHIITAKE POT ROAST

ASIAN BEEF & NOODLES

This yummy, economical dish takes only five ingredients—all of which are easy to keep on hand. Serve with a dash of soy sauce and a side of fresh pineapple slices. You can also try it with ground turkey instead of beef!
—*Laura Shull Stenberg, Wyoming, MN*

- -

TAKES: 20 min. • **MAKES:** 4 servings

- 1 lb. lean ground beef (90% lean)
- 2 pkg. (3 oz. each) Oriental ramen noodles, crumbled
- 2½ cups water
- 2 cups frozen broccoli stir-fry vegetable blend
- ¼ tsp. ground ginger
- 2 Tbsp. thinly sliced green onion

1. In a large skillet, cook beef over medium heat until no longer pink, breaking it into crumbles; drain. Add the contents of 1 ramen noodle flavoring packet; stir until dissolved. Remove beef; set aside.
2. In the same skillet, combine the water, vegetables, ginger, noodles and contents of remaining flavoring packet. Bring to a boil. Reduce heat; cover and simmer for 3-4 minutes or until noodles are tender, stirring occasionally. Return beef to the pan and heat through. Stir in onion.
1½ cups: 383 cal., 16g fat (7g sat. fat), 71mg chol., 546mg sod., 29g carb. (2g sugars, 2g fiber), 27g pro.

"My family really liked this, and their tastes range from wanting it bland to super spicy. I used a bag of frozen stir-fry veggies, and next time I'm going to use fresh ginger and add some pepper sauce."
—LANILEI, TASTEOFHOME.COM

STOUT & SHIITAKE POT ROAST

Mushrooms, onions and a bottle of Guinness add excellent flavor to my pot roast. This one-dish wonder may taste even better the next day.
—*Madeleine Bessette, Coeur d'Alene, ID*

- -

PREP: 30 min. • **COOK:** 1¾ hours
MAKES: 6 servings

- 3 Tbsp. olive oil, divided
- 1 boneless beef chuck roast (2 to 3 lbs.)
- 2 medium onions, sliced
- 1 garlic clove, minced
- 1 bottle (12 oz.) stout or nonalcoholic beer
- ½ oz. dried shiitake mushrooms (about ½ cup)
- 1 Tbsp. brown sugar
- 1 tsp. Worcestershire sauce
- ½ tsp. dried savory
- 1 lb. red potatoes (about 8 small), cut into 1-in. pieces
- 2 medium carrots, sliced
- ½ cup water
- ½ tsp. salt
- ¼ tsp. pepper

1. In a Dutch oven, heat 1 Tbsp. oil over medium heat. Brown roast on all sides; remove from pan.
2. In same pan, heat the remaining oil. Add onions and garlic; cook and stir until tender. Add the beer, stirring to loosen the browned bits from pan. Stir in the mushrooms, brown sugar, Worcestershire sauce and savory. Return roast to pan. Bring to a boil. Reduce heat; simmer, covered, 1½ hours.
3. Stir in remaining ingredients. Return to a boil. Reduce heat; simmer, covered, 15-25 minutes longer or until meat and vegetables are tender. If desired, skim fat and thicken cooking juices for gravy.
4 oz. cooked beef with 1 cup vegetables: 441 cal., 21g fat (7g sat. fat), 98mg chol., 293mg sod., 24g carb. (9g sugars, 3g fiber), 33g pro.

ASIAN BEEF
& NOODLES

BEEF & BEAN ENCHILADAS

These tried-and-true enchiladas are just what you need on a rushed weeknight. And leftovers reheat like a dream.
—*Myra Innes, Auburn, KS*

- -

TAKES: 30 min. • **MAKES:** 10 servings

1	lb. ground beef
2	cans (16 oz. each) refried beans
1½	tsp. dried minced onion
1	to 2 tsp. chili powder
½	tsp. salt
10	flour tortillas (8 in.), warmed
¼	cup chopped onion
1½	cups shredded cheddar cheese, divided
1	can (10 oz.) enchilada sauce, warmed
1	can (2½ oz.) sliced ripe olives, drained

1. In a large skillet, cook beef over medium heat until no longer pink, 5-7 minutes, breaking it into crumbles; drain. Stir in beans, dried minced onion, chili powder and salt; heat through.

2. Place about ⅓ cup down the center of each tortilla. Sprinkle each with onion and cheese. Fold bottom and sides over filling. Pour sauce over top; garnish with olives.

1 enchilada: 378 cal., 14g fat (6g sat. fat), 47mg chol., 993mg sod., 43g carb. (1g sugars, 6g fiber), 22g pro.

DIJON BEEF TENDERLOIN

I like having an ace recipe up my sleeve, and this tenderloin with Dijon is my go-to for birthdays, buffets and holidays.
—*Donna Lindecamp, Morganton, NC*

- -

TAKES: 20 min. • **MAKES:** 4 servings

4	beef tenderloin steaks (1 in. thick and 4 oz. each)
½	tsp. salt
¼	tsp. pepper
5	Tbsp. butter, divided
1	large onion, halved and thinly sliced
1	cup beef stock
1	Tbsp. Dijon mustard

1. Sprinkle steaks with salt and pepper. In a large skillet, heat 2 Tbsp. butter over medium-high heat. Add the steaks; cook 4-6 minutes on each side or until meat reaches desired doneness (for medium-rare, a thermometer should read 135°; medium, 140°; medium-well, 145°). Remove from pan; keep warm.

2. In the same pan, heat 1 Tbsp. butter over medium heat. Add onion; cook and stir 4-6 minutes or until tender. Stir in stock; bring to a boil. Cook 1-2 minutes or until liquid is reduced by half. Stir in mustard; remove from heat. Cube the remaining butter; stir into sauce just until blended. Serve with steaks.

1 steak with ¼ cup sauce: 317 cal., 21g fat (12g sat. fat), 88mg chol., 626mg sod., 5g carb. (2g sugars, 1g fiber), 26g pro.

DIJON
BEEF TENDERLOIN

GROUND BEEF CHOW MEIN

Here's a quick way to spice up ordinary burgers—our family sure enjoys the change of pace.

—Marjorie Nolan, Oakland, IL

- -

TAKES: 30 min. • **MAKES:** 8 servings

1 lb. ground beef
1 can (14½ oz.) diced tomatoes, undrained
1 tsp. Worcestershire sauce
1 to 2 tsp. chili powder
1 tsp. garlic salt
½ tsp. ground mustard
½ tsp. ground cumin
½ tsp. sugar
8 hamburger buns, split and toasted
1 cup shredded cheddar cheese
2 cups shredded lettuce

1. In a large skillet, cook beef over medium heat until no longer pink, 5-7 minutes, breaking it into crumbles; drain. Stir in tomatoes, Worcestershire sauce and the next 5 ingredients. Bring to a boil.
2. Reduce heat; simmer, uncovered, until thickened, 15-20 minutes. Spoon onto buns; top with cheese and lettuce.
1 serving: 280 cal., 11g fat (6g sat. fat), 43mg chol., 705mg sod., 26g carb. (5g sugars, 2g fiber), 17g pro.

GROUND BEEF CHOW MEIN

My grandma used to make a fabulous chop suey with pork, but I found this recipe that uses ground beef and has the same flavor. It's quick and tasty, and the leftovers are wonderful.

—Ann Nolte, Riverview, FL

- -

TAKES: 30 min. • **MAKES:** 5 servings

2 cups uncooked instant rice
1 lb. ground beef
1 can (14½ oz.) beef broth
1½ cups chopped celery
1 can (14 oz.) bean sprouts, drained
1 can (8 oz.) sliced water chestnuts, drained
1 jar (4½ oz.) sliced mushrooms, drained
1 jar (2 oz.) pimientos, drained and diced
2 Tbsp. soy sauce
½ tsp. ground ginger
2 Tbsp. cornstarch
3 Tbsp. water

1. Cook the instant rice according to the package directions.
2. Meanwhile, in a large skillet, cook beef over medium heat until no longer pink, breaking it into crumbles; drain. Add the broth, celery, bean sprouts, water chestnuts, mushrooms, pimientos, soy sauce and ginger. Bring to a boil. Reduce heat; cover and simmer for 10 minutes, stirring occasionally.
3. In a small bowl, combine cornstarch and water until smooth. Gradually stir into skillet. Bring to a boil; cook and stir 2 minutes, until thickened. Serve with rice.
1 cup chow mein with ¾ cup rice: 380 cal., 11g fat (4g sat. fat), 56mg chol., 949mg sod., 45g carb. (2g sugars, 4g fiber), 23g pro.

QUICK BEEF
VEGETABLE SOUP

QUICK BEEF VEGETABLE SOUP

At the end of a long day, you want to put something quick, warm and substantial on the table for your family. This hefty vegetable soup delivers. It will have you out of the kitchen in no time flat!

—D. M. Hillock, Hartford, MI

TAKES: 25 min.
MAKES: 4 servings

- 1 lb. ground beef
- ½ cup chopped onion
- 1 can (15 oz.) tomato sauce
- 1½ cups frozen mixed vegetables, thawed
- 1¼ cups frozen corn, thawed
- 1¼ cups beef broth
- 1 Tbsp. soy sauce
- 1 Tbsp. molasses

In a large skillet, cook the beef and onion over medium heat until meat is no longer pink, breaking it into crumbles; drain. Stir in the remaining ingredients. Bring to a boil. Reduce heat; cover and simmer for 10 minutes or until hot and bubbly.

Freeze option: Serve immediately, or cool and transfer to freezer containers. May be frozen for up to 3 months. To use frozen soup, thaw in the refrigerator overnight. Transfer to a saucepan. Cover and cook over medium heat until heated through.

1¾ cups: 318 cal., 11g fat (5g sat. fat), 56mg chol., 1099mg sod., 30g carb. (8g sugars, 5g fiber), 27g pro.

"After draining the ground beef, I browned a half roll of beef smoked sausage, cut lengthwise and then into bite-sized half-moon pieces. The sausage gave the soup a sweet yet earthy flavor. It is now a family favorite."
—ASSELSTINE, TASTEOFHOME.COM

SAUCY SKILLET STEAKS

SAUCY SKILLET STEAKS

These juicy ribeye steaks couldn't be easier. I prefer steak, but I've also cooked the recipe with chicken breasts, fish, veal and hamburgers, so use whatever meat or fish you have.

—Karen Haen, Sturgeon Bay, WI

TAKES: 30 min. • **MAKES:** 4 servings

- 4 beef ribeye steaks (¾ in. thick and 8 oz. each)
- ¼ cup butter
- 1 large onion, chopped
- 4 garlic cloves, minced
- ⅓ cup beef broth
- 2 Tbsp. Dijon mustard
  Salt and pepper to taste
- 1 Tbsp. minced fresh parsley

1. Heat a large nonstick skillet over medium heat. In batches, brown steaks, 1-2 minutes on each side. Remove from pan; set aside.

2. In same skillet, heat the butter over medium-high heat. Add onion; cook and stir until tender, 3-5 minutes. Add garlic; cook 1 minute longer. Stir in broth.

3. Return steaks to pan; cook 4 minutes. Brush tops with mustard; turn and cook until steaks reach desired doneness (for medium-rare, a thermometer should read 135°; medium, 140°; medium-well, 145°), 3-6 minutes longer. Season with salt and pepper to taste; sprinkle with parsley.

1 serving: 628 cal., 48g fat (22g sat. fat), 165mg chol., 479mg sod., 5g carb. (2g sugars, 1g fiber), 42g pro.

CABBAGE BUNDLES WITH KRAUT

In our area, cabbage rolls are a popular dish at potluck dinners. My family loves these bundles, which are cooked with plenty of sauerkraut.
—*Jean Kubley, Glidden, WI*

PREP: 30 min. • **COOK:** 1¼ hours
MAKES: 5 servings

- 1 large head cabbage
- 2 large eggs
- 1 medium onion, chopped
- ½ cup uncooked long grain rice
- 2 tsp. salt
- ¼ tsp. pepper
- 2 lbs. ground beef
- 1 can (27 oz.) sauerkraut, rinsed and drained
- 2 cups water

1. In a large saucepan, cook cabbage in boiling water just until leaves fall off the head. Set aside 10 large leaves for bundles (refrigerate remaining cabbage for another use). Cut out the thick vein from each reserved leaf, making a V-shaped cut; set aside.
2. In a bowl, combine the eggs, onion, rice, salt and pepper. Crumble the beef over mixture and mix well. Place about ½ cup meat mixture on each cabbage leaf; overlap cut ends of each leaf. Fold in the sides, beginning from the cut end. Roll up completely to enclose filling.
3. Place 5 bundles in a Dutch oven. Top with sauerkraut and remaining bundles. Pour water over all. Bring to a boil over medium heat. Reduce heat; cover and simmer until meat is no longer pink and cabbage is tender, 1¼-1½ hours.
2 bundles: 481 cal., 24g fat (9g sat. fat), 187mg chol., 2094mg sod., 28g carb. (5g sugars, 6g fiber), 38g pro.

TACO PASTA SALAD

TACO PASTA SALAD

I blend the best of two popular salads into one satisfying dish to share. Serve tortilla or corn chips on the side to make a complete meal.
—*Gert Rosenau, Pewaukee, WI*

TAKES: 30 min. • **MAKES:** 4 servings

- 2 cups uncooked spiral pasta
- 1 lb. ground beef
- 1 envelope taco seasoning
- 3 cups shredded lettuce
- 2 cups halved cherry tomatoes
- 1 cup shredded cheddar cheese
- ½ cup chopped onion
- ½ cup chopped green pepper
- ½ cup Catalina salad dressing
  Tortilla chips

1. Cook pasta according to package directions. Meanwhile, in a large skillet, cook beef over medium heat until no longer pink, breaking it into crumbles; drain. Stir in the taco seasoning; cool.

2. Drain pasta and rinse in cold water; stir into meat mixture. Add the lettuce, tomatoes, cheese, onion, green pepper and dressing; toss to coat. Serve with tortilla chips.

1 serving: 624 cal., 30g fat (12g sat. fat), 98mg chol., 1454mg sod., 55g carb. (13g sugars, 3g fiber), 33g pro.

TEST KITCHEN TIP

This is an easy and forgiving recipe. Pump up the veggies with whatever you have on hand.

MONGOLIAN BEEF

My family—including my husband, who is truly a meat-and-potatoes guy—just loves this meal-in-one option. The dish uses inexpensive ingredients to offer big flavor in a small amount of time.
—Heather Blum, Coleman, WI

TAKES: 25 min. • **MAKES:** 4 servings

- 1 Tbsp. cornstarch
- ¾ cup reduced-sodium chicken broth
- 2 Tbsp. reduced-sodium soy sauce
- 1 Tbsp. hoisin sauce
- 2 tsp. sesame oil
- 1 lb. beef top sirloin steak, cut into thin strips
- 1 Tbsp. olive oil, divided
- 5 green onions, cut into 1-in. pieces
- 2 cups hot cooked rice

1. In a small bowl, combine cornstarch and broth until smooth. Stir in the soy sauce, hoisin sauce and sesame oil; set aside. In a large nonstick skillet or wok, stir-fry beef in 1½ tsp. hot olive oil until no longer pink. Remove and keep warm.
2. In the same skillet, stir-fry the onions in remaining olive oil until crisp-tender, 3-4 minutes. Stir cornstarch mixture and add to the pan. Bring to a boil; cook and stir until thickened, about 2 minutes. Reduce heat; add beef and heat through. Serve with rice.

1 serving: 328 cal., 11g fat (3g sat. fat), 46mg chol., 529mg sod., 28g carb. (2g sugars, 1g fiber), 28g pro. **Diabetic exchanges:** 3 lean meat, 2 starch, 1 fat.

ONE-POT CHILIGHETTI

Grab your stockpot for my one-pot chili and spaghetti. I've got a large family, and this hearty pasta takes care of everybody.
—Jennifer Trenhaile, Emerson, NE

TAKES: 30 min. • **MAKES:** 8 servings

- 1½ lbs. ground beef
- 1 large onion, chopped
- 1 can (46 oz.) tomato juice
- 1 cup water
- 2 Tbsp. Worcestershire sauce
- 4 tsp. chili powder
- ½ tsp. salt
- ½ tsp. ground cumin
- ½ tsp. pepper
- 1 pkg. (16 oz.) spaghetti, broken into 2-in. pieces
- 2 cans (16 oz. each) kidney beans, rinsed and drained
  Sour cream
  Shredded cheddar cheese

1. In a 6-qt. stockpot, cook the beef and onion over medium-high heat until beef is no longer pink and onion is tender, 8-10 minutes, breaking the beef into crumbles; drain.
2. Stir in the tomato juice, water, Worcestershire sauce and seasonings; bring to a boil. Add spaghetti. Reduce heat; simmer, covered, until pasta is tender, 9-11 minutes. Stir in beans; heat through. Top servings with sour cream and cheese.

Freeze option: Freeze cooled pasta mixture in freezer containers. To use, partially thaw in refrigerator overnight. Heat through in a saucepan, stirring occasionally; add water if necessary.

1½ cups: 508 cal., 12g fat (4g sat. fat), 53mg chol., 903mg sod., 70g carb. (9g sugars, 9g fiber), 32g pro.

MONGOLIAN BEEF

Poultry

CHEESY CHICKEN
PARMIGIANA

CHEESY CHICKEN PARMIGIANA

My husband used to order chicken parmigiana at restaurants. Then I found this recipe in our local newspaper, adjusted it for two and began making the beloved dish at home. After more than 50 years of marriage, I still enjoy preparing his favorite recipes.
—Iola Butler, Sun City, CA

- -

PREP: 25 min. • **COOK:** 15 min.
MAKES: 2 servings

- 1 can (15 oz.) tomato sauce
- 2 tsp. Italian seasoning
- ½ tsp. garlic powder
- 1 large egg
- ¼ cup seasoned bread crumbs
- 3 Tbsp. grated Parmesan cheese
- 2 boneless skinless chicken breast halves (4 oz. each)
- 2 Tbsp. olive oil
- 2 slices part-skim mozzarella cheese
  Optional: Fresh basil leaves and additional Parmesan cheese

1. In a small saucepan, combine the tomato sauce, Italian seasoning and garlic powder. Bring to a boil. Reduce heat; cover and simmer for 20 minutes.

2. Meanwhile, in a shallow bowl, lightly beat the egg. In another shallow bowl, combine bread crumbs and Parmesan cheese. Dip chicken in egg, then coat with crumb mixture.

3. In a large skillet, cook chicken in oil over medium heat until a thermometer reads 165°, about 5 minutes on each side. Top with mozzarella cheese. Cover and cook until cheese is melted, 3-4 minutes longer. Serve with the tomato sauce. If desired, sprinkle with basil and additional Parmesan cheese.

1 chicken breast half: 444 cal., 26g fat (8g sat. fat), 166mg chol., 1496mg sod., 23g carb. (5g sugars, 3g fiber), 29g pro.

LARB GAI

TURKEY TORTELLINI TOSS

One night I had frozen cheese tortellini on hand but didn't have a clue about what I was going to make. I scanned my cupboards and refrigerator, and soon I was happily cooking away. So fresh-tasting and simple, this is a combination I turn to again and again!
—*Leo Parr, New Orleans, LA*

TAKES: 30 min. • **MAKES:** 4 servings

- 2 cups frozen cheese tortellini (about 8 oz.)
- 1 lb. ground turkey
- 2 medium zucchini, halved lengthwise and sliced
- 2 garlic cloves, minced
- 1½ cups cherry tomatoes, halved
- 1 tsp. dried oregano
- ½ tsp. salt
- ¼ tsp. crushed red pepper flakes
- 1 cup shredded Asiago cheese, divided
- 1 Tbsp. olive oil

1. Cook the tortellini according to the package directions.
2. Meanwhile, in a large skillet, cook the turkey, zucchini and garlic over medium heat until turkey is no longer pink, 7-9 minutes, breaking turkey into crumbles; drain. Add tomatoes, oregano, salt and pepper flakes; cook 2 minutes longer. Stir in ¾ cup cheese.
3. Drain tortellini; add to skillet and toss to combine. Drizzle with oil; sprinkle with remaining cheese.
1½ cups: 332 cal., 20g fat (8g sat. fat), 101mg chol., 449mg sod., 8g carb. (5g sugars, 2g fiber), 32g pro.

LARB GAI

Larb gai is a Thai dish made with ground chicken, chiles, mint and basil. Serve it as a main dish or an appetizer in lettuce cups. For a heartier version, serve it with rice.
—*Taste of Home Test Kitchen*

TAKES: 30 min. • **MAKES:** 4 servings

- 1 lb. ground chicken
- 2 Tbsp. canola oil
- 2 green or red fresh chiles, seeded and chopped
- 2 shallots, thinly sliced
- 2 garlic cloves, minced
- 2 Tbsp. lime juice
- 3 Tbsp. fish sauce
- 1 Tbsp. sweet chili sauce
- 2 tsp. brown sugar
- 1 to 2 tsp. Sriracha chili sauce
- ¼ cup fresh cilantro leaves
- 2 Tbsp. minced fresh mint
  Hot cooked sticky rice
  Boston lettuce leaves, optional

1. In a large skillet, cook the chicken over medium heat until no longer pink, 8-10 minutes, breaking it into crumbles; drain. In the same skillet, heat oil over medium heat. Add chiles and shallots; cook and stir until tender, 3-4 minutes. Add garlic; cook 1 minute longer.
2. Stir in cooked chicken, lime juice, fish sauce, chili sauce, brown sugar and Sriracha. Cook and stir until heated through. Stir in cilantro and mint. Serve with rice and, if desired, lettuce leaves.
Note: Wear disposable gloves when cutting hot peppers; the oils can burn skin. Avoid touching your face.
½ cup: 262 cal., 16g fat (3g sat. fat), 75mg chol., 1211mg sod., 10g carb. (6g sugars, 0 fiber), 20g pro.

THAI SLOPPY JOE
CHICKEN & WAFFLES

THAI SLOPPY JOE CHICKEN & WAFFLES

Since sloppy joes, Thai food, and chicken and waffles are all family favorites at my house, I decided to mix all three to create a tasty dish. The crunchy slaw with Asian peanut dressing adds crunch and flavor.
—Arlene Erlbach, Morton Grove, IL

TAKES: 30 min. • **MAKES:** 6 servings

¼ cup creamy peanut butter
½ cup minced fresh cilantro, divided
6 Tbsp. teriyaki sauce, divided
3 Tbsp. chili sauce, divided
2 Tbsp. lime juice
2 cups coleslaw mix
1 lb. ground chicken
⅓ cup canned coconut milk
1 tsp. ground ginger
¾ tsp. garlic powder
6 frozen waffles
Sliced green onions, optional

1. Place peanut butter, ¼ cup cilantro, 4 Tbsp. teriyaki sauce, 1 Tbsp. chili sauce and lime juice in a food processor; process until combined. Place coleslaw mix in a large bowl; add peanut butter mixture. Toss to coat; set aside.
2. In a large skillet, cook the chicken over medium heat until no longer pink, 6-8 minutes, breaking it into crumbles; drain. Stir in coconut milk, ginger, garlic powder, remaining ¼ cup cilantro and 2 Tbsp. teriyaki sauce. Cook and stir until heated through.
3. Meanwhile, prepare waffles according to package directions. Top waffles with chicken mixture and coleslaw. If desired, sprinkle with green onions.
1 serving: 314 cal., 17g fat (5g sat. fat), 55mg chol., 1046mg sod., 24g carb. (7g sugars, 2g fiber), 18g pro.

SPICY SAUSAGE & RICE SKILLET

SPICY SAUSAGE & RICE SKILLET

The spicy sausage in this quick skillet dish gives it a kick, and the sliced apples are a pleasant, tart surprise.
—Jamie Jones, Madison, GA

TAKES: 30 min. • **MAKES:** 6 servings

1 pkg. (12 oz.) fully cooked spicy chicken sausage links, halved lengthwise and cut into ½-in. slices
1 Tbsp. olive oil
2 medium yellow summer squash, chopped
2 medium zucchini, chopped
1 large sweet red pepper, chopped
1 medium onion, chopped
1 medium tart apple, cut into ¼-in. slices
1 garlic clove, minced
½ tsp. salt
1 pkg. (8.80 oz.) ready-to-serve brown rice
1 can (15 oz.) black beans, rinsed and drained
¼ to ½ cup water

1. In a large nonstick skillet, cook sausage over medium-high heat, turning occasionally, until lightly browned. Remove from skillet.
2. In the same skillet, heat oil over medium-high heat. Saute squash, zucchini, pepper, onion, apple, garlic and salt until the vegetables are tender, 5-7 minutes. Add rice, beans, ¼ cup water and sausage; cook and stir until heated through, about 5 minutes, adding more water if needed.
1⅓ cups: 285 cal., 8g fat (2g sat. fat), 43mg chol., 668mg sod., 34g carb. (9g sugars, 6g fiber), 17g pro. **Diabetic exchanges:** 2 starch, 2 lean meat, 1 vegetable, ½ fat.

TEST KITCHEN TIPS
• Skip the sausage and add more beans to create a meatless version of the dish.
• If making rice from scratch, you'll need about 2 cups cooked rice.

TURKEY & SWISS QUESADILLAS

My favorite sandwich is turkey with avocado, so I created this healthy quesadilla with ingredients I often have in the fridge and pantry.
—*Karen O'Shea, Sparks, NV*

TAKES: 20 min. • **MAKES:** 2 servings

- 2 Tbsp. reduced-fat Parmesan peppercorn ranch salad dressing
- 1 Tbsp. Dijon mustard
- 2 whole wheat tortillas (8 in.)
- 2 slices reduced-fat Swiss cheese, halved
- ½ medium ripe avocado, peeled and thinly sliced
- 6 oz. sliced cooked turkey breast
  Diced sweet red pepper, optional

1. In a small bowl, combine salad dressing and mustard; spread over 1 side of each tortilla. Place tortillas, spread side up, on a griddle coated with cooking spray.
2. Layer cheese, avocado and turkey over half of each tortilla. Fold over and cook over low heat for 1-2 minutes on each side or until cheese is melted. Garnish with red pepper if desired.

1 quesadilla: 421 cal., 16g fat (3g sat. fat), 86mg chol., 566mg sod., 32g carb. (2g sugars, 5g fiber), 38g pro. **Diabetic exchanges:** 4 lean meat, 2 starch, 2 fat.

CHICKEN CACCIATORE WITH POLENTA

CHICKEN CACCIATORE WITH POLENTA

The microwave makes quick work of homemade polenta, and the rest is done in one skillet. Save a little Parmesan for sprinkling on top before serving.
—*Yvonne Starlin, Westmoreland, TN*

TAKES: 30 min. • **MAKES:** 4 servings

- 3 cups water
- ¾ cup cornmeal
- ½ cup grated Parmesan cheese
- ¾ tsp. salt

CACCIATORE

- 1 lb. boneless skinless chicken thighs, cut into 1-in. pieces
- ⅛ tsp. salt
- ⅛ tsp. pepper
- 1 Tbsp. olive oil
- 1 large onion, sliced
- 1 garlic clove, minced
- 1 can (14½ oz.) fire-roasted crushed tomatoes
- ½ cup pitted Greek olives

1. In a microwave-safe bowl, whisk water and cornmeal; microwave, covered, on high for 6 minutes. Stir; cook, covered, 5-7 minutes longer or until polenta is thickened, stirring every 2 minutes. Stir in cheese and salt.
2. Meanwhile, sprinkle chicken with salt and pepper. In a large skillet, heat oil over medium-high heat. Add the chicken; cook and stir until browned. Remove with a slotted spoon.
3. Add onion to the same pan; cook and stir 2-4 minutes or until tender. Add garlic; cook 1 minute longer. Return chicken to pan; stir in tomatoes and olives. Bring to a boil. Reduce the heat; simmer, uncovered, 6-8 minutes or until chicken is no longer pink. Serve with polenta.

Freeze option: Do not prepare the polenta until later. Freeze cooled chicken mixture in freezer containers. To use, partially thaw in refrigerator overnight. Prepare polenta as directed. Meanwhile, in a saucepan, reheat chicken, stirring occasionally; add a little water if necessary. Serve with polenta.

1 cup chicken mixture with ¾ cup polenta: 448 cal., 19g fat (5g sat. fat), 84mg chol., 1214mg sod., 38g carb. (7g sugars, 4g fiber), 28g pro.

TURKEY PICCATA

With an appealing lemon flavor, this classic skillet supper never goes out of style. It can also be prepared with chicken or pork.

—*Perlene Hoekema, Lynden, WA*

PREP: 15 min. • **COOK:** 20 min.
MAKES: 8 servings

- 2 large eggs
- 2 Tbsp. whole milk
- 3½ cups fresh bread crumbs (from about 8 slices)
- 2 pkg. (17.6 oz. each) turkey breast cutlets
- ¾ cup butter
- 2 large lemons, divided
- 1½ cups water
- 2 tsp. chicken bouillon granules
- ½ tsp. salt
  Parsley sprigs

1. Beat eggs with milk in a shallow dish until well blended. Place bread crumbs on waxed paper. Dip cutlets in egg mixture and then in crumbs, coating both sides.
2. Melt the butter, as needed, in a 12-in. skillet over medium-high heat. Brown cutlets, in batches, 2-3 minutes on each side. Remove to a plate; keep warm.
3. Reduce heat to low. Squeeze juice of 1 lemon (about ¼ cup) into pan drippings in skillet; stir in the water, bouillon and salt until well mixed. Scrape brown bits from the bottom. Return the turkey to skillet; cover and simmer 15 minutes.
4. Thinly slice remaining lemon. To serve, arrange cutlets on large warm platter and garnish with lemon slices. Pour remaining sauce over cutlets; sprinkle with parsley.

5 oz. cooked turkey: 363 cal., 21g fat (12g sat. fat), 142mg chol., 682mg sod., 12g carb. (2g sugars, 1g fiber), 35g pro.

TURKEY ASPARAGUS STIR-FRY

Twenty minutes is all you need to create this quick stir-fry. Lean turkey breast, asparagus and mushrooms make it super nutritious, too.

—*Darlene Kennedy, Galion, OH*

TAKES: 20 min. • **MAKES:** 5 servings

- 1 Tbsp. olive oil
- 1 lb. boneless skinless turkey breast, cut into strips
- 1 lb. fresh asparagus, cut into 1-in. pieces
- 4 oz. fresh mushrooms, sliced
- 2 medium carrots, quartered lengthwise and cut into 1-in. pieces
- 4 green onions, cut into 1-in. pieces
- 2 garlic cloves, minced
- ½ tsp. ground ginger
- ⅔ cup cold water
- 2 Tbsp. reduced-sodium soy sauce
- 4 tsp. cornstarch
- 1 can (8 oz.) sliced water chestnuts, drained
- 3½ cups hot cooked white or brown rice
- 1 medium tomato, cut into wedges

1. In a large skillet or wok, heat oil over medium-high heat. Add turkey; stir-fry until no longer pink, about 5 minutes. Remove and keep warm.
2. Add the next 6 ingredients to pan; stir-fry until vegetables are crisp-tender, about 5 minutes. Combine water, soy sauce and cornstarch; add to skillet with water chestnuts. Bring to a boil; cook and stir 1-2 minutes or until sauce is thickened. Return the turkey to skillet and heat through. Serve with rice and tomato wedges.

1 cup with ¾ cup rice: 343 cal., 5g fat (1g sat. fat), 52mg chol., 363mg sod., 47g carb. (4g sugars, 4g fiber), 28g pro.
Diabetic exchanges: 3 starch, 3 lean meat, 1 vegetable, ½ fat.

TURKEY PICCATA

SAVORY ONION CHICKEN

FLAVORFUL CHICKEN FAJITAS

This chicken fajitas recipe is definitely on my weeknight dinner rotation. The marinated chicken in these popular wraps is mouthwatering. The fajitas go together in a snap and always get raves!
—*Julie Sterchi, Campbellsville, KY*

PREP: 20 min. + marinating
COOK: 10 min. • **MAKES:** 6 servings

- 4 Tbsp. canola oil, divided
- 2 Tbsp. lemon juice
- 1½ tsp. seasoned salt
- 1½ tsp. dried oregano
- 1½ tsp. ground cumin
- 1 tsp. garlic powder
- ½ tsp. chili powder
- ½ tsp. paprika
- ½ tsp. crushed red pepper flakes, optional
- 1½ lbs. boneless skinless chicken breasts, cut into thin strips
- ½ medium sweet red pepper, julienned
- ½ medium green pepper, julienned
- 4 green onions, thinly sliced
- ½ cup chopped onion
- 6 flour tortillas (8 in.), warmed
  Optional: Shredded cheddar cheese, taco sauce, salsa, guacamole, sliced red onions and sour cream

1. In a large bowl, combine 2 Tbsp. oil, lemon juice and seasonings; add the chicken. Turn to coat; cover. Refrigerate for 1-4 hours.
2. In a large cast-iron or other heavy skillet, saute the peppers and onions in remaining oil until crisp-tender. Remove and keep warm.
3. Drain chicken, discarding marinade. In the same skillet, cook chicken over medium-high heat until no longer pink, 5-6 minutes. Return pepper mixture to pan; heat through.
4. Spoon the filling down the center of tortillas; fold in half. Serve with toppings as desired.
1 fajita: 369 cal., 15g fat (2g sat. fat), 63mg chol., 689mg sod., 30g carb. (2g sugars, 1g fiber), 28g pro. **Diabetic exchanges:** 3 lean meat, 2 starch, 2 fat.`

SAVORY ONION CHICKEN

Dinner doesn't get any easier than this tasty onion chicken entree. Buy chicken that's already cut up to save even more time.
—*Julia Anderson, Ringgold, GA*

- -

TAKES: 30 min. • **MAKES:** 6 servings

- ¼ cup all-purpose flour, divided
- 1 broiler/fryer chicken (3 to 4 lbs.), cut up and skin removed
- 2 Tbsp. olive oil
- 1 envelope onion soup mix
- 1 bottle (12 oz.) beer or nonalcoholic beer

1. Place 2 Tbsp. flour in a shallow bowl. Add chicken, a few pieces at a time, and turn to coat. In a large skillet, heat oil over medium heat. Brown chicken on all sides; remove and keep warm.
2. Add soup mix and remaining flour, stirring to loosen browned bits from pan. Gradually whisk in beer. Bring to a boil; cook and stir for 2 minutes or until thickened.
3. Return chicken to the pan. Bring to a boil. Reduce heat; cover and simmer until chicken juices run clear, 12-15 minutes.
1 serving: 231 cal., 11g fat (2g sat. fat), 73mg chol., 469mg sod., 7g carb. (1g sugars, 0 fiber), 25g pro.

FLAVORFUL
CHICKEN FAJITAS

GRECIAN CHICKEN

The caper, tomato and olive flavors will whisk you away to the Greek isles. This easy skillet dish is perfect for hectic weeknights.
—Jan Marler, Murchison, TX

TAKES: 30 min. • **MAKES:** 4 servings

- 3 tsp. olive oil, divided
- 1 lb. chicken tenderloins
- 2 medium tomatoes, sliced
- 1 cup sliced fresh mushrooms
- ½ cup chopped onion
- 1 Tbsp. capers, drained
- 1 Tbsp. lemon-pepper seasoning
- 1 Tbsp. salt-free Greek seasoning
- 1 medium garlic clove, minced
- ½ cup water
- 2 Tbsp. chopped ripe olives
  Hot cooked orzo pasta, optional

1. In a large skillet, heat 2 tsp. oil over medium heat. Add chicken; saute until no longer pink, 7-9 minutes. Remove and keep warm.

2. In same skillet, heat remaining oil; add the next 6 ingredients. Cook and stir until onion is translucent, 2-3 minutes. Stir in garlic; cook 1 minute more. Add water; bring to a boil. Reduce heat; simmer, uncovered, until vegetables are tender, 3-4 minutes. Return chicken to skillet; add olives. Simmer, uncovered, until chicken is heated through, 2-3 minutes. If desired, serve with orzo.

1 serving: 172 cal., 5g fat (1g sat. fat), 56mg chol., 393mg sod., 6g carb. (3g sugars, 2g fiber), 28g pro. **Diabetic exchanges:** 3 lean meat, 1 vegetable, 1 fat.

CHICKEN AVOCADO WRAPS

I came up with this wrap while trying to figure out what to make for lunch one day. The recipe is now a favorite at my house.
—Shiva Houshidari, Plano, TX

PREP: 15 min. • **COOK:** 35 min.
MAKES: 4 servings

- 2 chicken leg quarters, skin removed
- 1 Tbsp. canola oil
- 1 can (14½ oz.) diced tomatoes, undrained
- ⅓ cup chopped onion
- ½ tsp. ground cumin
- ⅛ tsp. salt
  Dash cayenne pepper
- ½ medium ripe avocado
- 2 Tbsp. lime juice
- 4 whole wheat tortillas (8 in.), warmed
  Fresh cilantro leaves, optional

1. In a large skillet, brown chicken in oil. Stir in the tomatoes, onion, cumin, salt and cayenne. Bring to a boil. Reduce heat to low; cover and cook for 25-30 minutes or until a thermometer inserted in chicken reads 180°, stirring occasionally.

2. Remove chicken. When cool enough to handle, remove meat from bones; discard bones. Shred meat with 2 forks; return to skillet. Bring to a boil. Reduce heat; simmer, uncovered, for 8-10 minutes or until sauce is thickened.

3. Peel and slice avocado; drizzle with lime juice. Spoon ½ cup chicken mixture over each tortilla. Top with avocado and, if desired, cilantro; roll up.

1 wrap: 329 cal., 14g fat (2g sat. fat), 45mg chol., 416mg sod., 31g carb. (5g sugars, 5g fiber), 19g pro. **Diabetic exchanges:** 2 lean meat, 2 fat, 1½ starch, 1 vegetable.

CHICKEN AVOCADO WRAPS

NEW ORLEANS-STYLE STEWED CHICKEN

This dish is like a gumbo but with far less liquid and bigger pieces of meat. Don't let the ingredient list trick you into thinking it's a difficult recipe to cook. Most of the ingredients are herbs and spices that coat the chicken.

—Eric Olsson, Macomb, MI

PREP: 45 min. • **COOK:** 1 hour
MAKES: 4 servings

- 1 Tbsp. dried parsley flakes
- 2 tsp. salt
- 1¼ tsp. pepper, divided
- 1⅛ tsp. dried thyme, divided
- 1 tsp. garlic powder
- 1 tsp. onion powder
- ¼ tsp. white pepper
- ¼ tsp. cayenne pepper
- ¼ tsp. rubbed sage
- 1 lb. chicken drumsticks
- 1 lb. bone-in chicken thighs
- 2 Tbsp. plus ½ cup bacon drippings or olive oil, divided
- ½ cup all-purpose flour
- ½ lb. sliced fresh mushrooms
- 1 medium onion, chopped
- 1 medium green pepper, chopped
- 1 celery rib, chopped
- 1 jalapeno pepper, seeded and finely chopped
- 4 garlic cloves, minced
- 4 cups chicken stock
- 4 green onions, finely chopped
- 5 drops hot pepper sauce
  Hot cooked rice

NEW ORLEANS-STYLE STEWED CHICKEN

1. In a small bowl, mix parsley, salt, 1 tsp. pepper, 1 tsp. thyme, garlic powder, onion powder, white pepper, cayenne and sage; rub over chicken. In a Dutch oven, brown the chicken, in batches, in 2 Tbsp. bacon drippings; remove chicken from pan.

2. Add remaining ½ cup bacon drippings to the same pan; stir in flour until blended. Cook and stir over medium-low heat for 30 minutes or until browned (do not burn). Add mushrooms, onion, green pepper and celery; cook and stir for 2-3 minutes or until vegetables are crisp-tender. Add jalapeno pepper, garlic and remaining ⅛ tsp. thyme; cook 1 minute longer.

3. Gradually add stock. Return chicken to pan. Bring to a boil. Reduce heat; cover and simmer until chicken is very tender, about 1 hour.

4. Skim fat. Stir in green onions, hot pepper sauce and remaining ¼ tsp. pepper. Serve with rice.

Freeze option: Place individual portions of cooled stew in freezer containers and freeze. To use, partially thaw in refrigerator overnight. Heat through in a saucepan, stirring occasionally; add a little broth if necessary.

Note: Wear disposable gloves when cutting hot peppers; the oils can burn skin. Avoid touching your face.

1 serving: 680 cal., 48g fat (17g sat. fat), 131mg chol., 1847mg sod., 23g carb. (5g sugars, 3g fiber), 38g pro.

"This is a really good recipe. It reminds me of Thanksgiving with the sage and thyme. I would like to find a way to make it a bit healthier. At 680 calories, I would possibly use zoodles rather than rice and cut the bacon out or in half."

—GRANDMASCOOKING22, TASTEOFHOME.COM

CHIPOTLE CHICKEN WITH
SPANISH RICE

CHIPOTLE CHICKEN WITH SPANISH RICE

Here in Texas, we love southwestern cooking. Chipotle pepper adds smoky heat to this zesty chicken and rice dish. It's so quick and easy. Enjoy!
—Carolyn Collins, Freeport, TX

TAKES: 25 min. • MAKES: 4 servings

- 4 boneless skinless chicken thighs (about 1 lb.)
- ½ tsp. garlic salt
- 2 Tbsp. canola oil
- 1 can (15 oz.) black beans, rinsed and drained
- 1 cup chunky salsa
- 1 chipotle pepper in adobo sauce, finely chopped
- 2 pkg. (8.8 oz. each) ready-to-serve Spanish rice
- ½ cup shredded Mexican cheese blend or Monterey Jack cheese
- 2 Tbsp. minced fresh cilantro or parsley

1. Sprinkle chicken with garlic salt. In a large skillet, heat oil over medium-high heat. Brown chicken on both sides. Stir in beans, salsa and chipotle pepper; bring to a boil. Reduce heat; simmer, covered, 6-8 minutes or until a thermometer inserted into chicken reads 170°.
2. Meanwhile, prepare rice according to package directions. Serve chicken with rice; sprinkle with cheese and cilantro.
1 serving: 578 cal., 23g fat (5g sat. fat), 88mg chol., 1638mg sod., 57g carb. (5g sugars, 5g fiber), 32g pro.

TEST KITCHEN TIP

Canned chipotle peppers freeze wonderfully until needed for your next recipe. You may freeze the peppers individually in ice cube trays for easy retrieval or carefully cut pieces from frozen chipotles with a paring knife.

CRISPY BARBECUE CHICKEN TENDERS

CRISPY BARBECUE CHICKEN TENDERS

These crunch-coated chicken tenders are a little sweet, a little tangy and a whole lot of fun. In half an hour, your family's new favorite dish is ready to eat. When I have extra time, I roast garlic and add it to the sauce.
—Andreann Geise, Myrtle Beach, SC

TAKES: 30 min. • MAKES: 6 servings

- 1 cup sour cream
- ¼ cup minced fresh chives
- 2 garlic cloves, minced
- ½ tsp. salt

CHICKEN
- ¼ cup all-purpose flour
- 2 Tbsp. light brown sugar
- 1 tsp. ground mustard
- ¾ tsp. pepper
- ½ tsp. salt
- ¼ tsp. cayenne pepper
- 2 large eggs, lightly beaten
- 2 cups coarsely crushed barbecue potato chips
- 1½ lbs. chicken tenderloins
  Oil for frying

1. In a small bowl, mix sour cream, chives, garlic and salt. In a shallow bowl, mix flour, brown sugar and seasonings. Place eggs and potato chips in separate shallow bowls. Dip chicken in flour mixture to coat both sides; shake off excess. Dip in eggs, then in potato chips, patting to help coating adhere.
2. In a deep skillet, heat ¼ in. oil to 375°. Fry chicken, a few strips at a time, until golden brown, 2-3 minutes on each side. Drain on paper towels. Serve with sauce.
3 oz. cooked chicken with 2 Tbsp. sauce: 411 cal., 27g fat (6g sat. fat), 109mg chol., 492mg sod., 14g carb. (5g sugars, 1g fiber), 31g pro.

BUFFALO SLOPPY JOES

Lean ground turkey makes this a lighter sloppy joe than the standard ground beef version. A big splash of hot sauce and optional blue cheese provide that authentic Buffalo-style flavor.
—*Maria Regakis, Saugus, MA*

- -

TAKES: 30 min. • **MAKES:** 8 servings

- 2 lbs. extra-lean ground turkey
- 2 celery ribs, chopped
- 1 medium onion, chopped
- 1 medium carrot, grated
- 3 garlic cloves, minced
- 1 can (8 oz.) tomato sauce
- ½ cup chicken broth
- ¼ cup Louisiana-style hot sauce
- 2 Tbsp. brown sugar
- 1 Tbsp. Worcestershire sauce
- 2 Tbsp. red wine vinegar
- ¼ tsp. pepper
- 8 hamburger buns, split
  Crumbled blue cheese, optional

1. Cook the first 5 ingredients in a Dutch oven over medium heat until turkey is no longer pink, breaking it into crumbles. Stir in the tomato sauce, chicken broth, hot sauce, brown sugar, Worcestershire sauce, vinegar and pepper; heat through.
2. Serve on buns. If desired, sprinkle with blue cheese.
1 sandwich: 279 cal., 3g fat (0 sat. fat), 45mg chol., 475mg sod., 30g carb. (9g sugars, 2g fiber), 33g pro. **Diabetic exchanges:** 4 lean meat, 2 starch.

CHICKEN KORMA

CHICKEN KORMA

Chicken korma is a spiced Indian dish. It's not spicy-hot, but it's very flavorful from ingredients like cloves and ginger. Serve it with rice to soak in all the sauce.
—*Jemima Madhavan, Lincoln, NE*

- -

PREP: 20 min. • **COOK:** 25 min.
MAKES: 4 servings

- 1 large potato, peeled and cut into ½-in. cubes
- 1 large onion, chopped
- 1 cinnamon stick (3 in.)
- 1 bay leaf
- 3 whole cloves
- 1 Tbsp. canola oil
- 1 lb. boneless skinless chicken breasts, cut into ½-in. cubes
- 1 garlic clove, minced
- 1 tsp. curry powder
- ½ tsp. minced fresh gingerroot
- 2 medium tomatoes, seeded and chopped
- 1 tsp. salt
- ½ cup sour cream
  Hot cooked rice

1. Place potato in a small saucepan and cover with water. Bring to a boil. Reduce heat; cover and cook until tender, 10-15 minutes. Drain.
2. In a large skillet, saute the onion, cinnamon, bay leaf and cloves in oil until onion is tender. Add the chicken, garlic, curry and ginger; cook and stir 1 minute longer. Stir in the tomatoes, salt and potato.
3. Cover and cook until chicken is no longer pink, 10-15 minutes. Remove from the heat; discard cinnamon, bay leaf and cloves. Stir in sour cream. Serve with rice.
1 cup: 313 cal., 12g fat (5g sat. fat), 70mg chol., 665mg sod., 24g carb. (5g sugars, 4g fiber), 27g pro. **Diabetic exchanges:** 3 lean meat, 2 fat, 1½ starch.

HERB CHICKEN WITH HONEY BUTTER

When the whole family can use a heartwarming meal, this one fits the bill! You'll love how the honey's sweetness mixes perfectly with the herbs' salty flavor. It's a wonderful combination!
—Taste of Home *Test Kitchen*

TAKES: 25 min. • **MAKES:** 4 servings

- 1 large egg, lightly beaten
- ¾ cup seasoned bread crumbs
- 2 Tbsp. dried parsley flakes
- 1 tsp. Italian seasoning
- ¾ tsp. garlic salt
- ½ tsp. poultry seasoning
- 4 boneless skinless chicken breast halves (6 oz. each)
- 3 Tbsp. butter

HONEY BUTTER

- ¼ cup butter, softened
- ¼ cup honey

1. Place egg in a shallow bowl. In another shallow bowl, combine bread crumbs and seasonings. Dip the chicken in egg, then coat with bread crumb mixture.

2. In a large skillet over medium heat, cook the chicken in the butter until a thermometer reads 165°, 4-5 minutes on each side. Meanwhile, combine softened butter and honey. Serve with chicken.

1 chicken breast half with 2 Tbsp. honey butter: 485 cal., 25g fat (14g sat. fat), 171mg chol., 709mg sod., 27g carb. (18g sugars, 1g fiber), 38g pro.

Chicken with Sun-Dried Tomato Butter: Combine ⅓ cup butter, ¼ cup Parmesan cheese, 2 Tbsp. sun-dried tomato pesto and ¼ tsp. pepper. Substitute for the honey butter.

LEMON-BASIL CHICKEN ROTINI

My husband and our sons like to have meat with their meals, but I prefer more veggies. This combo is colorful and healthy, and it keeps everyone happy.
—Anna-Marie Williams, League City, TX

PREP: 25 min. • **COOK:** 20 min.
MAKES: 6 servings

- 3 cups uncooked whole wheat rotini
- 2 tsp. olive oil
- 1 lb. boneless skinless chicken breasts, cut into ¾-in. strips
- 1½ cups sliced fresh mushrooms
- 1½ cups shredded carrots
- 4 garlic cloves, thinly sliced
- 1 cup reduced-sodium chicken broth
- 3 oz. reduced-fat cream cheese
- 1 Tbsp. lemon juice
- 1½ cups frozen peas (about 6 oz.), thawed
- ⅓ cup shredded Parmesan cheese
- ¼ cup minced fresh basil
- 2 tsp. grated lemon zest
- ¼ tsp. salt
- ¼ tsp. pepper
- ¼ tsp. crushed red pepper flakes

1. Cook rotini according to the package directions. Meanwhile, in a large nonstick skillet, heat oil over medium heat. Add chicken; cook and stir until no longer pink. Remove from pan.

2. Add mushrooms and carrots to same skillet; cook and stir until tender. Add garlic; cook 1 minute longer. Stir in broth, cream cheese and lemon juice; stir until cheese is melted.

3. Drain rotini; add to vegetable mixture. Stir in chicken, peas, Parmesan cheese, basil, lemon zest, salt, pepper and red pepper flakes; heat through.

1⅓ cups: 308 cal., 8g fat (4g sat. fat), 56mg chol., 398mg sod., 31g carb. (5g sugars, 6g fiber), 27g pro. **Diabetic exchanges:** 3 lean meat, 2 starch, ½ fat.

HERB CHICKEN
WITH HONEY BUTTER

QUICK TURKEY CHOP SUEY

Whenever I serve this chop suey to relatives or friends, I'm asked for the recipe. Canned ingredients make it convenient to prepare.
—*Anne Powers, Munford, AL*

- -

TAKES: 25 min. • **MAKES:** 5 servings

- 1 lb. lean ground turkey
- ½ cup chopped onion
- 1 can (10½ oz.) condensed chicken broth, undiluted, divided
- 1 cup chopped celery
- 1 can (8 oz.) sliced water chestnuts, drained
- 1 jar (4½ oz.) sliced mushrooms, drained
- ¼ tsp. ground ginger
- 1 can (14 oz.) bean sprouts, drained
- 2 Tbsp. cornstarch
- 2 Tbsp. reduced-sodium soy sauce
  Hot cooked white or brown rice, optional

1. In a nonstick skillet or wok, cook turkey and onion over medium heat until the turkey is no longer pink, breaking it into crumbles; drain. Add 1 cup broth and the next 4 ingredients. Bring to a boil. Reduce heat; cover and simmer until celery is tender, 10-15 minutes.

2. Add bean sprouts. Combine the cornstarch, soy sauce and remaining broth; stir into turkey mixture. Bring to a boil; cook and stir until thickened, 2 minutes. If desired, serve over rice.

1 cup: 220 cal., 8g fat (2g sat. fat), 63mg chol., 801mg sod., 15g carb. (3g sugars, 3g fiber), 23g pro. **Diabetic exchanges:** 2 lean meat, 1 vegetable, ½ starch, ½ fat.

PECAN TURKEY CUTLETS WITH DILLED CARROTS

PECAN TURKEY CUTLETS WITH DILLED CARROTS

This recipe may look a bit long, but don't let that deter you. It's a simple dish, using the same everyday ingredients in several different ways.
—*Taste of Home Test Kitchen*

- -

TAKES: 30 min. • **MAKES:** 4 servings

- ¾ cup chopped pecans
- ½ cup grated Romano cheese
- ½ tsp. seasoned salt
- ½ tsp. dill weed
- 1 pkg. (17.6 oz.) turkey breast cutlets
- 3 Tbsp. butter, divided
- 2 garlic cloves, minced
- ½ cup chicken broth
- 1 tsp. cornstarch
- 2 Tbsp. lime juice
- ½ tsp. grated lime zest

CARROTS

- 1½ lbs. sliced fresh carrots
- 1½ tsp. butter
- ¾ tsp. grated lime zest
- ½ tsp. dill weed
- ¼ tsp. seasoned salt

1. Place pecans in a food processor; cover and process until ground. Combine the pecans, cheese, seasoned salt and dill in a shallow bowl. Coat turkey with the pecan mixture.

2. In a large skillet, heat 1 Tbsp. butter over medium heat. Add turkey in batches and cook until no longer pink, 3-4 minutes on each side. Remove and keep warm. In the same skillet, cook garlic in the remaining butter.

3. Combine the broth, cornstarch and lime juice until blended; gradually add to the skillet, stirring to loosen browned bits. Bring to a boil; cook and stir until thickened, 2 minutes. Stir in ½ tsp. lime zest. Remove from the heat; keep warm.

4. Meanwhile, place 1 in. of water in a saucepan; add carrots. Bring to a boil. Reduce heat; cover and simmer until crisp-tender, 7-9 minutes. Drain. Stir in the butter, lime zest, dill and seasoned salt. Serve with turkey and sauce.

3 oz. cooked turkey with 2 Tbsp. sauce and ¾ cup cooked carrots: 479 cal., 29g fat (10g sat. fat), 101mg chol., 900mg sod., 21g carb. (9g sugars, 7g fiber), 38g pro.

TURKEY CLUB ROULADES

Weeknights turn elegant when these short-prep roulades with familiar ingredients are on the menu. Not a fan of turkey? Substitute lightly pounded chicken breasts.
—Taste of Home *Test Kitchen*

PREP: 20 min. • **COOK:** 15 min.
MAKES: 8 servings

- ¾ lb. fresh asparagus, trimmed
- 8 turkey breast cutlets (about 1 lb.)
- 1 Tbsp. Dijon-mayonnaise blend
- 8 slices deli ham
- 8 slices provolone cheese
- ½ tsp. poultry seasoning
- ½ tsp. pepper
- 8 bacon strips

SAUCE

- ⅔ cup Dijon-mayonnaise blend
- 4 tsp. 2% milk
- ¼ tsp. poultry seasoning

1. Bring 4 cups water to a boil in a large saucepan. Add asparagus; cook, uncovered, for 3 minutes or until crisp-tender. Drain and immediately place asparagus in ice water. Drain and pat dry. Set aside.

2. Spread the turkey cutlets with Dijon-mayonnaise. Layer with ham, cheese and asparagus. Sprinkle with poultry seasoning and pepper. Roll up tightly and wrap with bacon.

3. Cook roulades in a large skillet over medium-high heat until bacon is crisp and turkey is no longer pink, turning occasionally, 12-15 minutes. Combine sauce ingredients; serve with roulades.

1 roulade with 1 Tbsp. sauce: 224 cal., 11g fat (5g sat. fat), 64mg chol., 1075mg sod., 2g carb. (1g sugars, 0 fiber), 25g pro.

TURKEY STROGANOFF WITH SPAGHETTI SQUASH

My twin sister and I came up with this entree after we both successfully lost weight but still wanted to indulge in comfort food. Spaghetti squash is a fantastic healthy alternative to pasta, and we use it in many recipes.
—Courtney Varela, Aliso Viejo, CA

PREP: 25 min. • **COOK:** 15 min.
MAKES: 6 servings

- 1 medium spaghetti squash (about 4 lbs.)
- 1 lb. lean ground turkey
- 2 cups sliced fresh mushrooms
- 1 medium onion, chopped
- 2 garlic cloves, minced
- ½ cup white wine or beef stock
- 3 Tbsp. cornstarch
- 2 cups beef stock
- 2 Tbsp. Worcestershire sauce
- 1 Tbsp. Montreal steak seasoning
- 1 tsp. minced fresh thyme or ¼ tsp. dried thyme
- ¼ cup half-and-half cream
  Optional: Grated Parmesan cheese and minced fresh parsley

1. Cut the squash in half lengthwise; discard seeds. Place the squash cut side down on a microwave-safe plate. Microwave, uncovered, on high until tender, 15-18 minutes.

2. Meanwhile, in a large nonstick skillet, cook the turkey, mushrooms and onion over medium heat until turkey is no longer pink, breaking it into crumbles; drain. Add garlic; cook 1 minute longer. Stir in wine.

3. Combine the cornstarch and stock until smooth. Add to pan. Stir in the Worcestershire sauce, steak seasoning and thyme. Bring to a boil; cook and stir until thickened, 2 minutes. Reduce heat. Stir in cream; heat through.

4. When squash is cool enough to handle, use a fork to separate strands. Serve with turkey mixture. If desired, sprinkle with cheese and parsley.

¾ cup meat mixture with ⅔ cup squash: 246 cal., 9g fat (3g sat. fat), 65mg chol., 677mg sod., 25g carb. (4g sugars, 4g fiber), 17g pro. **Diabetic exchanges:** 2 lean meat, 1½ starch.

TURKEY CLUB ROULADES

Pork

SPICY PLUM PORK MEATBALLS WITH BOK CHOY

I am a huge fan of sweet, salty and spicy, and now I'm trying to make healthier choices. This recipe is so satisfying and delicious, you won't miss any pasta or rice. If you don't want spiralized zucchini, any thin noodles will work.
—Susan Mason, Puyallup, WA

PREP: 30 min. • **COOK:** 30 min.
MAKES: 4 servings

- 1 jar (7 oz.) plum sauce
- ½ cup hoisin sauce
- 3 Tbsp. reduced-sodium soy sauce
- 2 Tbsp. rice vinegar
- 1 Tbsp. Sriracha chili sauce
- 1 large egg, lightly beaten
- 1½ cups panko bread crumbs, divided
- 1 lb. ground pork
- 4 Tbsp. olive oil, divided
- 2 medium zucchini, spiralized
- 1 lb. bok choy, trimmed and cut into 1-in. pieces
  Sesame seeds, optional

1. Whisk together the first 5 ingredients. Reserve 1¼ cups for sauce. Pour the remaining mixture into a large bowl; add egg and ½ cup bread crumbs. Add pork; mix lightly but thoroughly. Shape into 16 balls. Place remaining 1 cup bread crumbs in a shallow bowl. Roll meatballs in bread crumbs to coat.
2. In a large skillet, heat 3 Tbsp. oil over medium heat. In batches, cook meatballs until cooked through, turning occasionally. Remove and keep warm. Heat remaining 1 Tbsp. oil in the same skillet. Add zucchini and bok choy; cook and stir over medium-high heat until crisp-tender, 6-8 minutes. Add meatballs and the reserved sauce; heat through. If desired, sprinkle with sesame seeds.
1 serving: 647 cal., 34g fat (9g sat. fat), 123mg chol., 1656mg sod., 55g carb. (16g sugars, 4g fiber), 29g pro.

GREEK PITAS

These taste like gyros but can be made right at home! Plus, you can prepare the meat and yogurt sauce ahead of time for added convenience.
—*Lisa Hockersmith, Bakersfield, CA*

PREP: 20 min. + chilling • **COOK:** 5 min.
MAKES: 6 servings

   1   cup plain yogurt
   1   cup diced peeled cucumber
   1   tsp. dill weed
   ¼   tsp. seasoned salt
   ¼   cup olive oil
   ¼   cup lemon juice
   2   Tbsp. Dijon mustard
   2   garlic cloves, minced
   1½   tsp. dried oregano
   1   tsp. dried thyme
   1¼   lbs. lean boneless pork, thinly sliced
   12   pita pocket halves, warmed
   1   medium tomato, chopped
   2   Tbsp. chopped onion

1. In a small bowl, combine the yogurt, cucumber, dill and seasoned salt; cover and refrigerate for 6 hours or overnight.
2. Combine the oil, lemon juice, mustard, garlic, oregano and thyme in large bowl; add pork. Turn to coat; cover. Refrigerate for 6 hours or overnight, turning meat occasionally.
3. Drain pork, discarding marinade. In a large skillet, stir-fry pork until browned, about 4 minutes. Stuff into pita halves; top with cucumber sauce, tomato and onion.
2 pita halves: 362 cal., 12g fat (4g sat. fat), 60mg chol., 484mg sod., 35g carb. (4g sugars, 2g fiber), 26g pro. **Diabetic exchanges:** 3 lean meat, 2 starch, 1 fat.

"This is a staple at our house! Sometimes I buy the pork loin, slice it, put the marinade on it and freeze it—that much quicker and ready to go when I do cook it! Excellent recipe!"
—TWOLFMOM08, TASTEOFHOME.COM

COUNTRY HAM & POTATOES

COUNTRY HAM & POTATOES

Browned potatoes give simple ham a tasty touch. Not only do the potatoes pick up the flavor of the ham, but they look beautiful! Just add veggies or a salad and dinner is done.
—*Helen Bridges, Washington, VA*

TAKES: 30 min. • **MAKES:** 6 servings

   2   lbs. fully cooked sliced ham
        (about ½ in. thick)
   2   to 3 Tbsp. butter
   1½   lbs. potatoes, peeled, quartered
        and cooked
        Snipped fresh parsley

In a large heavy skillet, brown the ham over medium-high heat in butter on both sides until heated through. Move ham to 1 side of the skillet; brown potatoes in drippings until tender. Sprinkle potatoes with parsley.
1 serving: 261 cal., 9g fat (5g sat. fat), 64mg chol., 1337mg sod., 21g carb. (1g sugars, 1g fiber), 28g pro.

THAI PORK
SATAY

THAI PORK SATAY

I love this recipe since it can be made as a main dish or an appetizer. For appetizer portions, use short skewers and half the amount of pork.
—*Stephanie Butz, Portland, OR*

PREP: 30 min. + marinating
COOK: 10 min./batch • **MAKES:** 6 servings

- 1 cup coconut milk
- 3 garlic cloves, minced
- 2 Tbsp. ground cumin
- 1 Tbsp. ground coriander
- 1 Tbsp. brown sugar
- 4 Tbsp. canola oil, divided
- 1½ tsp. salt
- 1 tsp. paprika
- 1 tsp. curry powder
  Dash crushed red pepper flakes
- 1½ lbs. boneless pork,
  cut into ½-in. cubes

PEANUT DIPPING SAUCE
- 1 cup water
- ⅔ cup creamy peanut butter
- 1 garlic clove, minced
- 2 Tbsp. brown sugar
- 2 Tbsp. soy sauce
- 2 tsp. lemon juice
  Dash crushed red pepper flakes
  Hot cooked jasmine rice, optional

1. In a bowl or shallow dish, combine coconut milk, garlic, cumin, coriander, brown sugar, 1 Tbsp. oil, salt, paprika, curry and red pepper flakes; add pork and turn to coat. Cover; refrigerate overnight. Drain pork, discarding marinade.
2. For the sauce, in a small saucepan, combine the water, peanut butter and garlic. Cook and stir over medium heat until thickened, 2 minutes. Whisk in brown sugar, soy sauce, lemon juice and red pepper flakes until blended; keep warm.
3. Thread pork onto 12 metal or soaked wooden skewers. In a large skillet, heat remaining oil. Cook pork in batches until no longer pink, 8-10 minutes per batch, turning occasionally.
4. Serve skewers with peanut sauce and, if desired, rice.
2 skewers: 515 cal., 37g fat (13g sat. fat), 67mg chol., 1082mg sod., 16g carb. (10g sugars, 3g fiber), 32g pro.

PORK & MANGO
STIR-FRY

PORK & MANGO STIR-FRY

A recipe is special when everyone in your family raves about it. My finicky eaters each give a thumbs-up for this hearty, nutty stir-fry.
—*Kathy Specht, Clinton, MT*

TAKES: 25 min. • **MAKES:** 4 servings

- 1 pork tenderloin (1 lb.)
- 1 Tbsp. plus 2 tsp. canola oil, divided
- ¼ tsp. salt
- ½ tsp. crushed red pepper flakes, optional
- 6 oz. uncooked multigrain angel hair pasta
- 1 pkg. (8 oz.) fresh sugar snap peas
- 1 medium sweet red pepper, cut into thin strips
- ⅓ cup reduced-sugar orange marmalade
- ¼ cup reduced-sodium teriyaki sauce
- 1 Tbsp. packed brown sugar
- 2 garlic cloves, minced
- 1 cup chopped peeled mango
- ¼ cup lightly salted cashews, coarsely chopped

1. Cut tenderloin lengthwise in half; cut each half crosswise into thin slices. Toss pork with 1 Tbsp. oil, salt and, if desired, pepper flakes. Cook pasta according to package directions.
2. Place a large nonstick skillet over medium-high heat. Add half the pork; stir-fry 2-3 minutes or just until browned. Remove from the pan; repeat with the remaining pork.
3. Stir-fry snap peas and red pepper in remaining oil 2-3 minutes or just until crisp-tender. Stir in marmalade, teriyaki sauce, brown sugar and garlic; cook 1-2 minutes longer. Return pork to pan. Add mango and cashews; heat through, stirring to combine. Serve with pasta.
1½ cups pork mixture with ¾ cup pasta: 515 cal., 16g fat (3g sat. fat), 64mg chol., 553mg sod., 58g carb. (23g sugars, 6g fiber), 36g pro.

GOLDEN HAM CROQUETTES

Neighbors happened to drop in the first time I made this recipe, and they loved it. I often make the tasty favorite as a Sunday dinner for our family.
—*Peggy Anderjaska, Haigler, NE*

TAKES: 30 min. • **MAKES:** 10 servings

- 3 Tbsp. butter
- ¼ to ½ tsp. curry powder
- ¼ cup all-purpose flour
- ¾ cup whole milk
- 2 to 3 tsp. prepared mustard
- 1 tsp. grated onion
- 2 cups coarsely ground fully cooked ham
- ⅔ cup dry bread crumbs
- 1 large egg, room temperature, beaten
- 2 Tbsp. water
  Oil for deep-fat frying

CHEESE SAUCE
- 2 Tbsp. butter
- 2 Tbsp. all-purpose flour
- ¼ tsp. salt
  Dash pepper
- 1¼ cups whole milk
- ½ cup shredded cheddar cheese
- ½ cup shredded Swiss cheese

1. In a saucepan, melt the butter; stir in curry powder and flour. Gradually add milk. Bring to a boil; cook and stir until thickened, 2 minutes. Remove from the heat. Stir in mustard and onion; add ham and mix well. Cover and chill thoroughly.
2. With wet hands, shape the mixture into 10 balls. Roll balls in bread crumbs; shape each into a cone. Whisk together egg and water. Dip cones into egg mixture; roll again in crumbs.
3. Heat oil in an electric skillet or deep-fat fryer to 375°. Fry croquettes, a few at a time, until golden brown, 2-2½ minutes. Drain on paper towels; keep warm.
4. For the cheese sauce, melt butter in a saucepan; stir in flour, salt and pepper until smooth. Gradually add milk. Bring to a boil; cook and stir until thickened, 2 minutes. Reduce heat. Add cheeses; stir until melted. Spoon over croquettes.
1 croquette with about 2 Tbsp. sauce: 307 cal., 24g fat (9g sat. fat), 65mg chol., 603mg sod., 12g carb. (3g sugars, 1g fiber), 12g pro.

GLAZED PORK ON SWEET POTATO BEDS

When solving the what's-for-dinner puzzle, this maple-glazed pork tenderloin is often our top choice. Add sweet potatoes for a comfy side.
—*Jessie Grearson, Falmouth, ME*

PREP: 20 min. • **COOK:** 30 min.
MAKES: 6 servings

- 1½ lbs. sweet potatoes, peeled and cubed
- 1 medium apple, peeled and cut into 8 pieces
- 2 Tbsp. butter
- 1 Tbsp. lemon juice
- 2 tsp. minced fresh gingerroot
- ½ tsp. salt
- ½ tsp. pepper

PORK
- 1 tsp. water
- ½ tsp. cornstarch
- 3 Tbsp. maple syrup
- 2 tsp. wasabi mustard
- 2 tsp. soy sauce
- ½ tsp. pepper
- 1½ lbs. pork tenderloin, cut into 1-in. slices
- 1 Tbsp. olive oil
- 2 garlic cloves, minced

1. Place sweet potatoes and apple in a large saucepan with water to cover. Bring to a boil over high heat. Reduce heat to medium; cover and cook just until tender, 10-12 minutes. Drain. Mash potatoes and apple. Add the next 5 ingredients; keep warm.
2. Stir water into cornstarch until smooth; add the syrup, mustard, soy sauce and pepper. Add pork; stir to coat.
3. In a large skillet, heat oil over medium heat. Brown pork. Add garlic; cook until the meat is no longer pink, 3-5 minutes longer. Serve with sweet potatoes and pan juices.
3 oz. pork with ½ cup sweet potato mixture: 327 cal., 10g fat (4g sat. fat), 74mg chol., 473mg sod., 33g carb. (13g sugars, 4g fiber), 25g pro. **Diabetic exchanges:** 3 lean meat, 2 starch, 1 fat.

GLAZED PORK ON SWEET POTATO BEDS

PASTA WITH PROSCIUTTO, LETTUCE & PEAS

This elevated pasta dish will make your guests think you spent all day in the kitchen. It's the perfect company dish without a lot of work.
—*Amy White, Manchester, CT*

- -

PREP: 20 min. • **COOK:** 15 min.
MAKES: 8 servings

- 1 lb. uncooked campanelle pasta
- 2 Tbsp. butter
- 3 Tbsp. olive oil, divided
- 12 green onions, sliced
- 1 shallot, finely chopped
- ½ cup white wine or reduced-sodium chicken broth
- ½ cup reduced-sodium chicken broth
- ¼ tsp. salt
- ⅛ tsp. pepper
- 1 head Boston lettuce, cut into ¾-in. slices
- 2 cups fresh or frozen peas
- 1 cup grated Parmesan cheese
- 4 oz. thinly sliced prosciutto or deli ham, cut into ½-in. strips Additional Parmesan cheese, optional

1. Cook the pasta according to package directions for al dente.

2. Meanwhile, in a large skillet, heat butter and 2 Tbsp. oil over medium-high heat. Add green onions and shallot; cook and stir until tender. Stir in wine. Bring to a boil; cook and stir 6-8 minutes or until liquid is almost evaporated.

3. Add broth, salt and pepper. Bring to a boil. Reduce heat; stir in lettuce and peas. Cook and stir until lettuce is wilted. Drain pasta; add to pan. Stir in the cheese and prosciutto; drizzle with remaining oil. If desired, top with additional Parmesan.

1¼ cups: 220 cal., 13g fat (5g sat. fat), 29mg chol., 629mg sod., 14g carb. (5g sugars, 5g fiber), 13g pro.

PASTA WITH PROSCIUTTO, LETTUCE & PEAS

LAND OF
ENCHANTMENT
POSOLE

ZUCCHINI & SAUSAGE STOVETOP CASSEROLE

Gather zucchini from your garden or farmers market and start cooking. My family goes wild for this wholesome meal. You can grate the zucchini if you'd like.
—LeAnn Gray, Taylorsville, UT

TAKES: 30 min. • MAKES: 6 servings

1   lb. bulk pork sausage
1   Tbsp. canola oil
3   medium zucchini, thinly sliced
1   medium onion, chopped
1   can (14½ oz.) stewed tomatoes, cut up
1   pkg. (8.8 oz.) ready-to-serve long grain rice
1   tsp. prepared mustard
½   tsp. garlic salt
¼   tsp. pepper
1   cup shredded sharp cheddar cheese

1. In a large skillet, cook sausage over medium heat 5-7 minutes or until no longer pink, breaking it into crumbles. Drain and remove sausage from pan.
2. In the same pan, heat oil over medium heat. Add zucchini and onion; cook and stir 5-7 minutes or until tender. Stir in sausage, tomatoes, rice, mustard, garlic salt and pepper. Bring to a boil. Reduce heat; simmer, covered, 5 minutes to allow flavors to blend.
3. Remove from heat; sprinkle with cheese. Let stand, covered, 5 minutes or until cheese is melted.
1⅓ cups: 394 cal., 26g fat (9g sat. fat), 60mg chol., 803mg sod., 24g carb. (6g sugars, 2g fiber), 16g pro.

LAND OF ENCHANTMENT POSOLE

We usually make this spicy soup over the holidays when we have lots of family over. But be warned—we never have leftovers.
—Suzanne Caldwell, Artesia, NM

PREP: 30 min. • COOK: 45 min.
MAKES: 5 servings

1½ lbs. pork stew meat, cut into ¾-in. cubes
1   large onion, chopped
2   Tbsp. canola oil
2   garlic cloves, minced
3   cups beef broth
2   cans (15½ oz. each) hominy, rinsed and drained
2   cans (4 oz. each) chopped green chiles
1   to 2 jalapeno peppers, seeded and chopped, optional
½   tsp. salt
½   tsp. ground cumin
½   tsp. dried oregano
¼   tsp. pepper
¼   tsp. cayenne pepper
½   cup minced fresh cilantro
     Tortilla strips, optional

1. In a Dutch oven, cook pork and onion in oil over medium heat until meat is no longer pink. Add garlic; cook 1 minute longer. Drain. Stir in the broth, hominy, chiles, jalapeno if desired, salt, cumin, oregano, pepper and cayenne.
2. Bring to a boil. Reduce heat; cover and simmer for 45-60 minutes or until the meat is tender. Stir in cilantro. Serve with tortilla strips if desired.
1⅓ cups: 430 cal., 29g fat (9g sat. fat), 94mg chol., 1266mg sod., 14g carb. (2g sugars, 3g fiber), 27g pro.

DID YOU KNOW?

Sharp cheddar cheese has been aged longer than regular cheddar. As cheese ages, it loses moisture and its flavor becomes more pronounced. Using aged cheese in a recipe can add complexity and rich flavor, even to humble favorites like casseroles and mac and cheese. It's also wonderful in light cooking because you can get more flavor while using less.

ZUCCHINI & SAUSAGE
STOVETOP CASSEROLE

PORK CHOPS WITH DIJON SAUCE

Here's a main course that tastes rich yet isn't high in saturated fat. It's easy for weeknights, but the creamy sauce makes it special enough for weekends.
—Bonnie Brown-Watson, Houston, TX

TAKES: 25 min. • **MAKES:** 4 servings

- 4 boneless pork loin chops (6 oz. each)
- ¼ tsp. salt
- ¼ tsp. pepper
- 2 tsp. canola oil
- ⅓ cup reduced-sodium chicken broth
- 2 Tbsp. Dijon mustard
- ⅓ cup half-and-half cream

1. Sprinkle pork chops with salt and pepper. In a large skillet coated with cooking spray, brown chops in oil for 4-5 minutes on each side or until a thermometer reads 145°. Remove and keep warm.

2. Stir broth into skillet, scraping up any browned bits. Stir in mustard and half-and-half. Bring to a boil. Reduce the heat; simmer, uncovered, until thickened, 5-6 minutes, stirring occasionally. Serve with pork chops.

1 pork chop: 283 cal., 14g fat (5g sat. fat), 92mg chol., 432mg sod., 1g carb. (1g sugars, 0 fiber), 34g pro. **Diabetic exchanges:** 5 lean meat, 2 fat.

PARMESAN PORK CUTLETS

The aroma of these cutlets as they cook makes my kids eager to come to the dinner table. The dish is easy to make, and my whole family loves it.
—Julie Ahern, Waukegan, IL

PREP: 25 min. • **COOK:** 15 min.
MAKES: 4 servings

- 1 pork tenderloin (1 lb.)
- ⅓ cup all-purpose flour
- 2 large eggs, lightly beaten
- 1 cup dry bread crumbs
- ¼ cup grated Parmesan cheese
- 1 tsp. salt
- ¼ cup olive oil
  Lemon wedges

1. Cut pork diagonally into 8 slices; pound each to ¼-in. thickness. Place the flour and eggs in separate shallow bowls. In another shallow bowl, combine the bread crumbs, cheese and salt. Dip pork in the flour, eggs, then bread crumb mixture.

2. In a large skillet, heat oil over medium-high heat. Add the pork, in batches, and cook until a thermometer reads 145°, 2-3 minutes on each side. Remove and keep warm. Serve with lemon wedges.

2 cutlets: 376 cal., 21g fat (5g sat. fat), 162mg chol., 626mg sod., 15g carb. (1g sugars, 1g fiber), 29g pro.

PORK CHOPS WITH DIJON SAUCE

PORK CHOPS WITH NECTARINE SAUCE

MUSHROOM PORK

Seasoned with garlic, marjoram and a bit of lemon juice, this tender pork entree comes together easily. You can even make the mouthwatering gravy in the same skillet.
—*Kathy Mackey, Waterville, QC*

PREP: 15 min. • **COOK:** 25 min.
MAKES: 3 servings

- 1 pork tenderloin (about 1 lb.)
- 1 garlic clove, peeled
  Paprika
- 2 Tbsp. butter
- 1 cup sliced fresh mushrooms
- 2 to 3 tsp. lemon juice
- ¼ tsp. dried marjoram
  Salt and pepper to taste
- 1 Tbsp. all-purpose flour
- ¾ cup cold water
  Hot cooked rice

1. Rub pork on all sides with garlic; sprinkle with paprika. In a large skillet, heat butter over medium-high heat. Add pork; cook until browned. Add the mushrooms, lemon juice, marjoram, salt and pepper. Turn meat to coat with seasonings. Reduce heat; cover and simmer until a thermometer reads 145°, 25-30 minutes. Remove the meat and keep warm.

2. In a small bowl, combine the flour and cold water until smooth; stir into the pan juices. Bring to a boil; cook and stir until thickened, 2 minutes. Slice the pork; serve with gravy and rice.

1 serving: 261 cal., 13g fat (7g sat. fat), 105mg chol., 122mg sod., 3g carb. (1g sugars, 0 fiber), 31g pro. **Diabetic exchanges:** 4 lean meat, 2 fat.

"Easy to make, even on a weeknight. Good basic flavors that no one at your table should object to. I also used garlic powder instead of fresh. Make the seasoning adjustments you need so it's just right for your family. I had to double the recipe to feed a family of five, three of whom are guys!"
—LSHAW, TASTEOFHOME.COM

PORK CHOPS WITH NECTARINE SAUCE

As a dietitian, I am always looking for new ways to make meals healthy and delicious. These juicy chops are fast, too.
—*Suellen Pineda, Victor, NY*

TAKES: 30 min. • **MAKES:** 4 servings

- 4 boneless pork loin chops (6 oz. each)
- ½ tsp. salt
- ½ tsp. dried thyme
- ¼ tsp. pepper
- 3 Tbsp. all-purpose flour
- 1 Tbsp. canola oil
- 1 small onion, finely chopped
- 1 garlic clove, minced
- 3 medium nectarines or peeled peaches, cut into ½-in. slices
- ½ cup reduced-sodium chicken broth
- 1 Tbsp. honey, optional

1. Sprinkle pork chops with seasonings. Dredge lightly with flour. In a large skillet, heat the oil over medium heat; cook the chops until a thermometer reads 145°, 4-5 minutes per side. Remove from pan; keep warm.

2. Add onion to same pan; cook and stir over medium heat 2 minutes. Add garlic; cook and stir 1 minute. Add nectarines; cook until lightly browned on both sides. Stir in broth and, if desired, honey; bring to a boil. Reduce heat. Simmer, uncovered, until nectarines are softened and sauce is slightly thickened, about 5 minutes. Serve with chops.

1 pork chop with ½ cup sauce: 330 cal., 14g fat (4g sat. fat), 82mg chol., 414mg sod., 16g carb. (9g sugars, 2g fiber), 35g pro. **Diabetic exchanges:** 5 lean meat, 1 fruit, 1 fat.

DENVER
OMELET SALAD

DENVER OMELET SALAD

I love this recipe. It may not be your typical breakfast, but it has all the right elements. Plus, it's easy, healthy and quick to prep. Just turn your favorite omelet ingredients into a morning salad!
—*Pauline Custer, Duluth, MN*

- -

TAKES: 25 min. • **MAKES:** 4 servings

- 8   cups fresh baby spinach
- 1   cup chopped tomatoes
- 2   Tbsp. olive oil, divided
- 1½ cups chopped fully cooked ham
- 1   small onion, chopped
- 1   small green pepper, chopped
- 4   large eggs
     Salt and pepper to taste

1. Arrange spinach and tomatoes on a platter; set aside. In a large skillet, heat 1 Tbsp. olive oil over medium-high heat. Add ham, onion and green pepper; saute until the ham is heated through and the vegetables are tender, 5-7 minutes. Spoon over spinach and tomatoes.

2. In same skillet, heat remaining olive oil over medium heat. Break eggs, 1 at a time, into a small cup, then gently slide into the skillet. Immediately reduce heat to low; season with salt and pepper. To prepare sunny-side up eggs, cover pan and cook until whites are completely set and yolks thicken but are not hard. Top salad with fried eggs.

1 serving: 229 cal., 14g fat (3g sat. fat), 217mg chol., 756mg sod., 7g carb. (3g sugars, 2g fiber), 20g pro. **Diabetic exchanges:** 3 lean meat, 2 fat, 1 vegetable.

TEST KITCHEN TIP
Just about any omelet can be turned into a salad. It's time to get creative.

SPICY BRATWURST SUPPER

SPICY BRATWURST SUPPER

With a zesty sauce and shredded Gouda cheese melted over the top, this tasty bratwurst dish comes together quickly in a skillet.
— *Taste of Home Test Kitchen*

- -

TAKES: 25 min. • **MAKES:** 4 servings

- 6   bacon strips, diced
- ⅓   cup chopped onion
- 5   fully cooked bratwurst links, cut into ½-in. slices
- ½   lb. sliced fresh mushrooms
- 1   Tbsp. diced jalapeno pepper
- 2   cups meatless spaghetti sauce
- 2   oz. Gouda cheese, shredded
     Hot cooked rice

1. In a large skillet, cook bacon and onion over medium heat until bacon is almost crisp. Remove to paper towels to drain.

2. In the same skillet, saute the bratwurst, mushrooms and jalapeno for 3-4 minutes or until mushrooms are tender. Stir in the spaghetti sauce and bacon mixture.

3. Cover and cook 4-6 minutes or until heated through. Sprinkle with cheese. Serve with rice.

Note: Wear disposable gloves when cutting hot peppers; the oils can burn skin. Avoid touching your face.

1 cup: 630 cal., 51g fat (20g sat. fat), 103mg chol., 1525mg sod., 17g carb. (12g sugars, 3g fiber), 25g pro.

SMOKY MACARONI

Our two grandsons are big fans of macaroni and cheese. When they're hungry, I can have this tasty variation with little smoked sausages and peas on the table in about 20 minutes.
—*Perlene Hoekema, Lynden, WA*

TAKES: 25 min. • **MAKES:** 8 servings

- ¼ cup chopped sweet red pepper
- 2 Tbsp. chopped onion
- 1 can (10¾ oz.) condensed cheddar cheese soup, undiluted
- 1 cup 2% milk
- 1 pkg. (14 oz.) miniature smoked sausages
- 8 oz. Velveeta, cut into ½-in. cubes
- 1 cup frozen peas
- 4 cups cooked elbow macaroni

In a nonstick skillet, saute red pepper and onion until tender. Combine soup and milk; stir into skillet. Add sausage, cheese and peas. Reduce heat; simmer, uncovered, until the cheese is melted, 5-10 minutes, stirring occasionally. Add macaroni; cook until heated through, 5-10 minutes longer.

1 serving: 407 cal., 26g fat (11g sat. fat), 63mg chol., 1244mg sod., 27g carb. (7g sugars, 2g fiber), 19g pro.

TEST KITCHEN TIP
For an easy nutrition boost, double the red pepper and peas.

DOWN-HOME PORK CHOPS

A zippy sauce made of brown sugar, crushed red pepper flakes and soy sauce adds personality to this otherwise straightforward main dish.
—*Denise Hruz, Germantown, WI*

TAKES: 25 min. • **MAKES:** 4 servings

- 1 Tbsp. canola oil
- 4 boneless pork loin chops (4 oz. each)
- 1 garlic clove, minced
- ½ cup beef broth
- 2 Tbsp. brown sugar
- 1 Tbsp. soy sauce
- ¼ tsp. crushed red pepper flakes
- 2 tsp. cornstarch
- 2 Tbsp. cold water

1. In a large skillet, heat oil over medium-high heat. Add pork chops and brown on each side, 2-3 minutes. Remove and set aside. Add garlic to the pan; cook and stir for 1 minute. Stir in broth, brown sugar, soy sauce and red pepper flakes. Return chops to the pan; cover and simmer until a thermometer inserted in pork reads 145°, 6-8 minutes. Remove chops and keep warm.

2. Combine cornstarch and water until smooth; stir into broth mixture. Bring to a boil; cook and stir until thickened, about 2 minutes. Serve with chops.

1 pork chop with about 2 Tbsp. sauce: 219 cal., 10g fat (3g sat. fat), 55mg chol., 375mg sod., 8g carb. (7g sugars, 0 fiber), 23g pro. **Diabetic exchanges:** 3 lean meat, 1 fat, ½ starch.

BACON BOLOGNESE

Pasta with ground beef was a family staple while I was growing up. I've added bacon, ground pork, white wine and juicy tomatoes to make it a next-level meal.
—*Carly Terrell, Granbury, TX*

- -

PREP: 15 min. • **COOK:** 3¼ hours
MAKES: 10 servings

- ½ lb. ground beef
- ½ lb. ground pork
- ½ tsp. salt
- ¼ tsp. pepper
- 2 medium carrots, chopped
- 1 medium onion, chopped
- 6 thick-sliced bacon strips, chopped
- 8 garlic cloves, minced
- 1 cup dry white wine
- 1 can (28 oz.) whole tomatoes, crushed slightly
- 1½ cups chicken stock or reduced-sodium chicken broth
- 1 pkg. (16 oz.) spaghetti
- 3 Tbsp. butter, cubed
- 1 cup grated Parmesan cheese

1. In a 6-qt. stockpot, cook beef and pork over medium heat, 5-7 minutes, until no longer pink, breaking both into crumbles. Stir in salt and pepper. Remove from pot with a slotted spoon; pour off drippings.
2. Add carrots, onion and bacon to the same pot; cook and stir over medium heat 6-8 minutes or until vegetables are softened. Add garlic; cook 1 minute longer. Return meat to pot; add wine. Bring to a boil, stirring to loosen browned bits from pan; cook until liquid is almost evaporated.
3. Add the tomatoes and stock; return to a boil. Reduce the heat; simmer, covered, 3-4 hours to allow the flavors to blend, stirring occasionally.
4. To serve, cook the spaghetti according to package directions for al dente; drain. Stir butter into meat sauce; add spaghetti and toss to combine. Serve with cheese.
1 cup: 483 cal., 26g fat (11g sat. fat), 61mg chol., 686mg sod., 41g carb. (4g sugars, 3g fiber), 20g pro.

STUFFED PORK CHOPS WITH SHERRY SAUCE

This scrumptious pork chop recipe is one of my favorites. I like how easy it is to adapt for more than two people.
—*Dale Smith, Greensboro, NC*

- -

PREP: 20 min. • **COOK:** 30 min.
MAKES: 2 servings

- 2 bone-in pork loin chops (1 in. thick and 8 oz. each)
- 3 Tbsp. butter, divided
- ½ cup sliced fresh mushrooms
- ¼ cup chopped onion
- ¼ tsp. dried oregano
- ⅛ tsp. pepper
- 2 slices deli ham
- ½ cup sherry or chicken broth
- 2 tsp. cornstarch
- 1 Tbsp. cold water

1. Cut a pocket in each chop by slicing almost to the bone; set aside.
2. In a large skillet, heat 1 Tbsp. butter. Cook and stir mushrooms and onion until tender, 2-3 minutes. Remove from heat. Stir in oregano and pepper. Place a ham slice in the pocket of each chop; fill each with mushroom mixture.
3. In the same skillet, brown chops in remaining butter. Add sherry, stirring to loosen browned bits from pan. Bring to a boil. Reduce heat; cover and simmer 20-25 minutes or until a thermometer reads 145°. Remove to a serving platter.
4. Combine cornstarch and water until smooth; gradually stir into the pan. Bring to a boil; cook and stir until thickened, 2 minutes. Serve with pork chops.
1 stuffed pork chop with 2 Tbsp. gravy: 529 cal., 36g fat (18g sat. fat), 166mg chol., 399mg sod., 6g carb. (2g sugars, 1g fiber), 41g pro.

BACON BOLOGNESE

FRIED GREEN TOMATO STACKS

❄
BLACK-EYED PEA SAUSAGE STEW
I've always wanted to try black-eyed peas.
I happened to have some smoked sausage
on hand one night, so I invented this
full-flavored stew. It's the perfect way
to heat up a cold night without spending
a lot of time in the kitchen. I usually double
the seasonings because we enjoy our
food spicier.
—*Laura Wimbrow, Bridgeville, DE*

PREP: 15 min. • **COOK:** 30 min.
MAKES: 6 servings

- 1 pkg. (16 oz.) smoked sausage links, halved lengthwise and sliced
- 1 small onion, chopped
- 2 cans (15 oz. each) black-eyed peas, rinsed and drained
- 1 can (14½ oz.) diced tomatoes, drained
- 1 can (8 oz.) tomato sauce
- 1 cup beef broth
- ¼ tsp. garlic powder
- ¼ tsp. Cajun seasoning
- ¼ tsp. pepper
- ⅛ tsp. salt
- ⅛ tsp. cayenne pepper
- ⅛ tsp. hot pepper sauce
- 1½ cups frozen corn, thawed

1. In a Dutch oven or soup kettle, cook sausage and onion over medium heat until meat is no longer pink; drain. Stir in the peas, tomatoes, tomato sauce, broth, seasonings and hot pepper sauce.
2. Cook and stir for 10-12 minutes or until hot and bubbly. Stir in corn; cook 5 minutes longer or until heated through.
Freeze option: Freeze cooled stew in freezer containers. To use, partially thaw in refrigerator overnight. Heat through in a saucepan, stirring occasionally; add water if necessary.
1½ cups: 346 cal., 21g fat (7g sat. fat), 48mg chol., 1378mg sod., 25g carb. (6g sugars, 4g fiber), 16g pro.

🍎
FRIED GREEN TOMATO STACKS
This dish is for lovers of red and green tomatoes. When I ran across the recipe, I just had to try it. It proved to be so tasty!
—*Barbara Mohr, Millington, MI*

PREP: 20 min. • **COOK:** 15 min.
MAKES: 4 servings

- ¼ cup fat-free mayonnaise
- ¼ tsp. grated lime zest
- 2 Tbsp. lime juice
- 1 tsp. minced fresh thyme or ¼ tsp. dried thyme
- ½ tsp. pepper, divided
- ¼ cup all-purpose flour
- 2 large egg whites, lightly beaten
- ¾ cup cornmeal
- ¼ tsp. salt
- 2 medium green tomatoes
- 2 medium red tomatoes
- 2 Tbsp. canola oil
- 8 slices Canadian bacon

1. Mix the first 4 ingredients and ¼ tsp. pepper; refrigerate until serving. Place flour in a shallow bowl; place egg whites in a separate shallow bowl. In a third bowl, mix cornmeal, salt and remaining pepper.
2. Cut each tomato crosswise into 4 slices. Lightly coat each slice in flour; shake off excess. Dip in the egg whites, then in the cornmeal mixture.
3. In a large nonstick skillet, heat oil over medium heat. In batches, cook tomatoes until golden brown, 4-5 minutes per side.
4. In same pan, lightly brown Canadian bacon on both sides. For each serving, stack 1 slice each green tomato, bacon and red tomato. Serve with sauce.
1 stack: 284 cal., 10g fat (1g sat. fat), 16mg chol., 679mg sod., 37g carb. (6g sugars, 3g fiber), 12g pro. **Diabetic exchanges:** 2 starch, 1½ fat, 1 lean meat, 1 vegetable.

BLACK-EYED PEA
SAUSAGE STEW

Fish & Seafood

PINEAPPLE SHRIMP TACOS

PINEAPPLE SHRIMP TACOS

Taste the tropics with our cool, crispy take on shrimp tacos. Wrapping the shells in lettuce adds even more crunch while keeping the tacos tidy after you take a bite.
—Taste of Home *Test Kitchen*

- -

TAKES: 25 min. • **MAKES:** 4 servings

1	lb. uncooked shrimp (26-30 per pound), peeled and deveined
3	tsp. olive oil, divided
1	large sweet orange pepper, sliced
1	large sweet red pepper, sliced
1	small onion, halved and sliced
1	cup pineapple tidbits
1	envelope fajita seasoning mix
⅓	cup water
8	corn tortillas (6 in.), warmed
½	cup crumbled Cotija or shredded mozzarella cheese
8	large romaine lettuce leaves

1. Cook shrimp in 2 tsp. oil in a large cast-iron or other heavy skillet over medium heat until shrimp turn pink, 4-6 minutes. Remove and keep warm.
2. In the same skillet, saute the peppers, onion and pineapple in remaining oil until vegetables are tender. Add seasoning mix and water. Bring to a boil; cook and stir for 2 minutes. Return shrimp to the skillet; heat through. Spoon onto tortillas; top with cheese. Wrap lettuce around tortillas to serve.

2 tacos: 382 cal., 11g fat (4g sat. fat),153mg chol., 1123mg sod., 44g carb. (13g sugars, 6g fiber), 27g pro.

DID YOU KNOW?
Cotija is a cow's milk cheese from a town of the same name in western Mexico. Fresh Cotija is easily crumbled like feta and has a milky, salty taste. Aged Cotija cheese is drier and grates like Parmesan.

POACHED SALMON WITH CHIMICHURRI

CREAM OF MUSSEL SOUP

Every New England cook has a personal version of mussel soup, depending on favored regional herbs and cooking customs. Feel free to start with my recipe and develop your own luscious variation.
—*Donna Noel, Gray, ME*

- -

PREP: 35 min. • **COOK:** 10 min.
MAKES: 5 servings

- 3 lbs. fresh mussels (about 5 dozen), scrubbed and beards removed
- 2 medium onions, finely chopped
- 2 celery ribs, finely chopped
- 1 cup water
- 1 cup white wine or chicken broth
- 1 bottle (8 oz.) clam juice
- ¼ cup minced fresh parsley
- 2 garlic cloves, minced
- ¼ tsp. salt
- ¼ tsp. pepper
- 1 cup half-and-half cream

1. Tap mussels; discard any that do not close. Set aside. In a stockpot, combine onions, celery, water, wine or broth, clam juice, parsley, garlic, salt and pepper.
2. Bring to a boil. Reduce heat; add the mussels. Cover and simmer until mussels have opened, 5-6 minutes. Remove the mussels with a slotted spoon, discarding any unopened mussels; set aside opened mussels and keep warm.
3. Cool cooking liquid slightly. In a blender, cover and process cooking liquid in batches until blended. Return all to pan. Add cream and reserved mussels; heat through (do not boil).
1 serving: 368 cal., 11g fat (4g sat. fat), 102mg chol., 1043mg sod., 20g carb. (6g sugars, 2g fiber), 35g pro.

POACHED SALMON WITH CHIMICHURRI

Tender, flaky poached salmon gets a flavorful sauce in this elegant dish. Though it takes a little extra prep time, the entree is sure to satisfy.
—Taste of Home *Test Kitchen*

- -

PREP: 40 min. • **COOK:** 10 min.
MAKES: 4 servings

- 4 cups water
- ½ cup white wine or reduced-sodium chicken broth
- ½ cup white wine vinegar
- 1 medium carrot, coarsely chopped
- 1 celery rib with leaves, coarsely chopped
- 1 medium onion, coarsely chopped
- 4 sprigs fresh parsley
- 4 whole peppercorns
- 1 bay leaf
- 4 salmon fillets (4 oz. each)

CHIMICHURRI
- 2 Tbsp. lemon juice
- 1 Tbsp. white wine vinegar
- 1 Tbsp. olive oil
- 3 Tbsp. finely chopped onion
- 3 Tbsp. minced fresh parsley
- 1 garlic clove, minced
- ⅛ tsp. pepper
- ⅛ tsp. cayenne pepper

1. In a large Dutch oven, bring the first 9 ingredients to a boil. Reduce heat; simmer, uncovered, 15 minutes. Strain, reserving liquid (discard vegetables and spices).
2. Return liquid to the pan and bring to a boil. Reduce heat; add salmon. Poach, uncovered, until fish just begins to flake easily with a fork, 8-10 minutes.
3. Meanwhile, in a small bowl, whisk the lemon juice, vinegar and oil. Stir in the onion, parsley, garlic, pepper and cayenne. Serve with salmon.
1 fillet with 1 Tbsp. chimichurri: 246 cal., 16g fat (3g sat. fat), 67mg chol., 69mg sod., 2g carb. (1g sugars, 0 fiber), 23g pro.

**LINGUINE WITH
HERBED CLAM SAUCE**

IINDIAN-SPICED TILAPIA STICKS

These flavorful Indian-spiced fish sticks please my whole family. Serve them with the creamy dipping sauce.
—*Jessie Grearson, Falmouth, ME*

PREP: 35 min. • **COOK:** 20 min.
MAKES: 4 servings

    1   lb. tilapia fillets, cut into 1-in. strips
    ¼   tsp. pepper
    ⅛   tsp. salt
    ½   cup all-purpose flour
    ⅓   cup reduced-fat ranch
        salad dressing
    ¼   cup reduced-fat plain yogurt
  1½   cups panko bread crumbs
  1½   tsp. garam masala
    ½   tsp. ground cumin
    ½   tsp. cayenne pepper
    3   Tbsp. olive oil
SAUCE
    ½   cup reduced-fat plain yogurt
    3   Tbsp. fresh cilantro leaves
    ¼   tsp. ground cumin
    ¼   tsp. salt
    ¼   cup finely chopped peeled cucumber
    2   Tbsp. finely chopped sweet onion
    4   cups fresh baby spinach
    1   medium mango, peeled and sliced

1. Sprinkle tilapia with pepper and salt. Place flour in a shallow bowl. In a second shallow bowl, combine salad dressing and yogurt. In a third shallow bowl, combine the bread crumbs, garam masala, cumin and cayenne. Dip fish in the flour, dressing mixture, then bread crumb mixture.
2. In a large nonstick skillet heat oil over medium-high heat; cook fish in batches until fish just begins to flake easily with a fork, 2-3 minutes.
3. Meanwhile, for sauce, place yogurt, cilantro, cumin and salt in a food processor; cover and process until blended. Stir in cucumber and onion. Serve tilapia with spinach, mango and prepared sauce.

1 serving: 408 cal., 17g fat (3g sat. fat), 63mg chol., 548mg sod., 36g carb. (13g sugars, 3g fiber), 29g pro. **Diabetic exchanges:** 3 lean meat, 2 starch, 2 fat, 1 vegetable.

LINGUINE WITH
HERBED CLAM SAUCE

This impressive pasta looks and tastes so much like fancy restaurant fare that you'll want to serve it to guests. But the recipe is simple enough to prepare anytime.
—*Carolee Snyder, Hartford City, IN*

PREP: 20 min. • **COOK:** 15 min.
MAKES: 4 servings

    1   can (10 oz.) whole baby clams
    1   can (6½ oz.) minced clams
    ½   cup finely chopped onion
    ¼   cup olive oil
    ¼   cup butter
    ⅓   cup minced fresh parsley
    4   garlic cloves, minced
    2   Tbsp. cornstarch
    ½   cup white wine or chicken broth
    ¼   cup minced fresh basil or
        4 tsp. dried basil
        Dash pepper
        Dash cayenne pepper
        Hot cooked linguine
        Shredded Parmesan cheese

1. Drain baby and minced clams, reserving juice; set clams and juice aside. In a large skillet, saute onion in oil and butter until tender. Add parsley and garlic; saute for 2 minutes.
2. Add the drained clams; saute for 2 minutes longer.
3. Combine cornstarch and clam juice until smooth; stir into skillet with wine or broth. Bring mixture to a boil; cook and stir 1-2 minutes or until thickened. Stir in the basil, pepper and cayenne. Serve sauce over linguine; sprinkle with Parmesan cheese.
1⅔ cups: 328 cal., 26g fat (9g sat. fat), 73mg chol., 521mg sod., 10g carb. (1g sugars, 1g fiber), 10g pro.

INDIAN-SPICED
TILAPIA STICKS

CRISPY SCALLOPS WITH TARRAGON CREAM

You'll flip for these tender, crisp-coated scallops. The ridiculously easy, creamy tarragon sauce truly makes this dish a star. Utterly brilliant!
—*Karen Kuebler, Dallas, TX*

TAKES: 25 min. • **MAKES:** 4 servings

- 1 large egg
- 2 tsp. water
- ⅔ cup Italian-style panko bread crumbs
- ⅓ cup mashed potato flakes
- 1 lb. sea scallops
- ¼ cup olive oil
- 2 Tbsp. butter
- 1 Tbsp. all-purpose flour
- ¼ tsp. salt
- ⅛ tsp. pepper
- ¾ cup heavy whipping cream
- 2 Tbsp. minced fresh tarragon or 2 tsp. dried tarragon

1. In a shallow bowl, whisk egg and water. In another shallow bowl, combine bread crumbs and potato flakes. Dip scallops in egg mixture, then coat with the crumb mixture.

2. Heat oil in a large skillet over medium-high heat. Cook scallops in batches until golden brown, 2 minutes on each side.

3. Meanwhile, in a small saucepan, melt butter. Stir in the flour, salt and pepper until smooth; gradually add cream. Bring to a boil; cook and stir until thickened, 1-2 minutes. Stir in tarragon. Serve with scallops.

4 scallops with about 3 Tbsp. sauce: 503 cal., 40g fat (16g sat. fat), 166mg chol., 544mg sod., 13g carb. (0 sugars, 0 fiber), 23g pro.

JAMBALAYA RICE SALAD

JAMBALAYA RICE SALAD

My cold rice salad has a little hint of spice for a classic jambalaya-style kick. Shrimp, tomatoes, ham and peppers give the dish bright colors and a delightful texture.
—*Karen Rahn, Hixon, TN*

PREP: 20 min. • **COOK:** 15 min. + chilling
MAKES: 8 servings

- 1⅓ cups uncooked long grain rice
- 2 Tbsp. olive oil
- 2 cups cubed fully cooked ham
- ⅓ cup chopped onion
- 2 garlic cloves, minced
- 1 tsp. dried oregano
- 1 tsp. dried thyme
- ½ to 1 tsp. salt
- ¼ to ½ tsp. cayenne pepper
- ¼ tsp. pepper
- ⅓ cup red wine vinegar
- 1½ lbs. peeled and deveined cooked shrimp (31-40 per lb.)
- 2 celery ribs, thinly sliced
- 1 small green pepper, julienned
- 1 small sweet red pepper, julienned
- 1 pint cherry tomatoes, halved
- 2 green onions, sliced

1. Prepare rice according to package directions; cool. In a large skillet, heat oil over medium heat. Add ham and onion; cook and stir until onion is tender, about 5 minutes. Add the next 6 ingredients; cook and stir 2 minutes. Remove from heat; stir in vinegar.

2. Combine rice, ham mixture, shrimp, celery and peppers. Refrigerate, covered, at least 2 hours. Add tomatoes; toss to combine. Sprinkle with green onions.

1¼ cups: 309 cal., 7g fat (1g sat. fat), 150mg chol., 709mg sod., 32g carb. (2g sugars, 2g fiber), 28g pro. **Diabetic exchanges:** 4 lean meat, 2 starch, 1 vegetable, 1 fat.

SAUCY SKILLET FISH

The main industry here on Kodiak Island is fishing, so I'm always on the lookout for new seafood recipes. This is my favorite way to fix halibut since it's quick and tasty. I often get recipe requests when I serve this to guests.
—*Merle Powell, Kodiak, AK*

TAKES: 20 min. • **MAKES:** 8 servings

- ½ cup all-purpose flour
- 1¼ tsp. salt
- 1 tsp. paprika
- ⅛ tsp. pepper
- 2 lbs. halibut, haddock or salmon fillets or steaks
- 1 medium onion, sliced
- ⅓ cup butter, cubed
- 1½ cups sour cream
- 1 tsp. dried basil
- 1 Tbsp. minced fresh parsley

1. In a large bowl, combine the flour, salt, paprika and pepper. Add fish and toss to coat (if using fillets, cut into serving-sized pieces first).

2. In a large cast-iron or other heavy skillet, saute onion in butter until tender; remove and set aside. Add fish to the skillet, cook over medium heat until fish just begins to flake easily with a fork, 3-5 minutes on each side. Remove fish to a serving plate and keep warm.

3. Add the sour cream, basil and onion to the skillet; heat through (do not boil). Serve with fish. Garnish with parsley.

1 serving: 319 cal., 18g fat (10g sat. fat), 87mg chol., 531mg sod., 9g carb. (3g sugars, 1g fiber), 26g pro.

STIR-FRIED SCALLOPS & ASPARAGUS

Served over quick-cooking ramen noodles, this stir-fry is perfect for busy families on hurried weeknights. It comes together in about half an hour.
—*Barbara Schindler, Napoleon, OH*

TAKES: 25 min. • **MAKES:** 4 servings

- 1 pkg. (3 oz.) chicken ramen noodles
- 1 Tbsp. olive oil
- 1 lb. fresh asparagus, trimmed and cut into 1-in. pieces
- 1 medium sweet red pepper, julienned
- 3 green onions, thinly sliced
- 1 garlic clove, minced
- 1 lb. sea scallops, halved horizontally
- 1 Tbsp. lime juice
- 2 Tbsp. reduced-sodium soy sauce
- 1 tsp. sesame oil
- ¼ to 1 tsp. hot pepper sauce

1. Discard seasoning package from ramen noodles or save for another use. Cook ramen noodles according to package directions; keep warm.

2. Meanwhile, in a nonstick skillet or wok, heat oil over medium-high heat. Stir-fry asparagus and red pepper until the vegetables are crisp-tender, 2 minutes. Add green onions and garlic, stir-fry 1 minute longer. Add scallops. Stir-fry until scallops are firm and opaque, 3 minutes.

3. Combine the lime juice, soy sauce, sesame oil and hot pepper sauce; stir into skillet. Serve with ramen noodles.

1 cup: 269 cal., 9g fat (3g sat. fat), 37mg chol., 578mg sod., 22g carb. (2g sugars, 2g fiber), 24g pro. **Diabetic exchanges:** 3 lean meat, 1 starch, 1 vegetable, 1 fat.

SAUCY SKILLET FISH

SEARED SCALLOPS WITH
POLENTA & AVOCADO CREAM

SEARED SCALLOPS WITH POLENTA & AVOCADO CREAM

This is a really impressive dish. It's beautiful but simple and a wonderful dinner party entree. If you can find them, peppadew peppers add a bit of zing, but if you can't, roasted red peppers will work just fine. Shrimp can also be substituted for the scallops, if you prefer.
—*Katie Pelczar, West Hartford, CT*

PREP: 30 min. • **COOK:** 35 min.
MAKES: 4 servings

- 1 small onion, chopped
- 3 Tbsp. butter, divided
- ½ cup fresh corn or frozen corn, thawed
- ¼ cup roasted sweet red peppers, drained and chopped
- 4 cups reduced-sodium chicken broth
- ¾ tsp. salt, divided
- 1 cup yellow cornmeal
- ½ cup grated Parmesan cheese
- 1 medium ripe avocado, peeled and chopped
- ¼ to ½ cup water, divided
- 2 Tbsp. heavy whipping cream
- 8 sea scallops (about 1 lb.)
- ½ tsp. pepper

1. In a large skillet, saute onions in half the butter until tender, 5-7 minutes. Add corn and peppers; cook 4-5 minutes longer. Stir in broth and ¼ tsp. salt, bring to a boil. Reduce heat to a gentle boil; slowly whisk in cornmeal. Cook and stir with a wooden spoon until polenta is thickened and pulls away cleanly from the sides of the pan, 15-20 minutes. Stir in cheese. Remove from heat; set aside and keep warm.
2. Meanwhile, in a blender, combine the avocado, ¼ cup water, cream and ¼ tsp. salt. Blend until smooth, 30 seconds. Add additional water as needed to reach desired consistency. Cover and refrigerate until serving.
3. Sprinkle scallops with remaining salt and pepper. In a large skillet, saute the scallops in remaining butter until firm and opaque, 1-2 minutes per side. Serve with polenta and avocado cream.
2 scallops with 1 cup polenta and 2 Tbsp. avocado cream: 467 cal., 21g fat (10g sat. fat), 67mg chol., 1773mg sod., 46g carb. (4g sugars, 5g fiber), 24g pro.

SPINACH SHRIMP FETTUCCINE

SPINACH SHRIMP FETTUCCINE

I experimented for a couple of years before perfecting this colorful dish, and everyone raves about it. It is simple and light, and it fits into my busy schedule.
—*Kirstin Walker, Suffolk, VA*

TAKES: 20 min. • **MAKES:** 8 servings

- 1 lb. uncooked fettuccine
- 1 pkg. (6 oz.) baby spinach
- 2 Tbsp. olive oil
- 4 garlic cloves, minced
- 1 lb. uncooked shrimp (31-40 per pound), peeled and deveined
- 2 medium plum tomatoes, seeded and chopped
- ½ tsp. Italian seasoning
- ¼ tsp. salt
- ¼ cup shredded Parmesan cheese

1. Cook fettuccine according to package directions. Meanwhile, in a large skillet, saute spinach in oil for 2 minutes or until spinach begins to wilt. Add garlic; cook 1 minute longer.
2. Add shrimp, tomatoes, Italian seasoning and salt; saute 2-3 minutes or until the shrimp turn pink. Drain fettuccine and add to skillet; toss to coat. Sprinkle with cheese.
1¼ cups: 283 cal., 5g fat (1g sat. fat), 85mg chol., 209mg sod., 41g carb. (2g sugars, 3g fiber), 17g pro. **Diabetic exchanges:** 2 starch, 2 vegetable, 1½ lean meat.

LEMON-BUTTER TILAPIA WITH ALMONDS

Sometimes I want a nice meal without a ton of effort or wait time. Thankfully, I have this lemony, buttery fish that's super fast and totally tasty.
—*Ramona Parris, Canton, GA*

TAKES: 10 min. • **MAKES:** 4 servings

4 tilapia fillets (4 oz. each)
½ tsp. salt
¼ tsp. pepper
1 Tbsp. olive oil
¼ cup butter, cubed
¼ cup white wine or chicken broth
2 Tbsp. lemon juice
¼ cup sliced almonds

1. Sprinkle fillets with salt and pepper. In a large nonstick skillet, heat oil over medium heat. Add fillets; cook until fish just begins to flake easily with a fork, 2-3 minutes on each side. Remove and keep warm.
2. Add butter, wine and lemon juice to same pan; cook and stir until butter is melted. Serve with fish; sprinkle fish with almonds.

1 fillet with about 2 Tbsp. sauce and 2 Tbsp. almonds: 269 cal., 19g fat (8g sat. fat), 86mg chol., 427mg sod., 2g carb. (1g sugars, 1g fiber), 22g pro.

SAKE-STEAMED SOLE WITH SPICY SLAW

This healthy fish and zippy slaw can be prepared easily on a weeknight or for a special occasion. I like to serve the dish with steamed jasmine rice.
—*Donna Noel, Gray, ME*

PREP: 25 min. • **COOK:** 10 min.
MAKES: 4 servings

¾ cup chicken broth
½ cup sake
½ cup mirin (sweet rice wine)
¼ cup reduced-sodium soy sauce
2 Tbsp. sugar
⅛ tsp. salt
⅛ tsp. pepper
4 sole or whitefish fillets (4 oz. each)
SLAW
1½ cups shredded Chinese or napa cabbage
⅓ cup each julienned cucumber, radishes, carrot and sweet red pepper
2 jalapeno peppers, seeded and julienned
2 Tbsp. minced fresh cilantro
2 Tbsp. minced fresh mint
2 Tbsp. plus 2 tsp. rice vinegar
4½ tsp. reduced-sodium soy sauce
⅛ tsp. salt
⅛ tsp. pepper

1. In a large skillet, combine the first 7 ingredients. Bring to a boil; add fish. Reduce heat; cover and simmer until fish just begins to flake easily with a fork, 8-10 minutes.
2. Meanwhile, in a large bowl, combine cabbage, cucumber, radishes, carrot, red pepper, jalapenos, cilantro and mint. In a small bowl, combine the vinegar, soy sauce, salt and pepper; pour over vegetables and toss to coat. Serve slaw with fish.
Note: Wear disposable gloves when cutting hot peppers; the oils can burn skin. Avoid touching your face.

1 fillet with ⅔ cup slaw: 271 cal.,7g fat (1g sat. fat), 71mg chol., 1357mg sod., 19g carb. (15g sugars, 1g fiber), 25g pro.

SAKE-STEAMED SOLE WITH SPICY SLAW

SHRIMP WITH WARM GERMAN-STYLE COLESLAW

SOLE IN HERBED BUTTER

I often rely on seafood recipes for quick meals. This flavorful fish is easy to make and is ready in just a few minutes. I know your family will request this often throughout the year!
—*Marilyn Paradis, Woodburn, OR*

- -

TAKES: 25 min. • **MAKES:** 6 servings

- 4 Tbsp. butter, softened
- 1 tsp. dill weed
- ½ tsp. onion powder
- ½ tsp. garlic powder
- ½ tsp. salt, optional
- ¼ tsp. white pepper
- 2 lbs. sole fillets
  Optional: Fresh dill and lemon wedges

1. In a small bowl, combine the butter, dill, onion powder, garlic powder, salt if desired, and pepper.
2. In a large skillet, heat the butter mixture over medium heat until melted, 1-2 minutes. Add sole; cook until fish just begins to flake easily with a fork, 2-3 minutes on each side. If desired, garnish with dill and lemon.

1 serving: 256 cal., 12g fat (0 sat. fat), 72mg chol., 303mg sod., 0 carb. (0 sugars, 0 fiber), 35g pro.

"This is one of our family's favorites. It's super quick and tasty! We like to use the fish my husband and son catch (bluegill, crappie and bass) in place of the sole. It's sooo good!"
—ANNIESMAMA, TASTEOFHOME.COM

SHRIMP WITH WARM GERMAN-STYLE COLESLAW

We love anything that's tangy or has bacon. With fennel and tarragon, this is a super savory dish. I use the medley from Minute Rice if I don't have time to make my own.
—*Ann Sheehy, Lawrence, MA*

- -

TAKES: 30 min. • **MAKES:** 4 servings

- 6 bacon strips
- 2 Tbsp. canola oil, divided
- 3 cups finely shredded green cabbage
- ½ cup finely shredded carrot (1 medium carrot)
- 1 cup finely shredded red cabbage, optional
- ½ cup finely shredded fennel bulb, optional
- 6 green onions, finely chopped
- 3 Tbsp. minced fresh parsley
- 2 Tbsp. minced fresh tarragon or 2 tsp. dried tarragon
- ¼ tsp. salt
- ⅛ tsp. pepper
- ¼ cup red wine vinegar
- 1 lb. uncooked shrimp (26-30 per lb.), peeled and deveined
- 3 cups hot cooked rice or multigrain medley

1. In a large skillet, cook the bacon over medium heat until crisp. Remove to paper towels to drain. Pour off pan drippings, discarding all but 2 Tbsp. Crumble bacon.
2. In same skillet, heat 1 Tbsp. drippings with 1 Tbsp. oil over medium heat. Add green cabbage, carrot and, if desired, red cabbage and fennel; cook and stir until vegetables are just tender, 1-2 minutes. Remove to a bowl. Stir in green onions, parsley, tarragon, salt and pepper; toss with vinegar. Keep warm.
3. Add remaining drippings and remaining oil to skillet. Add the shrimp; cook and stir over medium heat until shrimp turn pink, 2-3 minutes. Remove from heat.
4. To serve, spoon rice and coleslaw into soup bowls. Top with shrimp; sprinkle with crumbled bacon.

1 serving: 472 cal., 20g fat (5g sat. fat), 156mg chol., 546mg sod., 44g carb. (2g sugars, 3g fiber), 28g pro.

COCONUT CITRUS SAUCED COD

I love to make this fusion meal on weeknights when I am short on time but want something big in flavor.
—Roxanne Chan, Albany, CA

TAKES: 30 min. • **MAKES:** 4 servings

- 4 cod fillets (6 oz. each)
- 1 Tbsp. cornstarch
- 1 cup canned coconut milk
- ½ cup orange juice
- 2 Tbsp. sweet chili sauce
- 1 tsp. minced fresh gingerroot
- 1 tsp. soy sauce
- 1 can (11 oz.) mandarin oranges, drained
- 1 green onion, chopped
- 2 Tbsp. sliced almonds
- 1 Tbsp. sesame oil
  Minced fresh cilantro

1. In a large saucepan, place a steamer basket over 1 in. water. Place cod in basket. Bring water to a boil. Reduce heat to maintain a low boil; steam, covered, until fish just begins to flake easily with a fork, 8-10 minutes.
2. Meanwhile, in a small saucepan, whisk cornstarch, coconut milk and orange juice until smooth. Add chili sauce, ginger and soy sauce. Cook and stir over medium heat until thickened, 1-2 minutes. Stir in oranges, green onion, almonds and sesame oil; heat through. Serve with cod; sprinkle with cilantro.
1 serving: 330 cal., 15g fat (10g sat. fat), 65mg chol., 316mg sod., 19g carb. (15g sugars, 1g fiber), 29g pro.

TEST KITCHEN TIP

Crystallized ginger is a good emergency stand-in when you don't have fresh ginger for your recipes. Just soak a few slices of ginger in hot water to soften it and remove excess sugar, then chop and use. Add about triple the amount of crystallized ginger in place of fresh.

CLASSIC CRAB BOIL

CLASSIC CRAB BOIL

Dig into Dungeness crab boiled in a special mix of flavorful spices.
—Matthew Hass, Ellison Bay, WI

PREP: 10 min. • **COOK:** 30 min.
MAKES: 2 servings

- 2 Tbsp. mustard seed
- 2 Tbsp. celery seed
- 1 Tbsp. dill seed
- 1 Tbsp. coriander seeds
- 1 Tbsp. whole allspice
- ½ tsp. whole cloves
- 4 bay leaves
- 8 qt. water
- ¼ cup salt
- ¼ cup lemon juice
- 1 tsp. cayenne pepper
- 2 whole live Dungeness crabs (2 lbs. each)
  Melted butter and lemon wedges

1. Place the first 7 ingredients on a double thickness of cheesecloth. Gather corners of cloth to enclose the seasonings; tie securely with string.
2. In a large stockpot, bring water, salt, lemon juice, cayenne and spice bag to a boil. Using tongs, add crab to stockpot; return to a boil. Reduce heat; simmer, covered, until shells turn bright red, about 15 minutes.
3. Using tongs, remove crab from pot. Run under cold water or plunge into ice water. Serve with melted butter and lemon wedges.
1 crab: 245 cal., 3g fat (0 sat. fat), 169mg chol., 956mg sod., 2g carb. (0 sugars, 0 fiber), 50g pro.

COCONUT CITRUS
SAUCED COD

SHRIMP FRIED RICE QUESADILLAS

Easy to make and always a treat, these fun quesadillas are bursting with flavor. The pepper jack cheese gives them a nice kick. To speed preparation even more, use leftover fried rice.
—Artland Campbell, Hyannis, MA

TAKES: 25 min. • **MAKES:** 2 servings

- ¼ lb. uncooked shrimp (41-50 per pound), peeled and deveined
- 2 Tbsp. chopped onion
- 2 Tbsp. chopped sweet red pepper
- 2 Tbsp. chopped green pepper
- 3 Tbsp. butter, divided
- 1 large egg, beaten
- ⅓ cup cooked long grain rice
- 1 Tbsp. reduced-sodium soy sauce
- 2 flour tortillas (8 in.)
- 2 slices pepper jack cheese (¾ oz. each)

1. In a small skillet, saute the shrimp, onion and peppers in 1 Tbsp. butter until shrimp turn pink; remove and keep warm.
2. In a small bowl, whisk the egg. In the same skillet, heat 1 Tbsp. butter until hot. Add egg; cook and stir over medium heat until egg is completely set. Stir in the rice, soy sauce and shrimp mixture.
3. Spread remaining butter over 1 side of each tortilla. Place tortillas butter side down, on a griddle. Place a slice of cheese on each tortilla. Sprinkle shrimp mixture over half of each tortilla. Fold over and cook over low heat until cheese is melted, 1-2 minutes on each side. Cut into wedges.
1 serving: 511 cal., 30g fat (16g sat. fat), 242mg chol., 903mg sod., 37g carb. (1g sugars, 1g fiber), 24g pro.

SHRIMP MOZAMBIQUE

SHRIMP MOZAMBIQUE

This recipe was passed down from my grandma and is one frequently made in our Portuguese culture. Variations include adding other seafood, such as clams, muscles or scallops. I've also made it with chicken since my kids will not eat seafood.
—Christina Souza, Brooksville, FL

PREP: 20 min. • **COOK:** 20 min.
MAKES: 6 servings

- 3 Tbsp. olive oil
- 1 medium onion, finely chopped
- 6 garlic cloves, minced
- 2 lbs. uncooked shell-on shrimp (16-20 per pound)
- 2 envelopes sazon with coriander and annatto
- 2 tsp. garlic salt
- 2 tsp. garlic powder
- 2 tsp. onion powder
- 1 tsp. paprika
- 1 bay leaf
- 1 bottle (12 oz.) beer or 1½ cups chicken broth
- 1 tsp. lemon juice
- ¼ cup ketchup
- 3 Tbsp. chopped fresh parsley
  Hot cooked rice

In a Dutch oven, heat oil over medium-high heat. Add onion; cook and stir until tender, 4-5 minutes. Add garlic and shrimp; cook 1 minute longer. Stir in seasonings. Add beer and lemon juice; bring to a boil. Reduce heat. Simmer, uncovered, until shrimp turn pink, 10-15 minutes. Stir in ketchup and parsley; discard bay leaf. Serve shrimp with rice.
1 serving: 223 cal., 9g fat (1g sat. fat), 184mg chol., 1190mg sod., 9g carb. (4g sugars, 1g fiber), 25g pro.

BLACKENED TILAPIA WITH ZUCCHINI NOODLES

I love quick and bright meals like this one-skillet wonder. Homemade pico de gallo is easy to make the night before.
—*Tammy Brownlow, Dallas, TX*

TAKES: 30 min. • **MAKES:** 4 servings

- 2 large zucchini (about 1½ lbs.)
- 1½ tsp. ground cumin
- ¾ tsp. salt, divided
- ½ tsp. smoked paprika
- ½ tsp. pepper
- ¼ tsp. garlic powder
- 4 tilapia fillets (6 oz. each)
- 2 tsp. olive oil
- 2 garlic cloves, minced
- 1 cup pico de gallo

1. Trim ends of zucchini. Using a spiralizer, cut zucchini into thin strands.
2. Mix cumin, ½ tsp. salt, smoked paprika, pepper and garlic powder; sprinkle generously onto both sides of tilapia. In a large nonstick skillet, heat oil over medium-high heat. In batches, cook tilapia until fish just begins to flake easily with a fork, 2-3 minutes per side. Remove from pan; keep warm.
3. In same pan, cook zucchini with garlic over medium-high heat until slightly softened, 1-2 minutes, tossing constantly with tongs (do not overcook). Sprinkle with remaining salt. Serve with tilapia and pico de gallo.
Note: If a spiralizer is not available, the zucchini may also be cut into ribbons using a vegetable peeler. Saute as directed, increasing time as necessary.
1 serving: 203 cal., 4g fat (1g sat. fat), 83mg chol., 522mg sod., 8g carb. (5g sugars, 2g fiber), 34g pro. **Diabetic exchanges:** 5 lean meat, 1 vegetable, ½ fat.

BLACKENED TILAPIA WITH ZUCCHINI NOODLES

WALNUT-CRUSTED FISH

A crispy, crunchy crust and moist, tender fish make this recipe a winner. The dipping sauce is salty-sweet and pairs beautifully with walnuts.
—*Taste of Home Test Kitchen*

TAKES: 25 min. • **MAKES:** 4 servings

- 4 tilapia or other mild fish fillets (5 oz. each)
- ½ tsp. salt
- ¼ tsp. pepper
- ¼ cup all-purpose flour
- 1 large egg, lightly beaten
- 1 cup finely chopped walnuts
- 3 Tbsp. seasoned bread crumbs
- 1 Tbsp. sesame seeds
- 1 Tbsp. dried parsley flakes
- 2 Tbsp. butter
- ¼ cup honey
- 1½ tsp. soy sauce

1. Sprinkle fillets with salt and pepper. Place flour and egg in separate shallow bowls. In another shallow bowl, combine the walnuts, bread crumbs, sesame seeds and parsley. Dip fish in flour, in egg, then in walnut mixture.
2. In a large skillet over medium heat, melt butter. Add fish; cook until fish just begins to flake easily with a fork, 2-3 minutes on each side. In a small bowl, whisk honey and soy sauce; serve with fish.
1 serving: 425 cal., 22g fat (5g sat. fat), 153mg chol., 633mg sod., 28g carb. (18g sugars, 2g fiber), 32g pro.

SOUTH SEAS
MANGO HALIBUT

SOUTH SEAS MANGO HALIBUT

Halibut marinated in aromatic spices, then stir-fried and combined with coconut milk and mango will transform a weeknight meal to a tropical delight!
—Taste of Home *Test Kitchen*

- -

PREP: 15 min. + marinating • **COOK:** 25 min.
MAKES: 6 servings

- 2 tsp. ground coriander
- 2 tsp. curry powder
- 1 tsp. chili powder
- ½ tsp. ground allspice
- ¼ tsp. salt
- ⅛ tsp. pepper
- 2 lbs. halibut fillets, cut into 1-in. pieces
- 2 large sweet red peppers, cut into 1-in. pieces
- 1 medium onion, cut into small wedges
- 5 Tbsp. canola oil, divided
- 1 can (13.66 oz.) light coconut milk
- 3 Tbsp. tomato paste
- 2 medium mangoes, peeled and chopped
- 1 pkg. (10 oz.) fresh spinach, torn

1. In a bowl or shallow dish, combine the first 6 ingredients. Add the halibut and turn to coat. Cover and refrigerate for 30 minutes. In a large skillet, stir-fry red peppers and onion in 1 Tbsp. oil until tender, 5 minutes. Remove from pan; set aside. Add 2 Tbsp. oil to pan; add halibut. Cook and stir until the fish just begins to flake easily with fork, 5-8 minutes. Stir in the milk, tomato paste, mangoes and reserved pepper mixture. Cook over medium heat for 5 minutes.
2. Meanwhile, in a Dutch oven, cook and stir spinach in remaining oil until wilted, 2 minutes. Serve fish over spinach.
1⅓ cups: 404 cal., 19g fat (5g sat. fat), 74mg chol., 285mg sod., 27g carb. (20g sugars, 5g fiber), 31g pro.

**LEMON & DILL
SHRIMP SANDWICHES**

LEMON & DILL
SHRIMP SANDWICHES

Our family took a once-in-a-lifetime trip to Norway, where we got to eat incredible shrimp sandwiches like these. The crustier the bread, the better.
—*Monica Kolva, Millville, NJ*

- -

TAKES: 20 min. • **MAKES:** 4 sandwiches

- 4 hoagie buns, split
- 1 Tbsp. butter
- 1 lb. uncooked shrimp (41-50 per lb.), peeled and deveined
- ½ cup mayonnaise
- 2 Tbsp. lemon juice
- 4 tsp. snipped fresh dill or 1¼ tsp. dill weed
- ½ tsp. salt
- ¼ tsp. pepper
   Optional: Lettuce leaves and sliced tomato

1. Hollow out bun bottoms, leaving a ½-in. shell (save removed bread for another use). In a large skillet, heat butter over medium heat. Add shrimp; cook and stir 3-4 minutes or until shrimp turn pink.
2. In a small bowl, mix mayonnaise, lemon juice, dill, salt and pepper until blended. Add shrimp; toss to coat. Spoon shrimp mixture into bun bottoms. If desired, top with lettuce and tomato. Replace bun tops.
1 sandwich: 534 cal., 31g fat (6g sat. fat), 156mg chol., 992mg sod., 36g carb. (5g sugars, 1g fiber), 27g pro.

JERK-SEASONED
MEAT LOAVES, PAGE 166

177

208

180

234

Oven Entrees

These are the kings of comfort food: hearty stews, potpies, pizzas, meat loaves and more fresh-baked creations. What's not to love about a meal that roasts hands-free? Turn the page to find 95 craveworthy baked dishes.

Beef & Ground Beef

JERK-SEASONED MEAT LOAVES

I wanted meat loaf but also something unique, so I decided to spice up my usual recipe by using Jamaican jerk seasoning. My family loved it! I completed the meal by serving it with string beans and yams.
—*Iris Cook, Batavia, IL*

PREP: 10 min. • **BAKE:** 40 min. + standing
MAKES: 2 loaves (6 servings each)

- 2 large eggs, lightly beaten
- 1 medium onion, finely chopped
- ½ cup dry bread crumbs
- 2 Tbsp. green pepper, finely chopped
- 1 Tbsp. Caribbean jerk seasoning
- 2 garlic cloves, minced
- 2 tsp. garlic powder
- 2 tsp. dried cilantro flakes
- 1 tsp. dried basil
- 3 lbs. ground beef

GLAZE
- ½ cup packed brown sugar
- 2 Tbsp. peach nectar or juice
- 2 Tbsp. ketchup
- 2 tsp. barbecue sauce
- Dash garlic powder
- Dash pepper

Preheat oven to 350°. In a large bowl, combine the first 9 ingredients. Add the beef; mix lightly but thoroughly. Transfer to 2 ungreased 9x5-in. loaf pans. Mix glaze ingredients; spread over tops. Bake until a thermometer reads 160°, 40-50 minutes. Let stand 10 minutes before slicing.

Freeze option: Securely wrap cooled meat loaf in foil, then freeze. To use, partially thaw in refrigerator overnight. Unwrap meat loaf; reheat on a greased 15x10x1-in. baking pan in a preheated 350° oven until heated through and a thermometer inserted in the center reads 165°.

1 slice: 283 cal., 14g fat (5g sat. fat), 101mg chol., 223mg sod., 15g carb. (11g sugars, 1g fiber), 22g pro.

JERK-SEASONED MEAT LOAVES

GARDEN-STUFFED ZUCCHINI BOATS

Not only are these boats a delightful way to get your veggies, they're basically a one-dish meal that covers all the bases—just grab your favorite garden goodies and add any spices or mix-ins you like.
—Janie Zirbser, Mullica Hill, NJ

PREP: 40 min. + cooling
BAKE: 25 min. • **MAKES:** 3 servings

- 3   medium zucchini
- ¾   lb. ground beef
- ¾   cup chopped onion
- ½   cup chopped green pepper
- 2   garlic cloves, minced
- 1½ cups water, divided
- ¾   cup canned fire-roasted diced tomatoes or chopped fresh tomatoes (with seeds and juices)
- ½   cup chopped roasted sweet red peppers
- ⅓   cup chopped fresh mushrooms
- ¼   cup uncooked ditalini or other small pasta
- 2   tsp. minced fresh thyme or 1 tsp. dried thyme
- ½   tsp. minced fresh oregano or ¼ tsp. dried oregano
- ¼   tsp. salt
- ¼   tsp. pepper
- ¼   cup grated Parmesan cheese
- 1   cup shredded Italian cheese blend, divided
      Pasta sauce, optional

1. Preheat oven to 350°. Halve zucchini lengthwise; place cut sides down in an ungreased 13x9-in. baking dish. Bake 10 minutes. When cool enough to handle, scoop out seeds, leaving a ¼-in. shell.
2. Meanwhile, in a large skillet, cook the beef, onion, green pepper and garlic over medium heat 8-10 minutes or until beef is no longer pink, breaking beef into crumbles; drain. Stir in 1 cup water, tomatoes, red peppers, mushrooms, pasta, thyme, oregano, salt and pepper. Cook until the mixture is thickened and pasta is al dente, 12-15 minutes. Stir in Parmesan cheese.
3. Spoon mixture into zucchini shells. Place in an ungreased 13x9-in. baking dish; sprinkle with ¾ cup Italian cheese blend. Pour the remaining water into bottom of dish. Bake, covered, 20 minutes.

GARDEN-STUFFED ZUCCHINI BOATS

Sprinkle with remaining cheese. Bake, uncovered, until zucchini is tender and cheese is melted, about 5 minutes longer. Serve with pasta sauce if desired.
2 stuffed zucchini halves: 489 cal., 24g fat (12g sat. fat), 103mg chol., 992mg sod., 28g carb. (10g sugars, 4g fiber), 36g pro.

TEST KITCHEN TIP
Fire-roasted tomatoes pack a rich, roasted flavor. You can freeze the remaining tomatoes for the next time you make this recipe.

SLOPPY JOE
PASTA

SLOPPY JOE PASTA

Since I found this quick-to-fix recipe a
few years ago, it's become a regular part
of my menu plans. Everyone loves the
combination of sloppy joe ingredients,
shell pasta and cheddar cheese.
—*Lynne Leih, Idyllwild, CA*

- -

PREP: 20 min. • **BAKE:** 30 min.
MAKES: 6 servings

- 1 lb. ground beef
- 1 envelope sloppy joe mix
- 1 cup water
- 1 can (8 oz.) tomato sauce
- 1 can (6 oz.) tomato paste
- 1 pkg. (7 oz.) small shell pasta,
  cooked and drained
- 1 cup 4% cottage cheese
- ½ cup shredded cheddar cheese

1. In a Dutch oven, cook beef over medium
heat until no longer pink, breaking it into
crumbles; drain. Stir in sloppy joe mix,
water, sauce and paste; heat through.
Remove from the heat; stir in pasta.
2. Spoon half the mixture into a greased
2½-qt. baking dish. Top with the cottage
cheese and remaining pasta mixture.
Sprinkle with cheddar cheese.
3. Bake, uncovered, at 350° until bubbly
and cheese is melted, 30-35 minutes.
1¼ cups: 291 cal., 11g fat (6g sat. fat),
55mg chol., 904mg sod., 24g carb. (7g
sugars, 2g fiber), 23g pro.

MIDWESTERN
MEAT PIES

MIDWESTERN MEAT PIES

When I moved to the Midwest in 1966, I
discovered many ethnic foods that I had
never heard of before. One of my friends
introduced me to meat pies, and they
quickly became a popular dish with
my family.
—*Dolly Croghan, Mead, NE*

- -

PREP: 35 min. + rising • **BAKE:** 20 min.
MAKES: 12 servings

- 4½ cups all-purpose flour, divided
- ½ cup sugar
- 2 pkg. (¼ oz. each) active dry yeast
- 1 tsp. salt
- ¾ cup 2% milk
- ½ cup water
- ½ cup shortening
- 2 large eggs

FILLING

- 1 lb. lean ground beef (90% lean)
- 2 small onions, chopped
- 4 cups chopped cabbage
- 1 tsp. salt
- ½ tsp. pepper

1. Place 1¾ cups flour and the sugar,
yeast and salt in a large bowl. Heat the
milk, water and shortening to 120°-130°.
Pour over flour mixture; add the eggs.
Beat with an electric mixer on low until
blended. Beat an additional 3 minutes
on high. Stir in remaining flour; knead
until smooth and elastic, 6-8 minutes.
2. Place dough in a greased bowl, turning
once to grease top. Cover and let rise in
a warm place until doubled, about 1 hour.
3. Meanwhile, in a large skillet, cook beef
and onion over medium heat until meat is
no longer pink, breaking it into crumbles;
drain. Add the cabbage, salt and pepper;
cook until cabbage is wilted.
4. Punch dough down; roll into twelve
6-in. squares. Top each square with
⅓ cup meat mixture. Fold into triangles.
Pinch edges tightly to seal, and place
on greased baking sheets. Bake at 350°
until golden brown, about 20 minutes.
Serve hot.
1 meat pie: 368 cal., 13g fat (4g sat. fat),
56mg chol., 443mg sod., 48g carb. (11g
sugars, 2g fiber), 14g pro.

BLUE CHEESE-TOPPED STEAKS

These juicy tenderloin steaks, lightly crusted with blue cheese and bread crumbs, are special enough for holiday dining. When drizzled with wine sauce, the beef melts in your mouth.
—*Tiffany Vancil, San Diego, CA*

TAKES: 30 min. • **MAKES:** 4 servings

- 2 Tbsp. crumbled blue cheese
- 4½ tsp. dry bread crumbs
- 4½ tsp. minced fresh parsley
- 4½ tsp. minced chives
  Dash pepper
- 4 beef tenderloin steaks (4 oz. each)
- 1½ tsp. butter
- 1 Tbsp. all-purpose flour
- ½ cup reduced-sodium beef broth
- 1 Tbsp. Madeira wine
- ⅛ tsp. browning sauce, optional

1. Preheat oven to 350°. In a small bowl, combine the blue cheese, bread crumbs, parsley, chives and pepper. Press onto 1 side of each steak.

2. In a large nonstick skillet, cook steaks over medium-high heat for 2 minutes on each side. Transfer to a 15x10x1-in. baking pan coated with cooking spray.

3. Bake 6-8 minutes or until the meat reaches desired doneness (for medium-rare, a thermometer should read 135°; medium, 140°; medium-well, 145°).

4. Meanwhile, in a small saucepan, melt the butter. Whisk in flour until smooth. Gradually whisk in broth and wine. Bring to a boil; cook and stir until thickened, 2 minutes. If desired, stir in browning sauce. Serve with steaks.

1 serving: 228 cal., 11g fat (5g sat. fat), 78mg chol., 197mg sod., 4g carb. (1g sugars, 0 fiber), 26g pro. **Diabetic exchanges:** 3 lean meat, ½ fat.

"I made this for my husband's birthday dinner, and it was perfect—delicious, tender, terrific combination of flavors. I did not have any wine, so I used a good-quality dark balsamic vinegar. The gravy was amazing."
—GEORGIAJAMMY, TASTEOFHOME.COM

TACOS DELUXE

TACOS DELUXE

I first tried this recipe in my junior high school home economics class more than 20 years ago. As an adult, I wrote home for the recipe and have enjoyed it ever since!
—*Katie Dreibelbis, Santa Clara, CA*

PREP: 25 min. • **BAKE:** 10 min.
MAKES: 8 servings

- 1 lb. ground beef
- 2 Tbsp. chopped onion
- 1 can (15 oz.) tomato sauce
- 1 tsp. white vinegar
- 1 tsp. Worcestershire sauce
- 2 to 3 drops hot pepper sauce
- 1 tsp. sugar
- 1 tsp. chili powder
- ½ tsp. garlic salt
- ¼ tsp. celery salt
- ¼ tsp. onion salt
- ⅛ tsp. ground allspice
- ⅛ tsp. ground cinnamon
  Dash pepper
- ½ cup shredded cheddar cheese
- 8 taco shells
  Shredded lettuce
  Chopped tomatoes

SWEET-AND-SOUR DRESSING
- 1 cup Miracle Whip
- ⅓ cup sugar
- 2 Tbsp. white vinegar
- ¼ tsp. salt
- ½ tsp. hot pepper sauce

1. In a large skillet, cook beef and onion over medium heat until the meat is no longer pink, breaking it into crumbles; drain. Add the next 12 ingredients to the meat mixture. Simmer, uncovered, for 10-15 minutes or until liquid is almost completely reduced, stirring occasionally. Cool slightly; stir in cheese.

2. Place taco shells open end up in a baking pan; place a scoop of meat mixture into each shell. Bake at 400° for 10-15 minutes until meat is hot and cheese is melted.

3. Sprinkle lettuce and tomatoes over the tacos. In a small bowl, combine dressing ingredients; drizzle over tacos.

1 taco: 312 cal., 19g fat (6g sat. fat), 44mg chol., 874mg sod., 21g carb. (12g sugars, 1g fiber), 13g pro.

EASY TEXAS BBQ BRISKET

My mom tried my brisket and said it was even better than the version we used to have back in Texas. What a compliment! Jazz up your sandwiches and tacos with the leftovers.
—Audra Rorick, Lyons, KS

PREP: 15 min. + chilling
BAKE: 4 hours + standing
MAKES: 10 servings

- 2 Tbsp. packed brown sugar
- 1 Tbsp. salt
- 1 Tbsp. onion powder
- 1 Tbsp. garlic powder
- 1 Tbsp. ground mustard
- 1 Tbsp. smoked paprika
- 1 Tbsp. pepper
- 2 fresh beef briskets (3½ lbs. each)
- 1 bottle (10 oz.) Heinz 57 steak sauce
- ½ cup liquid smoke
- ¼ cup Worcestershire sauce

1. In a small bowl, combine the first 7 ingredients. With a fork or sharp knife, prick holes in briskets. Rub the meat with the seasoning mixture. Cover and refrigerate overnight.
2. Preheat oven to 325°. Place briskets, fat sides up, in a roasting pan. In a small bowl, combine steak sauce, liquid smoke and Worcestershire sauce; pour over meat.
3. Cover tightly with foil; bake 4-5 hours or until tender. Let stand in juices for 15 minutes. To serve, thinly slice across the grain. Skim fat from pan juices; spoon over meat.

6 oz. cooked beef with about 2 Tbsp. juices: 456 cal., 14g fat (5g sat. fat), 135mg chol., 1283mg sod., 13g carb. (11g sugars, 1g fiber), 66g pro.

BAKED CHEESY MOSTACCIOLI

My friends and family often request this favorite. Because the sauce works well with several Italian meals, I make a large batch to use for weekday dinners or last-minute company.
—Dayna Brohm, Gold Canyon, AZ

PREP: 35 min. • **BAKE:** 25 min.
MAKES: 6 servings

- 3 cups uncooked mostaccioli
- 1 lb. ground beef
- ½ lb. bulk Italian sausage
- 1 small onion, chopped
- ½ cup chopped green pepper
- ½ cup chopped sweet red pepper
- ½ cup chopped fresh mushrooms
- 1 garlic clove, minced
- 1 can (15 oz.) crushed tomatoes
- 2 cans (8 oz. each) tomato sauce
- 1 Tbsp. Italian seasoning
- ½ tsp. sugar
- 2 cups shredded cheddar cheese, divided

1. Preheat oven to 350°. Cook mostaccioli according to the package directions for al dente; drain.
2. Meanwhile, in a 6-qt. stockpot, cook the beef, sausage, onion, peppers, mushrooms and garlic over medium-high heat until meat is no longer pink and vegetables are tender, 6-8 minutes, breaking meat into crumbles; drain.
3. Stir in the tomatoes, tomato sauce, Italian seasoning and sugar. Bring to a boil. Reduce heat; simmer, uncovered, 8-10 minutes to allow flavors to blend.
4. Stir in 1½ cups cheese and mostaccioli. Transfer to a greased 13x9-in. baking dish. Bake, covered, 20 minutes. Sprinkle with remaining cheese. Bake, uncovered, 5-10 minutes longer or until the cheese is melted.

1½ cups: 589 cal., 31g fat (13g sat. fat), 104mg chol., 1000mg sod., 45g carb. (8g sugars, 5g fiber), 35g pro.

EASY TEXAS BBQ BRISKET

CRESCENT BEEF CASSEROLE

This flavorful meal-in-one dish is all you need to serve a satisfying and quick weeknight dinner. It's on the table in just 30 minutes.
—Taste of Home *Test Kitchen*

TAKES: 30 min. • **MAKES:** 6 servings

- 1 lb. lean ground beef (90% lean)
- 2 tsp. olive oil
- 1 cup diced zucchini
- ¼ cup chopped onion
- ¼ cup chopped green pepper
- 1 cup tomato puree
- 1 tsp. dried oregano
- ¼ tsp. salt
- ⅛ tsp. pepper
- 1½ cups mashed potatoes
- 1 cup (4 oz.) crumbled feta cheese
- 1 tube (8 oz.) refrigerated crescent rolls
- 1 large egg, beaten, optional

1. Preheat the oven to 375°. In a large skillet, cook beef over medium heat until no longer pink, breaking it into crumbles; drain and set aside. In the same skillet, heat oil over medium-high heat. Add zucchini, onion and green pepper; cook and stir until crisp-tender, 4-5 minutes. Stir in beef, tomato puree, oregano, salt and pepper; heat through.

2. Spread mashed potatoes in an 11x7-in. baking dish coated with cooking spray. Top with beef mixture and sprinkle with feta cheese.

3. Unroll crescent dough. Separate into 4 rectangles; arrange 3 rectangles over the casserole. If desired, brush with the egg wash. Bake until the top is browned, 12-15 minutes. Roll the remaining dough into 2 crescent rolls; bake for another use.

1 serving: 443 cal., 22g fat (7g sat. fat), 67mg chol., 981mg sod., 31g carb. (6g sugars, 3g fiber), 26g pro.

SPINACH & FETA FLANK STEAK — caption on photo

SPINACH & FETA FLANK STEAK

While this dish may look difficult, it's actually very easy to prepare. The fancy spirals of flavor are perfect for holiday meals but are also easy enough for weeknight dinners.
—Josh Carter, Birmingham, AL

PREP: 15 min. • **BAKE:** 40 min.
MAKES: 6 servings

- 1 beef flank steak (1½ to 2 lbs.)
- 1 pkg. (10 oz.) frozen chopped spinach, thawed and squeezed dry
- 1 pkg. (4 oz.) crumbled feta cheese
- ⅓ cup minced fresh parsley
- 3 Tbsp. snipped fresh dill
- 3 Tbsp. chopped green onions
- 1 tsp. salt
- ½ tsp. pepper
- 1 Tbsp. olive oil

1. Cut steak horizontally from a long side to within ½ in. of opposite side. Open steak so it lies flat; flatten to ¼-in. thickness.

2. Combine the spinach, cheese, parsley, dill and onions. Spread over the steak to within 1 in. of edges. Roll up jelly-roll style, starting with a short side; tie with kitchen string. Sprinkle with salt and pepper.

3. In a large skillet, brown meat in oil on all sides; transfer to the greased rack of a shallow roasting pan. Bake at 400° until the meat reaches desired doneness (for medium-rare, a thermometer should read 135°; medium, 140°; medium-well, 145°), 40-45 minutes. Remove from oven and let stand 15 minutes. To serve, remove string; slice into 1-in.-thick slices.

2 slices: 242 cal., 14g fat (6g sat. fat), 58mg chol., 662mg sod., 3g carb. (0 sugars, 2g fiber), 24g pro. **Diabetic exchanges:** 3 lean meat, 2 fat.

CRESCENT BEEF
CASSEROLE

HERBED BEEF VEGETABLE CASSEROLE

If your family is resistant to eating vegetables, offer them this dish! Eggplant, zucchini, onion and yellow pepper are disguised in a beefy tomato sauce.
—*Betty Blandford, Johns Island, SC*

PREP: 20 min. • **BAKE:** 30 min.
MAKES: 10 servings

- 2 lbs. ground beef
- 1 medium eggplant, cubed
- 2 medium zucchini, cubed
- 1 medium onion, chopped
- 1 medium sweet yellow pepper
- 3 garlic cloves, minced
- 1 can (28 oz.) stewed tomatoes
- 1 cup cooked rice
- 1 cup shredded cheddar cheese, divided
- ½ cup beef broth
- ½ tsp. each oregano, savory and thyme
- ½ tsp. salt
- ¼ tsp. pepper

1. In a Dutch oven, cook beef over medium heat until no longer pink, breaking it into crumbles; drain. Add eggplant, zucchini, onion, yellow pepper and garlic; cook until tender. Add tomatoes, rice, ½ cup cheese, broth and seasonings; mix well.

2. Transfer to a greased 13x9-in. baking dish. Sprinkle with the remaining cheese. Bake, uncovered, at 350° for 30 minutes or until heated through.

1 serving: 257 cal., 12g fat (6g sat. fat), 56mg chol., 434mg sod., 18g carb. (8g sugars, 3g fiber), 21g pro.

"Labor intensive, but the results are good. I salted my eggplant and put it in a strainer for 45 minutes to draw out some of the bitterness; then I rinsed it well and let it drain. I cooked the ground beef with the onion and garlic. I also used 2 cups of cooked rice and no beef broth; I thought it was soupy enough from the veggies. In addition, I doubled the cheese. This is a good way to introduce vegetables to your family, which is why I made it."
—CHRISDD, TASTEOFHOME.COM

SLOW-SIMMERED BURGUNDY BEEF STEW

My mother-in-law shared this recipe with me about 25 years ago. Ever since then, it's been a go-to whenever I need a lot of food without a lot of fussing.
—*Mary Lou Timpson, Colorado City, AZ*

PREP: 30 min. • **BAKE:** 1¾ hours
MAKES: 4 servings

- 1½ lbs. beef stew meat (1¼-in. pieces)
- 3 Tbsp. all-purpose flour
- ¾ tsp. salt
- 2 to 4 tsp. canola oil, divided
- 2 tsp. beef bouillon granules
- 2 tsp. dried parsley flakes
- 1½ tsp. Italian seasoning
- 2 cups water
- 1 cup Burgundy wine or beef stock
- 3 medium potatoes (about 1⅓ lbs.), peeled and quartered
- 1 cup fresh mushrooms, halved
- 1 medium onion, cut into 8 wedges
- 2 medium carrots, cut into 1-in. pieces
- 2 celery ribs, cut into ½-in. pieces
  Additional water, optional

1. Preheat oven to 350°. Toss beef with flour and salt to coat lightly; shake off excess. In an ovenproof Dutch oven, heat 2 tsp. oil over medium heat. Brown the beef in batches, adding additional oil as needed. Remove from pan.

2. Add bouillon, parsley, seasoning, 2 cups water and wine to same pan; bring to a boil, stirring to loosen browned bits from pan. Add beef; return to a boil. Transfer to oven; bake, covered, 1 hour.

3. Stir in vegetables and, if desired, thin with additional water. Bake, covered, until beef and vegetables are tender, 45-60 minutes.

1½ cups: 419 cal., 15g fat (5g sat. fat), 106mg chol., 949mg sod., 33g carb. (5g sugars, 4g fiber), 37g pro.

SLOW-SIMMERED BURGUNDY BEEF STEW

ENCHILADA
CASSEROLE

LAYERED REUBEN CASSEROLE

This easy dish packs traditional Reuben taste, without all the bread. Sauerkraut fans will love this hearty layered casserole. Round out the meal for two with dinner rolls and a light fruit dessert.
—*Agnes Golian, Garfield Heights, OH*

PREP: 15 min. • **BAKE:** 25 min.
MAKES: 2 servings

- 1 can (8 oz.) sauerkraut, rinsed and well drained
- ⅛ tsp. caraway seeds
- 1 small tomato, cut into thin wedges
- 2 Tbsp. Thousand Island salad dressing
- 1 pkg. (2 oz.) thinly sliced deli corned beef
- ¼ cup shredded Swiss cheese
- ¼ cup cubed rye bread
- 2 tsp. butter, melted

1. Place the sauerkraut in an ungreased 3-cup baking dish; sprinkle with caraway seeds. Layer with the tomato wedges, salad dressing, corned beef and Swiss cheese. Toss bread cubes and butter; sprinkle over the top.
2. Bake, uncovered, at 375° until heated through, 25-30 minutes.
1 serving: 166 cal., 8g fat (3g sat. fat), 36mg chol., 1403mg sod., 14g carb. (6g sugars, 4g fiber), 12g pro.

ENCHILADA CASSEROLE

Every time I serve this dish, I get satisfied reviews—even from my father, who usually doesn't like Mexican food. Plus, it smells delicious while baking.
—*Nancy VanderVeer, Knoxville, IA*

PREP: 20 min. • **BAKE:** 30 min.
MAKES: 8 servings

- 1 lb. ground beef (90% lean)
- 1 can (10 oz.) enchilada sauce
- 1 cup salsa
- 6 flour tortillas (10 in.)
- 2 cups fresh or frozen corn
- 4 cups shredded cheddar cheese

1. Preheat oven to 350°. In a large skillet, cook beef over medium heat until no longer pink, breaking it into crumbles; drain. Stir in sauce and salsa; set aside.
2. Place 2 tortillas, overlapping as necessary, in the bottom of a greased 13x9-in. baking dish. Cover with a third of the meat mixture. Top with 1 cup corn; sprinkle with 1⅓ cups cheese. Repeat layers once, then top with the remaining tortillas, meat and cheese.
3. Bake casserole, uncovered, 30 minutes or until bubbly.
Freeze option: Cover and freeze unbaked casserole. To use, partially thaw in the refrigerator overnight. Remove from refrigerator 30 minutes before baking. Preheat oven to 350°. Bake casserole as directed, increasing time as necessary to heat through and for a thermometer inserted in center to read 165°.
1 cup: 418 cal., 17g fat (9g sat. fat), 65mg chol., 918mg sod., 36g carb. (4g sugars, 6g fiber), 28g pro.

TEST KITCHEN TIPS

- If you like authentic Mexican flavor, corn tortillas will sub in seamlessly.
- This recipe was made for mix-ins. We especially love to layer in black beans and corn for a nutritious boost.

SPECIAL OCCASION
BEEF BOURGUIGNON

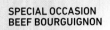

SPECIAL OCCASION BEEF BOURGUIGNON

I've found many rich and satisfying variations for beef bourguignon, including an intriguing peasant version that used beef cheeks for the meat and a rustic table wine. To make this stew gluten-free, use white rice flour instead of all-purpose.

—Leo Cotnoir, Johnson City, NY

PREP: 50 min. • BAKE: 2 hours
MAKES: 8 servings

- 4 bacon strips, chopped
- 1 beef sirloin tip roast (2 lbs.), cut into 1½-in. cubes and patted dry
- ¼ cup all-purpose flour
- ½ tsp. salt
- ½ tsp. pepper
- 1 Tbsp. canola oil
- 2 medium onions, chopped
- 2 medium carrots, coarsely chopped
- ½ lb. medium fresh mushrooms, quartered
- 4 garlic cloves, minced
- 1 Tbsp. tomato paste
- 2 cups dry red wine
- 1 cup beef stock
- 2 bay leaves
- ½ tsp. dried thyme
- 8 oz. uncooked egg noodles
  Minced fresh parsley

1. Preheat oven to 325°. In a Dutch oven, cook bacon over medium-low heat until crisp, stirring occasionally. Remove with a slotted spoon, reserving the drippings; drain on paper towels.
2. In batches, brown beef in drippings over medium-high heat; remove from pan. Toss with flour, salt and pepper.
3. In the same pan, heat 1 Tbsp. oil over medium heat; saute the onions, carrots and mushrooms until onions are tender, 4-5 minutes. Add the garlic and tomato paste; cook and stir 1 minute. Add wine and stock, stirring to loosen browned bits from pan. Add herbs, bacon and beef; bring to a boil.
4. Transfer to oven; bake, covered, until meat is tender, 2-2¼ hours.
5. Remove bay leaves. To serve, cook noodles according to package directions; drain. Serve stew with noodles; sprinkle with parsley.

Freeze option: Freeze cooled stew in freezer containers. To use, partially thaw in refrigerator overnight. Heat through in a saucepan, stirring occasionally; add a little stock or broth if necessary.

⅔ cup stew with ⅔ cup noodles: 422 cal., 14g fat (4g sat. fat), 105mg chol., 357mg sod., 31g carb. (4g sugars, 2g fiber), 31g pro. **Diabetic exchanges:** 4 lean meat, 2 fat, 1½ starch, 1 vegetable.

SLOPPY JOE CALZONES

It's a kid-friendly Friday night with these simple calzones. Chop the onion and pepper superfine for your really picky eaters.

—Taste of Home Test Kitchen

PREP: 20 min. • BAKE: 15 min.
MAKES: 4 servings

- 1 lb. ground beef
- 1 cup chopped onion
- 1 cup chopped green pepper
- 1 can (15 oz.) black beans, rinsed and drained
- 1 can (6 oz.) tomato paste
- ½ cup water
- ½ cup ketchup
- 1 tsp. dried oregano
- ¼ tsp. salt
- 2 tubes (8 oz. each) refrigerated crescent rolls
- 1 cup shredded cheddar cheese

1. Preheat oven to 375°. In a large skillet, cook beef, onion and pepper over medium heat until meat is no longer pink and onion is tender, 5-7 minutes, breaking meat into crumbles. Drain. Stir in the beans, tomato paste, water, ketchup, oregano and salt.
2. Separate the crescent roll dough into 4 rectangles; seal perforations. Spoon a fourth of the meat mixture onto half of each rectangle; sprinkle with cheese. Fold dough over filling; pinch edges to seal. Cut slits in tops.
3. Place on an ungreased baking sheet. Bake until golden brown, 13-15 minutes.

1 calzone: 961 cal., 47g fat (18g sat. fat), 116mg chol., 1900mg sod., 83g carb. (26g sugars, 8g fiber), 45g pro.

TEST KITCHEN TIP

Reach for no-salt-added black beans and eliminate the ¼ tsp. salt to slash this recipe's sodium content by nearly half.

SLOPPY JOE CALZONES

❄ ROAST BEEF POTPIE

Everyone in the family will want a piece
of this pie, and every home cook will
appreciate a helping hand from packaged
beef roast and refrigerated pie pastry.
—*Patricia Myers, Maryville, TN*

- -

PREP: 30 min. • **BAKE:** 30 min.
MAKES: 6 servings

- 10 fresh baby carrots, chopped
- 6 small red potatoes, cubed
- 1 medium onion, chopped
- 2 Tbsp. olive oil
- 1 pkg. (17 oz.) refrigerated beef roast
  au jus, coarsely chopped
- 2 Tbsp. minced fresh cilantro
- ¼ tsp. salt
- ¼ tsp. pepper
- ⅓ cup all-purpose flour
- 2¼ cups reduced-sodium beef broth
- 1 sheet refrigerated pie crust
- 1 large egg, beaten

1. Preheat oven to 375°. In a large skillet,
saute carrots, potatoes and onion in oil
until crisp-tender. Add the beef roast,
cilantro, salt and pepper. Combine flour
and broth until smooth; gradually stir
into the pan. Bring to a boil; cook and
stir until thickened, 2 minutes.
2. Transfer to a 9-in. deep-dish pie plate.
Place pie crust over the filling. Trim, seal
and flute edges. Cut slits in crust; brush
with egg. Bake pie until golden brown,
30-35 minutes.
Freeze option: Cover and freeze the
unbaked pie. To use, remove from freezer
30 minutes before baking (do not thaw).
Preheat the oven to 375°; bake until a
thermometer inserted in center reads
165° and the crust is golden brown,
70-80 minutes.
1 piece: 402 cal., 20g fat (7g sat. fat),
66mg chol., 700mg sod., 35g carb.
(6g sugars, 2g fiber), 20g pro.

BEEF STEW
WITH PASTA

BEEF STEW WITH PASTA

I have happy memories
of my mother's tomato-y
beef stew, so I combined
her recipe with a bunch of
fall veggies I needed to use.
The result was a fun, fill-you-up dinner.
—*Kristen Heigl, Staten Island, NY*

- -

PREP: 25 min. • **COOK:** 2¼ hours
MAKES: 12 servings (5 qt.)

- 3 Tbsp. olive oil, divided
- 2 lbs. beef stew meat
- 4 medium carrots, cut into 1-in. pieces
- 1 large onion, chopped
- 4 garlic cloves, minced
- 1 can (14½ oz.) diced tomatoes,
  drained
- 1 can (12 oz.) tomato paste
- ¾ tsp. salt
- ½ tsp. pepper
- 2 cartons (32 oz. each) chicken broth
- 2 Tbsp. minced fresh parsley, optional
- 2 lbs. potatoes (about 4 medium),
  peeled and cubed
- 1 can (15 oz.) cannellini beans,
  rinsed and drained
- ¼ cup grated Parmesan cheese
- 1½ cups uncooked ditalini or
  other small pasta
- 2 cups chopped fresh spinach

1. In a 7-qt. Dutch oven, heat 1 Tbsp. oil
over medium-high heat; brown half the
beef. Remove from pan. Repeat with the
additional oil and remaining beef.
2. In same pan, saute carrots and onion
in remaining oil until the onion is tender,
2-3 minutes. Add garlic; cook 1 minute
longer. Stir in the tomatoes, tomato paste,
salt, pepper, broth, beef and, if desired,
parsley; bring to a boil. Reduce heat;
simmer, covered, 1½ hours.
3. Stir in the potatoes, beans and cheese;
bring to a boil. Stir in pasta. Reduce heat;
simmer, uncovered, until the beef and
vegetables are tender, 15-20 minutes,
stirring occasionally. Stir in spinach
until wilted.
1⅔ cups: 342 cal., 10g fat (3g sat. fat),
52mg chol., 999mg sod., 40g carb.
(7g sugars, 5g fiber), 23g pro.

❄ ARGENTINE LASAGNA

My family is from Argentina, which has a strong Italian heritage and large cattle ranches. This all-in-one lasagna is packed with meat, cheese and veggies.
—*Sylvia Maenenr, Omaha, NE*

- -

PREP: 30 min.
BAKE: 55 min. + standing
MAKES: 12 servings

- 1 lb. ground beef
- 1 large sweet onion, chopped
- ½ lb. sliced fresh mushrooms
- 1 garlic clove, minced
- 1 can (15 oz.) tomato sauce
- 1 can (6 oz.) tomato paste
- ¼ tsp. pepper
- 4 cups shredded part-skim mozzarella cheese, divided
- 1 jar (15 oz.) Alfredo sauce
- 1 carton (15 oz.) ricotta cheese
- 2½ cups frozen peas, thawed
- 1 pkg. (10 oz.) frozen chopped spinach, thawed and squeezed dry
- 1 pkg. (9 oz.) no-cook lasagna noodles
  Fresh basil leaves and grated Parmesan cheese, optional

1. In a Dutch oven, cook the beef, onion, mushrooms and garlic over medium heat until meat is no longer pink, breaking it into crumbles; drain. Stir in the tomato sauce, tomato paste, pepper and 2 cups mozzarella cheese; set aside.
2. In a large bowl, combine the Alfredo sauce, ricotta cheese, peas and spinach.
3. Spread 1 cup meat sauce into a greased 13x9-in. baking dish. Layer with 4 noodles, 1¼ cups meat sauce and 1¼ cups spinach mixture. Repeat layers 3 times. Sprinkle with remaining mozzarella cheese.
4. Cover and bake at 350° for 45 minutes. Uncover; bake 10 minutes longer or until cheese is melted. Let stand for 10 minutes before cutting. Garnish with basil and, if desired, serve with Parmesan cheese.

Freeze option: Cover and freeze unbaked lasagna. To use, partially thaw in the refrigerator overnight. Remove from refrigerator 30 minutes before baking. Bake lasagna as directed, increasing time as necessary to heat through and for a thermometer to read 165°.
1 piece: 406 cal., 18g fat (10g sat. fat), 69mg chol., 598mg sod., 33g carb. (8g sugars, 4g fiber), 28g pro.

HOLLYWOOD PIZZA

My father and I used to order a pizza like this from a pizza place in Tinseltown. Here's my homemade version of that delicious pie.
—*Michael Williams, Moreno Valley, CA*

- -

PREP: 20 min. • **BAKE:** 20 min.
MAKES: 12 servings

- 1 loaf (1 lb.) frozen bread dough, thawed
- 2 Tbsp. olive oil
- ½ lb. lean ground beef (90% lean)
- 1 can (7 oz.) pizza sauce
- ½ cup sliced fresh mushrooms
- ½ cup chopped green pepper
- ¼ cup sliced seeded jalapeno peppers, optional
- 1 can (2¼ oz.) sliced ripe olives, drained
- 1 can (14½ oz.) stewed tomatoes, drained
- 2 cups shredded part-skim mozzarella cheese

1. Preheat oven to 400°. On a greased baking sheet, roll the bread dough into a 14x10-in. rectangle, building edges up slightly. Prick thoroughly with a fork. Brush crust with olive oil. Bake 10-12 minutes or until lightly browned.
2. Meanwhile, in a large skillet, cook beef over medium heat until no longer pink, breaking it into crumbles; drain. Spread pizza sauce over crust. Top with beef, mushrooms, green pepper, jalapeno peppers if desired, olives and tomatoes; sprinkle with cheese. Bake 20-25 minutes or until cheese is melted.
1 piece: 227 cal., 9g fat (3g sat. fat), 23mg chol., 464mg sod., 23g carb. (5g sugars, 2g fiber), 13g pro.

ARGENTINE LASAGNA

Poultry

BAKED CHICKEN CHIMICHANGAS

BAKED CHICKEN CHIMICHANGAS

I developed this quick and easy recipe through trial and error. My friends all love it when I cook these chimichangas, and they're much healthier than deep-fried.
—*Rickey Madden, Clinton, SC*

- -

PREP: 20 min. • **BAKE:** 20 min.
MAKES: 6 servings

1½ cups cubed cooked chicken breast
1½ cups picante sauce, divided
½ cup shredded reduced-fat cheddar cheese
⅔ cup chopped green onions, divided
1 tsp. ground cumin
1 tsp. dried oregano
6 flour tortillas (8 in.), warmed
1 Tbsp. butter, melted
Sour cream, optional

1. Preheat oven to 375°. In a small bowl, combine chicken, ¾ cup picante sauce, cheese, ¼ cup onions, cumin and oregano. Spoon ½ cup mixture down the center of each tortilla. Fold sides and ends over filling and roll up. Place seam side down in a 15x10x1-in. baking pan coated with cooking spray. Brush with butter.
2. Bake, uncovered, until heated through, 20-25 minutes. If desired, broil until browned, 1 minute. Top with remaining picante sauce and onions. If desired, serve with sour cream.

Freeze option: Cool baked chimichangas; wrap and freeze for up to 3 months. Place chimichangas on a baking sheet coated with cooking spray. Preheat oven to 400°. Bake until heated through, 10-15 minutes.

1 chimichanga: 269 cal., 8g fat (3g sat. fat), 39mg chol., 613mg sod., 31g carb. (3g sugars, 1g fiber), 17g pro. **Diabetic exchanges:** 2 lean meat, 1½ starch, 1 vegetable, ½ fat.

CASSOULET FOR TODAY

French cassoulet is traditionally cooked for hours. This version of the rustic dish offers the same homey taste in less time. It's easy on the wallet, too.
—*Virginia Anthony, Jacksonville, FL*

PREP: 45 min. • **BAKE:** 50 min.
MAKES: 6 servings

- 6 boneless skinless chicken thighs (about 1½ lbs.)
- ¼ tsp. salt
- ¼ tsp. coarsely ground pepper
- 3 tsp. olive oil, divided
- 1 large onion, chopped
- 1 garlic clove, minced
- ½ cup white wine or chicken broth
- 1 can (14½ oz.) diced tomatoes, drained
- 1 bay leaf
- 1 tsp. minced fresh rosemary or ¼ tsp. dried rosemary, crushed
- 1 tsp. minced fresh thyme or ¼ tsp. dried thyme
- 2 cans (15 oz. each) cannellini beans, rinsed and drained
- ¼ lb. smoked turkey kielbasa, chopped
- 3 bacon strips, cooked and crumbled

TOPPING
- ½ cup soft whole wheat bread crumbs
- ¼ cup minced fresh parsley
- 1 garlic clove, minced

1. Preheat oven to 325°. Sprinkle chicken with salt and pepper. In a broiler-safe Dutch oven, heat 2 tsp. oil over medium heat; brown the chicken on both sides. Remove from pan.

2. In same pan, saute onion in remaining oil over medium heat until crisp-tender. Add garlic; cook 1 minute. Add wine; bring to a boil, stirring to loosen browned bits from pan. Add the tomatoes, herbs and chicken; return to a boil.

3. Transfer to oven; bake, covered, 30 minutes. Stir in beans and kielbasa; bake, covered, until chicken is tender, 20-25 minutes longer.

4. Remove from oven; preheat broiler. Discard bay leaf; stir in bacon. Toss bread crumbs with parsley and garlic; sprinkle over top. Place in oven so surface of the cassoulet is 4-5 in. from heat; broil until crumbs are golden brown, 2-3 minutes.

1 serving: 394 cal., 14g fat (4g sat. fat), 91mg chol., 736mg sod., 29g carb. (4g sugars, 8g fiber), 33g pro. **Diabetic exchanges:** 4 lean meat, 2 starch, ½ fat.

CASSOULET FOR TODAY

TEST KITCHEN TIP
Adding pulses such as cannellini beans to a meat-based main dish bumps up the fiber and protein without adding saturated fat.

CURRY CHICKEN POPOVER PIE

SHEET-PAN CHICKEN
CURRY DINNER

SHEET-PAN CHICKEN CURRY DINNER

My husband loves anything curry and will even eat veggies when they have a curry sauce. This is a quick, minimal-fuss, one-pan way to get a meal on the table that everyone loves and that is healthy to boot. Add more curry if desired. The dish is wonderful with jasmine rice.
—*Trisha Kruse, Eagle, ID*

PREP: 20 min. • **COOK:** 40 min.
MAKES: 6 servings

- 2 **lbs. sweet potato, peeled and cubed**
- 2 **cups fresh cauliflowerets**
- 1 **large onion, chopped**
- 3 **garlic cloves, minced**
- 2 **Tbsp. olive oil**
- 2 **tsp. curry powder, divided**
- 1¼ **tsp. salt, divided**
- 1 **tsp. lemon-pepper seasoning, divided**
- 6 **bone-in chicken thighs (about 2¼ lbs.), skin removed**
- 1 **tsp. smoked paprika**
- ¼ **cup chicken broth**

1. Preheat the oven to 425°. Line a 15x10x1-in. baking pan with foil. Place sweet potatoes, cauliflower, onion and garlic on prepared pan. Drizzle with oil; sprinkle with 1 tsp. curry powder, ¾ tsp. salt and ½ tsp. lemon pepper; toss to coat.
2. Arrange chicken over vegetables. In a small bowl, mix paprika and remaining 1 tsp. curry powder, ½ tsp. salt and ½ tsp. lemon pepper; sprinkle over the chicken. Roast until vegetables are almost tender, 30-35 minutes. Drizzle with broth; bake until thermometer inserted in chicken reads 170°-175° and vegetables are tender, 7-10 minutes longer.
1 serving: 409 cal., 14g fat (3g sat. fat), 87mg chol., 686mg sod., 42g carb. (17g sugars, 6g fiber), 28g pro. **Diabetic exchanges:** 4 lean meat, 3 starch, 1 fat.

CURRY CHICKEN
POPOVER PIE

CURRY CHICKEN POPOVER PIE

My cast-iron skillet is one of my favorite pans to use for cooking. This flavorful curry chicken potpie has Indian influences. It is perfect to cook in the skillet and then serve at the table puffed, golden and piping hot.
—*Roxanne Chan, Albany, CA*

PREP: 25 min. • **BAKE:** 30 min.
MAKES: 6 servings

- 1½ **cups cubed cooked chicken breast**
- ½ **cup canned cooked lentils**
- ¼ **cup finely chopped green onions**
- ¼ **cup shredded carrots**
- 4 **large eggs**
- 1 **cup all-purpose flour**
- 1 **cup light coconut milk**
- 2 **Tbsp. minced fresh cilantro**
- 2 **tsp. curry powder**
- 1 **garlic clove, halved**
- 1 **tsp. minced fresh gingerroot**
- ½ **tsp. salt**
- ¼ **tsp. pepper**
  Grated lemon zest
  Optional: Sliced green onions and cilantro

1. Preheat oven to 425°. Place chicken, lentils, green onions and carrots in a greased 10-in. cast-iron skillet. Place the eggs, flour, coconut milk, cilantro, curry powder, garlic, ginger, salt and pepper in a blender; cover and process until blended. Pour into skillet.
2. Bake until puffy, browned and cooked through, 30-35 minutes. Sprinkle with lemon zest before serving. If desired, top with green onions and cilantro.
1 serving: 232 cal., 7g fat (3g sat. fat), 151mg chol., 271mg sod., 22g carb. (1g sugars, 3g fiber), 18g pro.

SHEET-PAN CHICKEN CURRY DINNER

CREAMY GREEN CHILE CHICKEN COBBLER

A biscuity crumb topping takes this family-friendly combo of rotisserie chicken and cheesy, creamy green enchilada sauce over the top.
—*Johnna Johnson, Scottsdale, AZ*

- -

PREP: 30 min. • **BAKE:** 35 min.
MAKES: 8 servings

- 2 cups all-purpose flour
- ½ cup grated Parmesan cheese
- 2 tsp. baking powder
- 6 Tbsp. cold butter, cubed
- ¾ cup plus 2 Tbsp. heavy whipping cream
- 3 oz. cream cheese, softened
- ½ cup sour cream
- 1 can (10½ oz.) condensed cream of chicken soup, undiluted
- 1 can (10 oz.) green enchilada sauce
- 2 cans (4 oz. each) chopped green chiles
- 2½ cups shredded rotisserie chicken (about 10 oz.)
- 1½ cups shredded Colby-Monterey Jack cheese

1. Preheat oven to 450°. For crumb topping, whisk together flour, cheese and baking powder. Cut in butter until mixture resembles coarse crumbs. Add cream; stir just until moistened. On a lightly greased 15x10x1-in. pan, crumble mixture into ½- to 1-in. pieces.
2. Bake on an upper oven rack until light golden brown, 8-10 minutes. Reduce oven setting to 350°.
3. In a large bowl, mix cream cheese and sour cream until smooth. Stir in soup, enchilada sauce, green chiles and chicken. Transfer to an 11x7-in. baking dish; sprinkle with cheese. Add crumb topping (dish will be full).
4. Place dish on a baking sheet. Bake, uncovered, on a lower oven rack until topping is deep golden brown and filling is bubbly, 35-40 minutes.
1¼ cups: 581 cal., 39g fat (22g sat. fat), 132mg chol., 1076mg sod., 33g carb. (3g sugars, 2g fiber), 25g pro.

SPINACH-PESTO TURKEY TENDERLOINS

SPINACH-PESTO TURKEY TENDERLOINS

My husband and I are avid trail runners who get hungry after long runs. We love the taste of turkey tenderloin stuffed with spinach and goat cheese.
—*Hayley Long, Oxford, AL*

- -

PREP: 20 min. • **BAKE:** 25 min.
MAKES: 4 servings

- 6 cups fresh baby spinach (about 6 oz.), coarsely chopped
- 1 cup crumbled goat cheese
- 2 garlic cloves, minced
- 2 turkey breast tenderloins (8 oz. each)
- ⅓ cup prepared pesto
- ¼ cup shredded Parmesan cheese

1. Preheat oven to 350°. In a large saucepan, bring ½ in. water to a boil. Add spinach; cover and boil 3-5 minutes or until wilted. Drain well.
2. In a small bowl, combine spinach, cheese and garlic. Cut a pocket in each tenderloin by slicing horizontally to within ½ in. of opposite side. Fill with cheese mixture; tie with kitchen string if necessary.
3. Place tenderloins on a greased 15x10x1-in. baking pan; brush with pesto. Bake 20 minutes. Sprinkle with Parmesan cheese. Bake 5-10 minutes longer or until a thermometer reads 165°. Cut each tenderloin into 4 slices.
2 slices cooked turkey: 306 cal., 19g fat (8g sat. fat), 87mg chol., 458mg sod., 5g carb. (0 sugars, 3g fiber), 32g pro.

CREAMY OLIVE-STUFFED CHICKEN

Guess what? This 7-ingredient stuffed chicken entree not only is a cinch to prepare but is good for you, too. In less than an hour, you can have dinner on the table and feel good knowing that each serving has less than 300 calories.
—Taste of Home *Test Kitchen*

PREP: 20 min. • **BAKE:** 20 min.
MAKES: 4 servings

- 4 boneless skinless chicken breast halves (6 oz. each)
- 4 oz. fat-free cream cheese
- 1 can (2¼ oz.) sliced ripe olives, drained
- ⅛ tsp. dried oregano
- ⅛ tsp. pepper
- ½ cup seasoned bread crumbs
- 1 Tbsp. olive oil

1. Preheat oven to 350°. Flatten chicken to ¼-in. thickness. In a small bowl, combine cream cheese, olives, oregano and pepper. Spoon 2 Tbsp. down center of each chicken breast. Fold chicken over the filling; secure with toothpicks, then roll in bread crumbs.

2. In a large ovenproof skillet, brown chicken in oil. Bake until a thermometer reads 165°, 20-25 minutes . Discard the toothpicks.

1 serving: 286 cal., 10g fat (2g sat. fat), 96mg chol., 483mg sod., 8g carb. (0 sugars, 1g fiber), 40g pro. **Diabetic exchanges:** 5 lean meat, 1 fat, ½ starch.

Mascarpone-Pesto Chicken Rolls: Omit cream cheese, olives, oregano and pepper. Sprinkle flattened chicken breasts with ¾ tsp. garlic salt. Mix ½ cup mascarpone cheese and ¼ cup prepared pesto. Fill, brown and bake chicken as recipe directs. Serve with buttered cooked fettuccine if desired.

DEVILED CHICKEN THIGHS

I make this dish when I invite my next-door neighbor over for supper. It's just enough for the two of us. The tasty chicken is tender and moist with a bit of crunch from the cashews.
—Bernice Morris, Marshfield, MO

TAKES: 30 min. • **MAKES:** 2 servings

- 1 tsp. butter, softened
- 1 tsp. cider vinegar
- 1 tsp. prepared mustard
- 1 tsp. paprika
   Dash pepper
- 2 boneless skinless chicken thighs (about ½ lb.)
- 3 Tbsp. soft bread crumbs
- 2 Tbsp. chopped cashews

1. In a large bowl, combine the butter, vinegar, mustard, paprika and pepper. Spread over chicken thighs. Place in a greased 11x7-in. baking dish. Sprinkle with bread crumbs.

2. Bake chicken, uncovered, at 400° for 15 minutes. Sprinkle with cashews. Bake until chicken juices run clear and topping is golden brown, 7-12 minutes longer.

1 chicken thigh: 246 cal., 14g fat (4g sat. fat), 81mg chol., 189mg sod., 6g carb. (1g sugars, 1g fiber), 23g pro. **Diabetic exchanges:** 3 lean meat, 1 fat, ½ starch.

DEVILED
CHICKEN THIGHS

CHICKEN MARSALA EN CROUTE

I love puff pastry and chicken Marsala, so I decided to combine the two. The result is a very special meal perfect for Sunday dinner or any special occasion. Be sure to keep the puff pastry chilled so it is easier to work with.
—*Lorraine Russo, Mahwah, NJ*

PREP: 35 min. + chilling • **BAKE:** 20 min.
MAKES: 4 servings

- 3   Tbsp. butter
- ½   lb. sliced baby portobello mushrooms
- 2   shallots, finely chopped
- 3   garlic cloves, minced
- 1   Tbsp. all-purpose flour
- ¼   cup beef broth
- ⅔   cup Marsala wine
- 4   boneless skinless chicken breast halves (5 oz. each)
- 1   Tbsp. large egg
- 1   Tbsp. water
- 1   sheet frozen puff pastry, thawed
- ½   tsp. salt
- ¼   tsp. pepper
      Fresh thyme, optional

1. In a large skillet, heat butter over medium-high heat; saute mushrooms and shallots until tender, 3-4 minutes. Add garlic; cook and stir 1 minute longer. Stir in flour until blended. Gradually stir in broth and wine; bring to a boil, stirring constantly. Reduce the heat; simmer, uncovered, until slightly thickened, 2-3 minutes, stirring occasionally. Remove to a bowl; cool slightly. Refrigerate, covered, until cold.
2. Preheat oven to 425°. Pound chicken breasts with a meat mallet to even thickness. Whisk together egg and water. On a lightly floured surface, roll pastry sheet into a 14-in. square. Cut into four 7-in. squares. Place 1 chicken breast on center of each square. If desired, fold narrow end under to fit pastry square; sprinkle with salt and pepper. Top each with 1 rounded Tbsp. mushroom mixture. Lightly brush pastry edges with egg mixture. Fold pastry over filling; press the edges with a fork to seal. Place on a rimmed parchment-lined baking sheet.
3. Brush tops with egg mixture. Bake until golden brown and a thermometer inserted in chicken reads 165°, 18-23 minutes. Reheat remaining mushroom mixture; serve with pastries. If desired, garnish with thyme.
1 pastry: 599 cal., 29g fat (10g sat. fat), 115mg chol., 703mg sod., 45g carb. (3g sugars, 5g fiber), 36g pro.

CHICKEN MARSALA
EN CROUTE

TEST KITCHEN TIP

Marsala is a fortified (higher alcohol) wine from Sicily that's popular in Italian cooking. It's made in dry and sweet styles. Use dry or cooking Marsala in this recipe. You could also prepare it with sherry if you don't have Marsala.

❄ TURKEY MUSHROOM CASSEROLE

My mother developed this recipe years ago. The flavor, cheese and splash of sherry make it elegant enough to serve at a dinner party.
—*Peggy Kroupa, Leawood, KS*

PREP: 50 min. • **COOK:** 30 min.
MAKES: 2 casseroles (4 servings each)

- 1 lb. uncooked spaghetti
- ½ lb. sliced fresh mushrooms
- 1 cup chopped onion
- 2 Tbsp. olive oil
- ½ tsp. minced garlic
- 3 cans (10¾ oz. each) condensed cream of mushroom soup, undiluted
- 3 cups cubed cooked turkey
- 1 cup chicken broth
- ⅓ cup sherry or additional chicken broth
- 1 tsp. Italian seasoning
- ¾ tsp. pepper
- 2 cups grated Parmesan cheese, divided

1. Preheat oven to 350°. Cook spaghetti according to package directions.
2. Meanwhile, in a Dutch oven, saute mushrooms and onion in oil until tender. Add garlic; cook 1 minute longer. Stir in soup, turkey, broth, sherry, Italian seasoning, pepper and 1 cup cheese. Drain spaghetti; stir into turkey mixture.
3. Transfer to 2 greased 8-in. square baking dishes. Sprinkle with remaining cheese. Cover and bake 1 casserole until heated through, 30-40 minutes.
Freeze option: Cover and freeze the remaining casserole for up to 3 months. Thaw in refrigerator overnight. Remove from refrigerator 30 minutes before baking. Preheat oven to 350°. Cover and bake 45 minutes. Uncover; bake until bubbly, 5-10 minutes longer.
1½ cups: 534 cal., 19g fat (6g sat. fat), 63mg chol., 1286mg sod., 55g carb. (4g sugars, 4g fiber), 33g pro.

BREADED RANCH CHICKEN

BREADED RANCH CHICKEN

A crunchy coating of cornflakes and Parmesan cheese adds delectable flavor to this zesty ranch chicken. The golden, crispy chicken is a mainstay dish I can always count on.
—*Launa Shoemaker, Landrum, SC*

PREP: 10 min. • **BAKE:** 45 min.
MAKES: 8 servings

- ¼ cup unsalted butter, melted
- ¾ cup crushed cornflakes
- ¾ cup grated Parmesan cheese
- 1 envelope ranch salad dressing mix
- 8 boneless skinless chicken breast halves (4 oz. each)

1. Preheat oven to 350°. Place butter in a shallow bowl. In another shallow bowl, combine the cornflakes, cheese and salad dressing mix. Dip chicken in butter, then roll in cornflake mixture to coat.
2. Place in a greased 13x9-in. baking dish. Bake, uncovered, about 45 minutes, until a thermometer reads 165°.
1 chicken breast half: 254 cal., 10g fat (5g sat. fat), 84mg chol., 959mg sod., 13g carb. (1g sugars, 0 fiber), 26g pro.

TEST KITCHEN TIP

Unless otherwise specified, *Taste of Home* recipes are tested with lightly salted butter. Unsalted, or sweet, butter is sometimes used to achieve a buttery flavor, such as in shortbread cookies or buttercream frosting. In these recipes, added salt would detract from the buttery taste desired.

CRANBERRY TURKEY BURGERS WITH ARUGULA SALAD

These healthy burgers taste just like the holidays, all in one bite. They are a little sweet and a little savory, and they're delicious over a bed of peppery arugula.
—*Nicole Stevens, Charleston, SC*

- -

TAKES: 25 min. • **MAKES:** 4 servings

- ¾ lb. ground turkey
- ⅓ cup dried cranberries
- ⅓ cup gluten-free soft bread crumbs
- 3 green onions, finely chopped
- 2 to 3 Tbsp. crumbled goat cheese
- 2 Tbsp. pepper jelly
- 3 garlic cloves, minced
- 1 large egg yolk
- ¼ tsp. salt
- ¼ tsp. pepper
- 4 cups fresh arugula
- 1 Tbsp. grapeseed oil or olive oil
- 1 Tbsp. honey

1. Preheat oven to 375°. Combine the first 10 ingredients, mixing lightly but thoroughly. Shape into four ½-in.-thick patties; transfer to a greased baking sheet. Bake 12 minutes. Heat broiler; broil until a thermometer inserted in burgers reads 165°, about 5 minutes.
2. Meanwhile, toss arugula with oil. Drizzle with honey; toss to combine. Top salad with turkey burgers.
1 burger with 1 cup salad: 281 cal., 12g fat (3g sat. fat), 107mg chol., 240mg sod., 26g carb. (21g sugars, 2g fiber), 19g pro.

QUINOA-STUFFED ACORN SQUASH

Here's an amazingly flavorful (and healthy) recipe that my family will actually eat. You can omit the sausage if you want to make it a side dish or an even lighter meal.
—*Valarree Osters, Lodi, OH*

- -

PREP: 15 min. • **BAKE:** 45 min.
MAKES: 4 servings

- 2 small acorn squash (about 1½ lbs. each)
- 1 Tbsp. olive oil
- 1 tsp. Italian seasoning, divided
- ½ tsp. salt, divided
- ¼ tsp. garlic powder
- 2 Italian turkey sausage links (about 8 oz.), casings removed
- 1 small onion, finely chopped
- 2 garlic cloves, minced
- ¼ tsp. pepper
- ¾ cup quinoa, rinsed
- 1½ cups chicken stock
- 1 large egg, lightly beaten
- 1 Tbsp. minced fresh parsley
   Shredded Parmesan cheese
   Additional minced fresh parsley

1. Preheat oven to 400°. Cut squash crosswise in half; discard seeds. Cut a thin slice from bottom of each half to allow them to lie flat. Place on a baking sheet, hollow side up; brush tops with oil. Mix ½ tsp. Italian seasoning, ¼ tsp. salt and garlic powder; sprinkle over top. Bake until almost tender, 25-30 minutes.
2. Meanwhile, in a large skillet, cook and crumble sausage with onion over medium heat until no longer pink, 4-6 minutes. Add garlic, pepper and the remaining Italian seasoning and salt; cook and stir 1 minute. Stir in quinoa and stock; bring to a boil. Reduce heat; simmer, covered, until liquid is absorbed, 15-20 minutes. Cool slightly. Stir in egg and parsley; spoon into squash.
3. Bake until filling is heated through and squash is tender, 20-25 minutes. Sprinkle with cheese and additional parsley.
1 stuffed squash half: 351 cal., 10g fat (2g sat. fat), 67mg chol., 740mg sod., 53g carb. (7g sugars, 7g fiber), 16g pro.

CRANBERRY TURKEY BURGERS
WITH ARUGULA SALAD

CAPRESE CHICKEN WITH BACON

KABOBLESS CHICKEN & VEGETABLES

As the primary caregiver for my grandma, I am trying to cook healthier for her. I am fascinated with Mediterranean cuisine. It is much easier to have chicken and vegetables off the kabob, which inspired this sheet-pan dinner.
—Chelsea Madren, Fullerton, CA

- -

PREP: 10 min. + marinating
BAKE: 45 min. • **MAKES:** 6 servings

- ½   cup olive oil
- ½   cup balsamic vinegar
- 2   tsp. lemon-pepper seasoning
- 2   tsp. Italian seasoning
- 2   lbs. boneless skinless chicken breasts, cut into 1-in. pieces
- 2   medium yellow summer squash, sliced
- 2   medium zucchini, sliced
- 1   medium carrot, sliced
- 1   cup grape tomatoes

1. In a large bowl, combine oil, vinegar, lemon pepper and Italian seasoning. Pour half the marinade into a separate bowl or shallow dish. Add chicken; turn to coat. Cover and refrigerate overnight. Cover and refrigerate remaining marinade.
2. Preheat the oven to 350°. Line a 15x10x1-in. baking pan with foil. Drain chicken, discarding that marinade. Place squash, zucchini, carrot and tomatoes in pan in a single layer. Place chicken on top of the vegetables; pour reserved marinade over top. Cook until chicken is no longer pink and vegetables are tender, 45-60 minutes. Let stand 5 minutes before serving.
1 serving: 305 cal., 15g fat (3g sat. fat), 84mg chol., 158mg sod., 9g carb. (7g sugars, 2g fiber), 32g pro. **Diabetic exchanges:** 4 lean meat, 2 fat, 1 vegetable.

CAPRESE CHICKEN WITH BACON

Smoky bacon, fresh basil, ripe tomatoes and gooey mozzarella top these appealing chicken breasts. The aroma as the chicken bakes is irresistible!
—Tammy Hayden, Quincy, MI

- -

PREP: 20 min. • **BAKE:** 20 min.
MAKES: 4 servings

- 8   bacon strips
- 4   boneless skinless chicken breast halves (6 oz. each)
- 1   Tbsp. olive oil
- ½   tsp. salt
- ¼   tsp. pepper
- 2   plum tomatoes, sliced
- 6   fresh basil leaves, thinly sliced
- 4   slices part-skim mozzarella cheese

1. Preheat oven to 400°. Place bacon in an ungreased 15x10x1-in. baking pan. Bake until partially cooked but not crisp, 8-10 minutes. Remove to paper towels to drain.
2. Place chicken in an ungreased 13x9-in. baking pan; brush with oil and sprinkle with salt and pepper. Top with tomatoes and basil. Wrap each in 2 bacon strips, arranging bacon in a crisscross.
3. Bake, uncovered, until a thermometer reads 165°, 15-20 minutes. Top each piece with cheese; bake until melted, 1 minute longer.
1 chicken breast half: 373 cal., 18g fat (7g sat. fat), 123mg chol., 821mg sod., 3g carb. (1g sugars, 0 fiber), 47g pro.

z

CAPRESE CHICKEN WITH BACON

190   TASTEOFHOME.COM

KABOBLESS
CHICKEN & VEGETABLES

STUFFED CORNISH HENS

With a golden and flavorful stuffing, these tender hens are a special-occasion entree perfect for two.
—*Wanda Jean Sain, Hickory, NC*

PREP: 45 min. + cooling
BAKE: 1 hour • **MAKES:** 2 servings

- 2 Tbsp. finely chopped onion
- ⅓ cup uncooked long grain rice
- 4 Tbsp. butter, divided
- ¾ cup water
- ½ cup condensed cream of celery soup, undiluted
- 1 Tbsp. lemon juice
- 1 tsp. minced chives
- 1 tsp. dried parsley flakes
- 1 tsp. chicken bouillon granules
- 2 Cornish game hens (20 to 24 oz. each)
  Salt and pepper to taste
- ½ tsp. dried tarragon

1. In a small skillet, saute onion and rice in 2 Tbsp. butter until rice is browned. Add water, soup, lemon juice, chives, parsley and bouillon. Bring to a boil. Reduce heat; cover and simmer for 25 minutes or until rice is tender and liquid is absorbed. Remove from heat and cool slightly. Preheat oven to 375°.
2. Sprinkle hen cavities with salt and pepper; stuff with rice mixture. Place with breast side up on a rack in an ungreased 13x9-in. baking pan. Melt remaining butter and add tarragon; brush some over the hens.
3. Cover loosely and bake for 30 minutes. Uncover and bake until a thermometer reads 170° for hens and 165° for stuffing, 30-45 minutes longer, basting frequently with tarragon butter.
1 hen: 1076 cal., 75g fat (29g sat. fat), 415mg chol., 1097mg sod., 33g carb. (1g sugars, 2g fiber) 63g pro.

"Cornish hens were moist and tender. Very flavorful! Stuffing was delicious. Will definitely make again."
—MELODIOUS88, TASTEOFHOME.COM

TERIYAKI PINEAPPLE DRUMSTICKS

We have a large family and love to throw big parties, so I look for ways to free my husband from the grill. Roasted drumsticks keep everyone happy.
—*Erica Allen, Tuckerton, NJ*

PREP: 35 min. • **BAKE:** 1½ hours
MAKES: 12 servings

- 1 Tbsp. garlic salt
- 1 Tbsp. minced chives
- 1½ tsp. paprika
- 1½ tsp. pepper
- ½ tsp. salt
- 24 chicken drumsticks
- ½ cup canola oil
- 1 can (8 oz.) crushed pineapple
- ½ cup water
- ¼ cup packed brown sugar
- ¼ cup Worcestershire sauce
- ¼ cup yellow mustard
- 4 tsp. cornstarch
- 2 Tbsp. cold water

1. Preheat oven to 350°. Mix the first 5 ingredients; sprinkle over chicken. In a large skillet, heat oil over medium-high heat. Brown the drumsticks in batches. Transfer to a roasting pan.
2. Meanwhile, combine pineapple, ½ cup water, brown sugar, Worcestershire sauce and mustard; pour over chicken. Cover; bake until tender, 1½-2 hours, uncovering during the last 20-30 minutes of baking to let skin crisp.
3. Remove drumsticks to a platter; keep warm. Transfer cooking juices to a small saucepan; skim fat. Bring juices to a boil. In a small bowl, mix cornstarch and cold water until smooth; stir into the cooking juices. Return to a boil; cook and stir until thickened, 1-2 minutes. Serve with the drumsticks.
2 drumsticks: 360 cal., 22g fat (4g sat. fat), 95mg chol., 540mg sod., 11g carb. (8g sugars, 1g fiber), 29g pro.

TERIYAKI PINEAPPLE DRUMSTICKS

CHICKEN POTPIE CASSEROLE

CHICKEN & RICE DINNER

The chicken in this recipe bakes to a beautiful golden brown while the moist rice is packed with flavor. The taste is simply unbeatable!
—Denise Baumert, Dalhart, TX

PREP: 15 min. • **BAKE:** 50 min.
MAKES: 6 servings

- 1 broiler/fryer chicken (3½ to 4 lbs.), cut up
- ¼ to ⅓ cup all-purpose flour
- 2 Tbsp. canola oil
- 2⅓ cups water
- 1½ cups uncooked long grain rice
- 1 cup milk
- 1 tsp. salt
- 1 tsp. poultry seasoning
- ½ tsp. pepper
   Minced fresh parsley

1. Preheat oven to 350°. Dredge chicken in flour. In a large skillet, brown chicken in oil on all sides over medium heat.
2. In a large bowl, combine the water, rice, milk, salt, poultry seasoning and pepper. Pour into a greased 13x9-in. baking dish. Top with chicken.
3. Cover and bake until chicken juices run clear, 50-55 minutes. Sprinkle with parsley.
1 serving: 541 cal., 23g fat (6g sat. fat), 108mg chol., 504mg sod., 43g carb. (2g sugars, 1g fiber), 38g pro.

TEST KITCHEN TIP

If you don't have poultry seasoning on hand, you can make your own with ¾ teaspoon rubbed sage and ¼ teaspoon dried marjoram or thyme.

CHICKEN POTPIE CASSEROLE

I always have leftover chicken broth on hand and use it for many things, including this comforting family favorite. You can bake your own biscuits as I do or buy them at the store. I like to bake extra biscuits to eat with butter and jam.
—Liliane Jahnke, Cypress, TX

PREP: 40 min. • **BAKE:** 15 min.
MAKES: 8 servings

- ⅓ cup butter, cubed
- 1½ cups sliced fresh mushrooms
- 2 medium carrots, sliced
- ½ medium onion, chopped
- ¼ cup all-purpose flour
- 1 cup chicken broth
- 1 cup 2% milk
- 4 cups cubed cooked chicken
- 1 cup frozen peas
- 1 jar (2 oz.) diced pimientos, drained
- ½ tsp. salt

BISCUIT TOPPING
- 2 cups all-purpose flour
- 4 tsp. baking powder
- 2 tsp. sugar
- ½ tsp. salt
- ½ tsp. cream of tartar
- ½ cup cold butter, cubed
- ⅔ cup 2% milk

1. Preheat the oven to 400°. In a large saucepan, heat butter over medium heat. Add mushrooms, carrots and onion; cook and stir until tender.
2. Stir in flour until blended; gradually stir in broth and milk. Bring to a boil, stirring constantly; cook and stir 2 minutes or until thickened. Stir in the chicken, peas, pimientos and salt; heat through. Transfer to a greased 11x7-in. baking dish.
3. For the topping, in a large bowl, whisk flour, baking powder, sugar, salt and cream of tartar. Cut in butter until mixture resembles coarse crumbs. Add milk; stir just until moistened.
4. Turn onto a lightly floured surface; knead gently 8-10 times. Pat or roll dough to ½-in. thickness; cut with a floured 2½-in. biscuit cutter. Place over chicken mixture. Bake, uncovered, 15-20 minutes or until biscuits are golden brown.
1 serving: 489 cal., 26g fat (14g sat. fat), 118mg chol., 885mg sod., 36g carb. (6g sugars, 3g fiber), 27g pro.

**ROASTED TUSCAN
CHICKEN DINNER**

ROASTED TUSCAN CHICKEN DINNER

When an Italian friend shared many years ago that she often added Italian sausages to her pan of baked chicken, I had to give it a try! The sausages give the chicken an amazing flavor. Over the years, I've turned her idea into a one-dish meal by adding potatoes, onions and peppers. It has become a family favorite that I often use for holidays, spur-of-the-moment company and Sunday dinners.
—*Teri Lindquist, Gurnee, IL*

PREP: 20 min. • **BAKE:** 1¼ hours
MAKES: 6 servings

- 6 medium red potatoes, cut into wedges
- 3 Tbsp. olive oil, divided
- 6 bone-in chicken thighs (about 2 lbs.)
- 3 sweet Italian sausage links (4 oz. each), cut in half lengthwise
- 1 large onion, cut into wedges
- 1 large green pepper, cut into 1-in. pieces
- 1 large sweet red pepper, cut into 1-in. pieces
- 1 tsp. garlic salt
- 1 tsp. dried oregano
- 1 tsp. dried thyme
- 1 tsp. dried rosemary, crushed
- 1 tsp. paprika
- 1 tsp. pepper

1. Preheat oven to 425°. Place potatoes in a shallow roasting pan; drizzle with 1 Tbsp. oil and toss to coat. Rub chicken and sausage with 1 Tbsp. oil; arrange over potatoes.
2. In a large bowl, toss onion and peppers with remaining oil; spoon over chicken and sausage. Sprinkle with seasonings.
3. Bake, uncovered, until a meat thermometer inserted into chicken reads 170°-175° and potatoes are tender, 1¼-1½ hours.
1 serving: 673 cal., 44g fat (13g sat. fat), 149mg chol., 1181mg sod., 26g carb. (5g sugars, 4g fiber), 43g pro.

MAMA MIA MEATBALL TAQUITOS

MAMA MIA MEATBALL TAQUITOS

We love lasagna, but it takes too long on weeknights. My solution: meatball taquitos. My kids get the flavors they want, and I get a meal on the table in a hurry.
—*Lauren Wyler, Dripping Springs, TX*

TAKES: 30 min. • **MAKES:** 6 servings

- 12 frozen fully cooked Italian turkey meatballs, thawed
- 2 cups shredded part-skim mozzarella cheese
- 1 cup whole-milk ricotta cheese
- 1 tsp. Italian seasoning
- 12 flour tortillas (8 in.)
  Cooking spray
  Warm marinara sauce

1. Preheat oven to 425°. Place meatballs in a food processor; pulse until finely chopped. Transfer to a large bowl; stir in cheeses and Italian seasoning.
2. Spread about ¼ cup meatball mixture down center of each tortilla. Roll up tightly. Place in a greased 15x10x1-in. baking pan, seam sides down; spritz taquitos with cooking spray.
3. Bake 16-20 minutes or until golden brown. Serve with marinara sauce.
2 taquitos: 617 cal., 28g fat (11g sat. fat), 94mg chol., 1069mg sod., 60g carb. (3g sugars, 3g fiber), 33g pro.

HONEY-GLAZED CHICKEN

My family raves over this nicely browned chicken. The rich honey glaze gives each luscious piece a spicy tang. This dish is simple enough to prepare for a family dinner and delightful enough to serve to guests.

—*Ruth Andrewson, Leavenworth, WA*

- -

PREP: 15 min. • **BAKE:** 1¼ hours
MAKES: 6 servings

- ½ cup all-purpose flour
- 1 tsp. salt
- ½ tsp. cayenne pepper
- 1 broiler/fryer chicken (about 3 lbs.), cut up
- ½ cup butter, melted, divided
- ¼ cup packed brown sugar
- ¼ cup honey
- ¼ cup lemon juice
- 1 Tbsp. reduced-sodium soy sauce
- 1½ tsp. curry powder

1. Preheat oven to 350°. In a bowl or shallow dish, combine the flour, salt and cayenne pepper; add the chicken pieces and turn to coat. Pour 4 Tbsp. butter into a 13x9-in. baking pan; place chicken in pan, turning pieces once to coat.
2. Bake, uncovered, 30 minutes. Combine brown sugar, honey, lemon juice, soy sauce, curry powder and remaining butter; pour over chicken. Bake until juices run clear, 45 minutes, basting several times with pan drippings.
1 serving: 501 cal., 29g fat (13g sat. fat), 128mg chol., 781mg sod., 30g carb. (20g sugars, 1g fiber), 29g pro.

BREADED CURRY CHICKEN DRUMMIES

These drumsticks are crispy with just the right amount of zing to get your mouth watering for more! They are easy to make and are baked rather than fried so they save on fat but not on flavor. Boneless skinless chicken breasts or assorted chicken parts can be used instead of all drumsticks.

—*Lynn Kaufman, Mount Morris, IL*

- -

PREP: 20 min.
BAKE: 45 min.
MAKES: 8 servings

BREADED CURRY CHICKEN DRUMMIES

- 1½ cups seasoned bread crumbs
- 1½ tsp. kosher salt
- 1½ tsp. onion powder
- 1½ tsp. garlic powder
- 1 tsp. curry powder
- 1 tsp. smoked paprika
- 1 tsp. dried parsley flakes
- ½ tsp. ground turmeric
- ¼ tsp. pepper
- ⅛ tsp. cayenne pepper
- ½ cup butter, cubed
- 3 Tbsp. lemon juice
- 16 chicken drumsticks (about 4 lbs.)

1. Preheat oven to 375°. In a shallow bowl, mix bread crumbs and seasonings. In a microwave, melt butter with lemon juice. Brush drumsticks with butter mixture, then coat with crumb mixture. Place on greased racks in two 15x10x1-in. pans.
2. Bake until coating is golden brown and a thermometer reads 170°-175°, 45-55 minutes, rotating pans halfway through baking.
2 drumsticks: 380 cal., 24g fat (11g sat. fat), 125mg chol., 535mg sod., 9g carb. (1g sugars, 1g fiber), 31g pro.

TEST KITCHEN TIP

These drumsticks are fantastic on their own, but if you'd like to serve with a dip or sauce, make raita, which is a simple combination of plain yogurt, chopped and seeded cucumber, cilantro and salt.

❄ TERRIFIC TURKEY ENCHILADAS

Enchiladas are a favorite dish in our home. Our little girl, who calls them laladas, especially loves them. This is a really tasty take on the classic southwestern dish.
—*Jenn Tidwell, Fair Oaks, CA*

- -

PREP: 35 min. • **BAKE:** 35 min.
MAKES: 3 servings

- 1¼ cups frozen corn, thawed
- 1 can (4 oz.) chopped green chiles
- 1 cup fresh cilantro leaves
- ⅓ cup heavy whipping cream
- ¼ tsp. salt
- ¼ tsp. pepper

ENCHILADAS

- ¾ lb. ground turkey
- ⅓ cup chopped onion
- 1 garlic clove, minced
- 1 Tbsp. olive oil
- ¾ cup salsa
- 1 Tbsp. cornmeal
- 2 tsp. chili powder
- 1½ tsp. ground cumin
- 1 tsp. dried oregano
- ⅛ tsp. salt
- ⅛ tsp. pepper
- 6 flour tortillas (8 in.), warmed
- 1¼ cups shredded Mexican cheese blend, divided
- ¼ cup sliced ripe olives

1. Preheat oven to 350°. Place the first 6 ingredients in a food processor; cover and pulse until blended.

2. In a large skillet, cook turkey, onion and garlic in oil over medium heat until meat is no longer pink, breaking it into crumbles. Remove from heat; stir in salsa, cornmeal and seasonings.

3. Spoon ⅓ cup turkey mixture down center of each tortilla; top with 2 Tbsp. cheese. Roll up and place seam sides down in a greased 11x7-in. baking dish. Spoon corn mixture over top; sprinkle with olives and remaining cheese.

4. Cover and bake 30 minutes. Uncover; bake 5-10 minutes longer or until heated through. If desired, top with additional chopped cilantro.

Freeze option: Cover and freeze unbaked enchiladas. To use, partially thaw in refrigerator overnight. Remove from refrigerator 30 minutes before baking. Preheat oven to 350°. Cover casserole with foil; bake until casserole is heated through, sauce is bubbling and cheese is melted, 30-35 minutes. Serve as directed.

2 enchiladas: 968 cal., 55g fat (23g sat. fat), 155mg chol., 1766mg sod., 81g carb. (4g sugars, 5g fiber), 41g pro.

"I've made this recipe a few times and love the spices and taste. To combat any dryness, I add up to 1 cup of taco sauce to the turkey mixture. This tastes amazing."
—*PALOMA, TASTEOFHOME.COM*

TERRIFIC TURKEY ENCHILADAS

POBLANOS STUFFED WITH
CHIPOTLE TURKEY CHILI

ROTISSERIE-STYLE CHICKEN

My mother used to fix this chicken when I lived at home, and we called it Church Chicken because Mom would put it in the oven Sunday morning before we left for church. When we got home, the aroma of the roasted chicken would hit us as we opened the door.
—*Brian Stevenson, Grand Rapids, MI*

PREP: 15 min. + chilling
BAKE: 1¼ hours + standing
MAKES: 6 servings

    2 tsp. salt
 1¼ tsp. paprika
    1 tsp. brown sugar
   ¾ tsp. dried thyme
   ¾ tsp. white pepper
   ¼ tsp. cayenne pepper
   ¼ tsp. pepper
    1 broiler/fryer chicken (3 to 4 lbs.)
    1 medium onion, quartered

1. Mix the first 7 ingredients. Rub over the outside and inside of chicken. Place in a large resealable plastic bag. Refrigerate 8 hours or overnight.
2. Preheat oven to 350°. Place chicken on rack in a shallow roasting pan, breast side up. Tuck wings under chicken; tie drumsticks together. Place onion around chicken in pan.
3. Roast until a thermometer inserted in thickest part of thigh reads 170°-175°, 1¼-1½ hours. Baste occasionally with pan drippings. (Cover loosely with foil if chicken browns too quickly.)
4. Remove chicken from oven; tent with foil. Let stand 15 minutes before slicing.
5 oz. cooked chicken: 306 cal., 17g fat (5g sat. fat), 104mg chol., 878mg sod., 3g carb. (2g sugars, 1g fiber), 33g pro.

POBLANOS STUFFED WITH CHIPOTLE TURKEY CHILI

As an emergency room doctor, I stay pretty busy. But when I'm home, I enjoy cooking dishes that are healthy yet full of flavor. Using two varieties of peppers in this dish really punches up the taste.
—*Sonali Ruder, New York, NY*

PREP: 35 min. • **BAKE:** 10 min.
MAKES: 4 servings

    8 poblano peppers
    1 pkg. (20 oz.) lean ground turkey
    1 medium onion, chopped
    3 garlic cloves, minced
    2 tsp. olive oil
    1 can (14½ oz.) fire-roasted diced tomatoes, undrained
    1 can (8¾ oz.) whole kernel corn, drained
    1 Tbsp. minced chipotle pepper in adobo sauce
    2 tsp. adobo sauce
   ½ tsp. salt
   ½ tsp. ground cumin
   ½ tsp. chili powder
   ¼ tsp. pepper
    3 Tbsp. minced fresh cilantro, divided
    1 cup shredded Mexican cheese blend
   ½ cup reduced-fat sour cream

1. Broil peppers 4 in. from the heat until skins blister, about 5 minutes. With tongs, rotate peppers a quarter turn. Broil and rotate until all sides are blistered and blackened. Immediately place peppers in a large bowl; cover and let stand for 20 minutes.
2. Meanwhile, in a large nonstick skillet over medium heat, cook turkey, onion and garlic in oil until meat is no longer pink, breaking it into crumbles; drain. Add the tomatoes, corn, chipotle pepper, adobo sauce, salt, cumin, chili powder and pepper; heat through. Remove from heat; stir in 2 Tbsp. cilantro. Set aside.
3. Preheat oven to 375°. Peel off and discard charred skins from poblanos. Cut a lengthwise slit down each pepper, leaving stem intact; remove membranes and seeds. Fill each pepper with ½ cup turkey mixture.
4. Place peppers in a greased 13x9-in. baking dish. Sprinkle with the cheese. Bake, uncovered, until cheese is melted, 10-15 minutes. Sprinkle with remaining cilantro. Serve with sour cream.
2 stuffed peppers: 539 cal., 28g fat (11g sat. fat), 147mg chol., 1180mg sod., 33g carb. (15g sugars, 7g fiber), 38g pro.

ROTISSERIE-STYLE
CHICKEN

CHICKEN & WILD RICE STRUDELS

I wanted the buttery crunch of layered pastry without the sweet filling of strudel. Using rotisserie chicken from the store, I found my savory answer.
—*Johnna Johnson, Scottsdale, AZ*

- -

TAKES: 30 min. • **MAKES:** 6 servings

1	pkg. (8.8 oz.) ready-to-serve long grain and wild rice
1½	cups coarsely chopped rotisserie chicken
½	cup shredded Swiss cheese
½	tsp. Italian seasoning
¼	tsp. salt
¼	tsp. pepper
12	sheets phyllo dough (14x9-in. size)
6	Tbsp. butter, melted

1. Preheat the oven to 400°. Place the first 6 ingredients in a large bowl; toss to combine.
2. Place 1 sheet of phyllo dough on a work surface; brush lightly with melted butter. Layer with 5 additional sheets, brushing each layer. (Keep remaining phyllo covered with a damp towel to prevent it from drying out.)
3. Spoon half rice mixture down center of phyllo dough to within 1 in. of ends. Fold up short sides to enclose filling. Roll up tightly, starting with a long side.
4. Transfer to a parchment-lined 15x10x1-in. baking pan, seam side down. Brush with additional butter. Repeat with remaining ingredients. Bake 20-25 minutes or until golden brown and heated through.
1 serving: 323 cal., 18g fat (10g sat. fat), 70mg chol., 550mg sod., 25g carb. (1g sugars, 1g fiber), 16g pro.

❄ PARMESAN CHICKEN NUGGETS

My 3-year-old went through a chicken-nuggets-and-french-fries-only stage, so I made these golden nuggets for him. Even the grown-ups like them!
—*Amanda Livesay, Mobile, AL*

- -

TAKES: 30 min. • **MAKES:** 8 servings

¼	cup butter, melted
1	cup panko bread crumbs
½	cup grated Parmesan cheese
½	tsp. kosher salt
1½	lbs. boneless skinless chicken breasts, cut into 1-in. cubes
	Marinara sauce, optional

1. Place butter in a shallow bowl. Combine bread crumbs, cheese and salt in another shallow bowl. Dip chicken in butter, then roll in crumbs.
2. Place nuggets in a single layer in two 15x10x1-in. baking pans. Bake at 375° for 15-18 minutes or until no longer pink, turning once. Serve with marinara sauce if desired.
Freeze option: Cool chicken nuggets. Freeze in freezer containers. To use, partially thaw in refrigerator overnight. Place on a baking sheet and reheat in a preheated 375° oven 7-12 minutes or until heated through.
6 nuggets: 191 cal., 9g fat (5g sat. fat), 67mg chol., 309mg sod., 5g carb. (0 sugars, 0 fiber), 20g pro.
Spicy Chicken Nuggets: Add ¼-½ tsp. ground chipotle pepper to the bread crumb mixture.
Italian Seasoned Chicken Nuggets: Add 2 tsp. Italian seasoning to the bread crumb mixture.
Ranch Chicken Nuggets: Substitute crushed cornflakes for bread crumbs. Toss chicken cubes with ⅓ cup ranch salad dressing, then roll chicken in cornflake mixture. Serve with additional ranch dressing.

PARMESAN CHICKEN NUGGETS

CHICKEN
BISCUIT POTPIE

CAJUN CHICKEN FETTUCCINE

For this quick-mix casserole, I combine two pasta sauces and add Cajun seasoning for kick. Using frozen onions and peppers speeds things up even more. You could even try adding mushrooms or peas.
—Rebecca Reece, Henderson, NV

PREP: 25 min. • **BAKE:** 25 min.
MAKES: 8 servings

    8   oz. uncooked fettuccine
    1   large sweet onion, halved and sliced
    1   medium green pepper,
        cut into ¼-in. strips
    1   medium sweet red pepper,
        cut into ¼-in. strips
    2   Tbsp. olive oil
    2   cups cubed cooked chicken
    4   tsp. Cajun seasoning
    1   tsp. minced garlic
    1   jar (15 oz.) Alfredo sauce
    ½   cup spaghetti sauce
    2   cups shredded part-skim
        mozzarella cheese
    ½   cup grated Parmesan cheese

1. Preheat oven to 375°. Cook fettuccine according to the package directions. Meanwhile, in a large skillet, saute onion and peppers in oil until tender. Add the chicken, Cajun seasoning and garlic; heat through. Transfer to a large bowl. Drain fettuccine; add to chicken mixture. Stir in Alfredo and spaghetti sauces.
2. Transfer to a greased 13x9-in. baking dish. Sprinkle with cheeses. Cover and bake for 15 minutes. Uncover; bake until golden brown, 10-15 minutes longer.
Freeze option: Before baking, cover and freeze the casserole for up to 3 months. Remove casserole from freezer 30 minutes before baking (do not thaw). Cover and bake at 350° for 70 minutes. Uncover; bake 5-10 minutes longer or until heated through. Let casserole stand 10 minutes before serving.
1 cup: 401 cal., 19g fat (9g sat. fat), 69mg chol., 898mg sod., 30g carb. (5g sugars, 3g fiber), 27g pro.

CHICKEN BISCUIT POTPIE

This hearty meal in one takes just 10 minutes to assemble before you can pop it in the oven.
—Dorothy Smith, El Dorado, AR

PREP: 10 min. • **BAKE:** 25 min.
MAKES: 4 servings

    1⅔ cups frozen mixed vegetables,
        thawed
    1½ cups cubed cooked chicken
    1   can (10¾ oz.) condensed
        cream of chicken soup, undiluted
    ¼   tsp. dried thyme
    1   cup biscuit/baking mix
    ½   cup 2% milk
    1   large egg

1. Preheat oven to 400°. In a large bowl, combine the vegetables, chicken, soup and thyme. Pour into an ungreased deep-dish 9-in. pie plate. Combine the biscuit mix, milk and egg; spoon over chicken mixture.
2. Bake until topping is golden brown and toothpick inserted in center comes out clean, 25-30 minutes.
1 serving: 376 cal., 14g fat (4g sat. fat), 103mg chol., 966mg sod., 38g carb. (5g sugars, 5g fiber), 23g pro.

CHICKEN-PROSCIUTTO
PINWHEELS IN WINE SAUCE

CHICKEN-PROSCIUTTO PINWHEELS IN WINE SAUCE

We host a large group for holiday meals, and these pinwheels always go over well alongside the regular dishes. I often double this recipe and use two 13x9-in. pans.
—*Johnna Johnson, Scottsdale, AZ*

- -

PREP: 30 min. + chilling • **BAKE:** 30 min.
MAKES: 6 servings

- 6 boneless skinless chicken breast halves (6 oz. each)
- 6 thin slices prosciutto or deli ham
- 6 slices part-skim mozzarella cheese
- 2 large eggs, lightly beaten
- ½ cup Italian-style panko bread crumbs
- ½ cup butter, cubed
- 1 shallot, finely chopped
- 2 garlic cloves, minced
- 3 cups Madeira wine

1. Pound chicken breasts with a meat mallet to ¼-in. thickness; layer with the prosciutto and mozzarella. Roll up chicken from a short side; secure with toothpicks.
2. Place the eggs and bread crumbs in separate shallow bowls. Dip chicken in eggs, then roll in the crumbs to coat. Cut each chicken breast crosswise into 3 slices; place in a greased 13x9-in. baking dish, cut side down. Refrigerate, covered, overnight.
3. Preheat oven to 350°. Remove chicken from refrigerator; uncover and let stand while oven heats. In a small saucepan, heat butter over medium-high heat. Add shallot and garlic; cook and stir until tender, 1-2 minutes. Add wine. Bring to a boil; cook until the liquid is reduced to 1½ cups. Pour over chicken.
4. Bake, uncovered, until a thermometer reads 165°, 30-35 minutes. Discard toothpicks before serving.
3 pinwheels: 581 cal., 30g fat (15g sat. fat), 227mg chol., 827mg sod., 15g carb. (5g sugars, 0 fiber), 48g pro.

**TURKEY BISCUIT
SKILLET**

TURKEY BISCUIT SKILLET

My mother always made this while I was growing up. Now I make it for my husband and kids. I cut the biscuits into smaller pieces so they will brown nicely on top. I also sometimes add mushrooms to this recipe because my family likes them so much.
—*Keri Boffeli, Monticello, IA*

- -

TAKES: 30 min. • **MAKES:** 6 servings

- 1 Tbsp. butter
- ⅓ cup chopped onion
- ¼ cup all-purpose flour
- 1 can (10½ oz.) condensed chicken broth, undiluted
- ¼ cup fat-free milk
- ⅛ tsp. pepper
- 2 cups cubed cooked turkey breast
- 2 cups frozen peas and carrots (about 10 oz.), thawed
- 1 tube (12 oz.) refrigerated buttermilk biscuits, quartered

1. Preheat oven to 400°. Melt butter in a 10-in. cast-iron or other ovenproof skillet over medium-high heat. Add onion; cook and stir until tender, 2-3 minutes.
2. In a small bowl, mix flour, broth, milk and pepper until smooth; stir into pan. Bring to a boil, stirring constantly; cook and stir until thickened, 1-2 minutes. Add the turkey and frozen vegetables; heat through. Arrange biscuits over stew. Bake until the biscuits are golden brown, 15-20 minutes.
1 serving: 319 cal., 10g fat (4g sat. fat), 43mg chol., 878mg sod., 36g carb. (4g sugars, 2g fiber), 22g pro.

TEST KITCHEN TIPS

- This is a perfect use for leftover turkey during the holiday season. It also works well with chicken.
- The biscuits are plentiful, making this hearty dish just right for chilly weather.

Pork

SPINACH-ARTICHOKE
PORK TENDERLOIN

SPINACH-ARTICHOKE PORK TENDERLOIN

Stuffed with spinach and artichoke hearts, these pork medallions look fancy for guests. A sweet-sour sauce enhances the entree.
—*Linda Rae Lee, San Francisco, CA*

- -

PREP: 25 min. • **BAKE:** 25 min. + standing
MAKES: 4 servings

- 2 cups torn fresh baby spinach
- ½ cup frozen artichoke hearts, thawed and chopped
- ⅓ cup shredded Parmesan cheese
- ¼ tsp. dried rosemary, crushed
- 1 pork tenderloin (1 lb.)
- ½ tsp. salt, divided
- ⅛ tsp. pepper

SAUCE

- ½ cup thawed apple-cranberry juice concentrate
- ¼ cup balsamic vinegar
- 1 Tbsp. sugar

1. In a large cast-iron or other ovenproof skillet, cook the spinach in ¼ cup water over medium heat for 3-4 minutes or until wilted; drain well. In a large bowl, combine the spinach, artichokes, Parmesan cheese and rosemary; set aside.
2. Cut a lengthwise slit down center of tenderloin to within ½ in. of bottom. Open meat so it lies flat; cover with plastic wrap. Flatten to ¼-in. thickness; remove plastic. Sprinkle meat with ¼ tsp. salt; top with spinach mixture.
3. Close meat; tie with kitchen string and secure ends with toothpicks. Sprinkle with pepper and remaining salt. Place in skillet. Bake at 425° for 15 minutes.
4. Meanwhile, in a small saucepan, combine the sauce ingredients. Bring to a boil over medium heat. Reduce heat; simmer, uncovered, for 15 minutes. Pour over the meat. Bake until a thermometer reads 145°, 10 minutes longer. Let stand for 10 minutes before slicing. Discard the toothpicks.
1 serving: 259 cal., 6g fat (3g sat. fat), 68mg chol., 485mg sod., 24g carb. (21g sugars, 1g fiber), 26g pro.

SAUSAGE-STUFFED
PUMPKINS

GREEN BEAN HAM QUICHE

Here's a delicious, healthful way to use up leftover ham. Green beans make the dish fresh and snappy. Cheddar cheese works perfectly in this, too, if it's what you have on hand.

—Sandy Flick, Toledo, OH

PREP: 20 min. • BAKE: 35 min.
MAKES: 8 servings

- ½ lb. fresh green beans, trimmed and cut into 1-in. pieces
- 1 cup cubed fully cooked ham
- 1 jar (6 oz.) sliced mushrooms, drained
- 1 cup shredded Swiss cheese
- ½ cup finely chopped onion
- ⅛ tsp. garlic powder
- 3 large eggs, lightly beaten
- 1½ cups 2% milk
- ¾ cup biscuit/baking mix
- ½ tsp. salt
- ¼ tsp. pepper

1. Preheat oven to 400°. Place beans in a large saucepan and cover with water. Bring to a boil; cook, uncovered, until crisp-tender, 5 minutes.
2. Meanwhile, in a large bowl, combine the ham, mushrooms, cheese, onion and garlic powder. Drain beans; stir into ham mixture. Transfer to a 9-in. deep-dish pie plate coated with cooking spray.
3. In a small bowl, combine the eggs, milk, biscuit mix, salt and pepper just until blended; pour over ham mixture.
4. Bake until a knife inserted near the center comes out clean, 35-40 minutes. Let stand for 5 minutes before cutting.
1 slice: 198 cal., 10g fat (5g sat. fat), 108mg chol., 686mg sod., 14g carb. (4g sugars, 2g fiber), 13g pro.

"Wonderful recipe. We were doubtful about green beans in a quiche, but I had a ton of leftover ham to use up. The meal was awesome! I left out the mushrooms, and it turned out fine."
—CASEYJACIE, TASTEOFHOME.COM

SAUSAGE-STUFFED PUMPKINS

Baking a meal in a pumpkin is such a fun fall idea! To serve the dish, cut the pumpkin into wedges, giving each person both pumpkin and stuffing.

—Rebecca Baird, Salt Lake City, UT

PREP: 50 min. • BAKE: 1¼ hours
MAKES: 8 servings

- 2 cups water
- 1 cup uncooked brown rice
- 2 tsp. chicken bouillon granules
- ½ tsp. curry powder
- 1 lb. bulk Italian sausage
- 4 cups sliced fresh mushrooms
- 1 small onion, chopped
- 2 shallots, minced
- 1 garlic clove, minced
- 5 Tbsp. dried currants
- ¼ cup chicken broth
- 1 tsp. poultry seasoning
- ½ tsp. rubbed sage
- ¼ tsp. dried marjoram
- 2 medium pie pumpkins (2½ lbs. each)
- ½ tsp. salt
- ½ tsp. garlic powder

1. In a large saucepan, bring the water, rice, bouillon and curry powder to a boil. Reduce the heat; cover and simmer 45-50 minutes or until tender.
2. Meanwhile, in a large skillet, cook the sausage over medium heat until no longer pink, breaking it into crumbles; drain and set aside. In the same skillet, saute the mushrooms, onion and shallots 3-5 minutes or until vegetables are tender. Add garlic; cook 1 minute longer.
3. Reduce heat; add the currants, broth, poultry seasoning, sage and marjoram. Return sausage to the pan. Cook and stir 5-7 minutes or until liquid is absorbed. Remove from the heat; stir in rice.
4. Wash the pumpkins; cut a 3-in. circle around each stem. Remove tops and set aside. Remove and discard loose fibers; save seeds for another use. Prick inside each pumpkin with a fork; sprinkle with salt and garlic powder. Stuff with sausage mixture; replace tops.
5. Place in a 13x9-in. baking dish; add ½ in. water. Bake, uncovered, at 350° for 30 minutes. Cover loosely with foil; bake 45-50 minutes longer or until tender. Cut each pumpkin into 4 wedges to serve.
1 slice: 337 cal., 13g fat (4g sat. fat), 31mg chol., 744mg sod., 46g carb. (9g sugars, 4g fiber), 13g pro.

PROSCIUTTO
PESTO PIZZA

PROSCIUTTO PESTO PIZZA

I developed this pizza for my young grandson who hasn't acquired a taste for veggies yet. He scarfs it up and doesn't even notice the edamame. It's also a hit with my other grandkids and nieces—not to mention all of their parents!
—Don Manzagol, Campbell, CA

- -

TAKES: 25 min. • **MAKES:** 6 servings

- 1 tube (11 oz.) refrigerated thin pizza crust
- ¼ cup prepared pesto
- 2 cups shredded Monterey Jack cheese
- 3 oz. thinly sliced prosciutto, cut into bite-sized pieces
- ½ cup frozen shelled edamame, thawed
- ½ cup sliced almonds

Preheat oven to 400°. Unroll and press the dough onto bottom of a greased 15x10x1-in. baking pan. Spread pesto over pizza dough; sprinkle with cheese, prosciutto, edamame and almonds. Bake until cheese is melted and crust is golden brown, 15-18 minutes.

2 pieces: 419 cal., 25g fat (10g sat. fat), 46mg chol., 922mg sod., 28g carb. (4g sugars, 2g fiber), 21g pro.

RHUBARBECUE

This simmered sauce is a roller-coaster ride for your tongue. It is a wonderful blend of complex flavors that goes with any meat.
—R.D. Stendel-Freels, Albuquerque, NM

- -

PREP: 45 min. • **BAKE:** 2½ hours
MAKES: 8 servings

- 1½ tsp. salt
- 1½ tsp. paprika
- 1 tsp. coarsely ground pepper
- 3 to 4 lbs. boneless country-style pork ribs

SAUCE
- 3 cups sliced fresh or frozen rhubarb (about 7 stalks)
- 2 cups fresh strawberries, halved
- 2 to 3 Tbsp. olive oil
- 1 medium onion, chopped
- 1 cup packed brown sugar
- ¾ cup ketchup

RHUBARBECUE

- ½ cup red wine vinegar
- ½ cup bourbon
- ¼ cup reduced-sodium soy sauce
- ¼ cup honey
- 2 Tbsp. Worcestershire sauce
- 2 tsp. garlic powder
- 1 tsp. crushed red pepper flakes
- 1 tsp. coarsely ground pepper

1. Preheat oven to 325°. Mix the salt, paprika and pepper; sprinkle over ribs. Refrigerate, covered, while preparing the sauce.

2. In a large saucepan, combine rhubarb and strawberries; add water to cover. Bring to a boil. Cook, uncovered, until rhubarb is tender, 8-10 minutes. Drain; return to pan. Mash until blended.

3. In a Dutch oven, heat 1 Tbsp. oil over medium heat. Brown ribs in batches, adding more oil as needed. Remove from pan.

4. Add onion to same pan; cook and stir until tender, 4-6 minutes. Add remaining ingredients; stir in rhubarb mixture. Return ribs to pan, turning to coat. Bring to a boil. Cover; bake until ribs are tender, about 2 hours. Bake, uncovered, until the sauce is slightly thickened, 30-35 minutes.

4 oz. cooked pork with ⅓ cup sauce: 533 cal., 19g fat (6g sat. fat), 98mg chol., 1158mg sod., 52g carb. (45g sugars, 2g fiber), 31g pro.

TEST KITCHEN TIP

Country-style ribs come from the loin end close to the shoulder. They're generally considered the meatiest type of rib. Country-style ribs are sold as a bone-in rack and as single ribs, with bones or boneless.

STUFFED APPLE PORK CHOPS

My family has used apples for many fabulous dishes, including this pork chop recipe from my grandmother that uses apples, apple butter and apple cider. I adapted the meal for two. My boyfriend loves it served with a baked sweet potato and a green salad.
—*Heather Kenney, Arlington, VA*

- -

PREP: 30 min. • **BAKE:** 15 min.
MAKES: 2 servings

- 2 Tbsp. apple butter
- 2 Tbsp. cider vinegar
- 1 Tbsp. Dijon mustard
- 2 to 3 tsp. minced fresh rosemary
- 2 boneless butterflied pork chops (6 oz. each)
- ¾ tsp. salt
- ¼ tsp. pepper
- 1 large tart apple, chopped
- ⅓ cup chopped sweet onion
- 2 Tbsp. butter
- ¾ cup apple cider or juice

1. Preheat oven to 350°. In a small bowl, combine apple butter, vinegar, mustard and rosemary. Flatten pork chops to ½-in. thickness; sprinkle with salt and pepper. Brush with apple butter mixture.
2. Combine apple and onion; place over 1 side of each pork chop. Fold other side of pork over filling and secure with toothpicks.
3. In a small ovenproof skillet, brown the chops in butter on each side, 3-4 minutes. Add cider.
4. Bake, uncovered, until apples and onions are tender and a thermometer reads 145°, 15-20 minutes. Remove chops and keep warm. Bring pan juices to a boil; cook until reduced by half. Discard toothpicks. Serve pork with sauce.
1 serving: 440 cal., 17g fat (8g sat. fat), 102mg chol., 1203mg sod., 40g carb. (31g sugars, 4g fiber), 35g pro.

PINEAPPLE-ONION
PORK CHOPS

PINEAPPLE-ONION PORK CHOPS

I prepared these tender pork chops for my teenage grandson's birthday meal. Brown sugar and pineapple provide sweetness for the onion-topped entree.
—*Marjorie Bruner, Parchment, MI*

- -

PREP: 25 min. • **BAKE:** 25 min.
MAKES: 6 servings

- ¼ cup all-purpose flour
- ½ tsp. salt
- ¼ tsp. pepper
- 6 boneless pork loin chops (¾ in. thick)
- 3 Tbsp. butter
- ½ cup water
- 1 medium onion, sliced
- 1½ cups pineapple juice
- 2 Tbsp. brown sugar
- 2 Tbsp. honey mustard

1. In a large shallow bowl, combine the flour, salt and pepper. Add pork chops and toss to coat. In a skillet, brown the chops on both sides in butter. Transfer to a greased 13x9-in. baking dish. Add water to dish. Place onion over chops. Cover and bake at 350° for 20 minutes.
2. Meanwhile, in a saucepan, combine the pineapple juice, brown sugar and mustard. Bring to a boil. Reduce heat; simmer, uncovered, 10 minutes. Pour over pork. Bake, uncovered, 5-10 minutes or until meat juices run clear.
1 pork chop: 294 cal., 13g fat (6g sat. fat), 70mg chol., 332mg sod., 22g carb. (16g sugars, 1g fiber), 23g pro.

CHORIZO & CHIPOTLE STUFFED CABBAGE CUPS

Our family and friends enjoy Polish recipes, and my hubby loves Mexican, too. I created delicious cabbage rolls that highlight the warm and inviting flavors of both cultures.
—Brenda Watts, Gaffney, SC

PREP: 45 min. • **BAKE:** 15 min.
MAKES: 6 servings

8   oz. pepper jack cheese, divided
2   finely chopped chipotle peppers in adobo sauce plus 1 Tbsp. sauce, divided
1   can (15 oz.) crushed tomatoes
½   cup chili sauce
1   medium head cabbage
2   Tbsp. olive oil
8   oz. bulk pork sausage
8   oz. fresh chorizo
⅔   cup chopped onion
1   jalapeno pepper, seeded and finely chopped
2   garlic cloves, minced
½   cup dry bread crumbs

1. Preheat oven to 350°. Grease 12 muffin cups. Shred a fourth of the cheese; cut remaining cheese into 12 cubes. Set aside.
2. In a small saucepan, bring 1 chipotle in adobo sauce, crushed tomatoes and chili sauce to a boil over medium heat. Reduce heat; simmer, uncovered, 5 minutes. Reserve ½ cup; cover remaining sauce and keep warm.
3. Meanwhile, core cabbage head. In a Dutch oven, cook cabbage, stem side down, in boiling water to cover just until outer leaves begin to separate from head, about 2 minutes. Carefully remove the outer leaves and repeat until there are 12 leaves. (Refrigerate remaining cabbage for another use.) Pat leaves dry. Trim the thick vein from the bottom of each leaf, making a V-shaped cut. Set aside.
4. In a large nonstick skillet, heat oil over medium-high heat. Add sausage and chorizo; cook and stir, crumbling meat, 3-4 minutes. Stir in onion, jalapeno and remaining chipotle; cook until meat is no longer pink and vegetables are tender. Add garlic; cook 1 minute longer. Stir in bread crumbs and reserved sauce.
5. To assemble, spoon 2 tsp. sauce onto a cabbage leaf; add about 3 Tbsp. sausage mixture. Top with a cheese cube. Pull together cabbage edges to overlap; fold over filling. Place folded side down in prepared muffin cup. Repeat with remaining cabbage leaves. Top with remaining sauce. Bake until heated through, 15-20 minutes. Sprinkle with shredded cheese.

Freeze option: Cover and freeze baked cabbage cups on waxed paper-lined baking sheets until firm. Transfer to resealable freezer containers; return to freezer. To use, bake cabbage cups as directed, increasing time as necessary to heat through. Top with cheese.

Note: Wear disposable gloves when cutting hot peppers; the oils can burn skin. Avoid touching your face.

2 cabbage cups: 521 cal., 37g fat (14g sat. fat), 94mg chol., 1464mg sod., 24g carb. (10g sugars, 3g fiber), 25g pro.

CHORIZO & CHIPOTLE STUFFED CABBAGE CUPS

BROCCOLI SCALLOPED
POTATOES

TANGY TENDER PORK CHOPS

I have used this recipe for many years and always get compliments when I serve it. The saucy onion-and-pepper topping compliments the chops.
—*Thomas Maust, Berlin, PA*

PREP: 30 min. • **BAKE:** 20 min.
MAKES: 6 servings

- 6 bone-in pork loin chops (7 oz. each)
- 2 tsp. canola oil
- 2 celery ribs, finely chopped
- 1 small onion, finely chopped
- 1 Tbsp. butter
- ½ cup ketchup
- ¼ cup water
- 2 Tbsp. cider vinegar
- 1 Tbsp. brown sugar
- 1 Tbsp. lemon juice
- 1 Tbsp. Worcestershire sauce
- ¼ tsp. salt
- ⅛ tsp. pepper
- 1 small onion, thinly sliced
- 1 large green pepper, cut into rings

1. Preheat oven to 350°. In a large nonstick skillet, brown chops in oil in batches. Transfer to a 13x9-in. baking dish coated with cooking spray.
2. In the same pan, saute celery and chopped onion in butter until tender. Stir in ketchup, water, vinegar, brown sugar, lemon juice, Worcestershire sauce, salt and pepper. Bring to a boil. Reduce heat; cover and simmer until slightly reduced, 15-20 minutes.
3. Pour sauce over chops. Top with sliced onion and pepper rings. Cover and bake until a thermometer reads 145°, 20-25 minutes.
Freeze option: Place pork chops in freezer containers; top with sauce. Cool and freeze. To use, partially thaw in refrigerator overnight. Heat through in a covered saucepan, gently stirring sauce; add a little water if necessary.
1 pork chop: 284 cal., 12g fat (4g sat. fat), 91mg chol., 469mg sod., 12g carb. (10g sugars, 1g fiber), 31g pro. **Diabetic exchanges:** 4 lean meat, 1 starch, ½ fat.

BROCCOLI SCALLOPED POTATOES

The combination of ham and Swiss creates a wonderfully rich, smoky flavor. I also love that I can cook an entire meal—veggie and all—in one standout dish.
—*Denell Syslo, Fullerton, NE*

PREP: 25 min. • **BAKE:** 1 hour
MAKES: 8 servings

- ¼ cup butter, cubed
- 2 Tbsp. chopped onion
- 4 garlic cloves, minced
- 5 Tbsp. all-purpose flour
- ¼ tsp. white pepper
- ⅛ tsp. salt
- 2½ cups whole milk
- 2 cups shredded Swiss cheese, divided
- 2 lbs. potatoes, peeled and thinly sliced (about 4 cups)
- 2 cups julienned fully cooked ham
- 2 cups frozen broccoli florets, thawed and patted dry

1. Preheat oven to 350°. In a Dutch oven, heat butter over medium-high heat. Add onion and garlic; cook and stir until tender, 2-3 minutes. Stir in flour, white pepper and salt until blended; gradually whisk in milk. Bring to a boil, stirring constantly; cook and stir until thickened, 2 minutes.
2. Stir in 1 cup cheese. Reduce heat; cook until cheese is melted (sauce will be thick), 1-2 minutes. Remove from heat.
3. Add the potatoes, ham and broccoli to sauce; stir gently to coat. Transfer to 8 greased 8-oz. ramekins.
4. Bake, covered, 40 minutes. Sprinkle with remaining cheese. Bake, uncovered, until potatoes are tender and cheese is melted, 20-25 minutes longer.
1 serving: 309 cal., 17g fat (10g sat. fat), 61mg chol., 626mg sod., 23g carb. (3g sugars, 2g fiber), 17g pro.

TANGY TENDER
PORK CHOPS

BAKED PORK CHIMICHANGAS

Lean shredded pork and pinto beans combine with south-of-the-border green chiles and picante sauce.
—*LaDonna Reed, Ponca City, OK*

PREP: 15 min. + standing
BAKE: 1 hour 25 min. + standing
MAKES: 2½ dozen

- 1 lb. dried pinto beans
- 1 boneless pork loin roast (3 lbs.)
- 3 cans (4 oz. each) chopped green chiles
- 1 large onion, chopped
- ⅓ cup chili powder
- ½ cup reduced-sodium chicken broth
- 30 flour tortillas (6 in.)
- 4 cups shredded reduced-fat cheddar cheese
- 2 cups picante sauce
- 1 large egg white
- 2 tsp. water

1. Place beans in a stockpot; add water to cover by 2 in. Bring to a boil; boil for 2 minutes. Remove from heat; cover and let stand 1 hour. Drain and rinse beans.
2. Preheat oven to 350°. Place roast in a Dutch oven. Combine the chiles, onion, chili powder and beans. Spoon over roast. Cover and bake 30 minutes. Stir in broth; cover and bake until a thermometer reads 145°, 30-45 minutes longer.
3. Remove meat; let stand 10 minutes. Shred with 2 forks; set aside. Mash bean mixture; stir in shredded pork.
4. Spoon ⅓ cup mixture down the center of each tortilla; top with 2 Tbsp. cheese and 1 Tbsp. picante sauce. Fold sides and ends over filling and roll up. Place seam sides down on two 15x10x1-in. baking pans coated with cooking spray.
5. In a small bowl, whisk egg white and water; brush over tops. Bake, uncovered, until heated through, 25-30 minutes. Serve immediately.
Freeze option: Cool, wrap and freeze for up to 3 months. Place chimichangas on a baking sheet coated with cooking spray. Bake at 400° until heated through, 10-15 minutes.
1 serving: 276 cal., 8g fat (4g sat. fat), 36mg chol., 475mg sod., 30g carb. (0 sugars, 6g fiber), 20g pro. **Diabetic exchanges:** 2 starch, 2 lean meat.

HAM & PINEAPPLE KABOBS

For a twist on the usual holiday fare, my family turns ham and pineapple into juicy kabobs. The marinade gets its unique zip from hoisin, teriyaki and soy sauces.
—*Chandra Lane Sirois, Kansas City, MO*

PREP: 30 min. + marinating • **BAKE:** 15 min.
MAKES: 12 servings

- ¼ cup hoisin sauce
- ¼ cup unsweetened pineapple juice
- ¼ cup teriyaki sauce
- 1 Tbsp. honey
- 1½ tsp. rice vinegar
- 1½ tsp. reduced-sodium soy sauce

KABOBS
- 2 lbs. fully cooked boneless ham, cut into 1-in. pieces
- 1 large fresh pineapple, peeled, cored and cut into 1-in. cubes (about 4 cups)

1. In a large shallow dish, combine the first 6 ingredients. Add ham; turn to coat. Refrigerate, covered, overnight.
2. Preheat oven to 350°. Drain ham, reserving marinade. For glaze, pour marinade into a small saucepan; bring to a boil. Reduce heat; simmer, uncovered, 5-7 minutes or until slightly thickened, stirring occasionally. Remove from heat.
3. Meanwhile, on 12 metal or soaked wooden skewers, alternately thread ham and pineapple; place in a foil-lined 15x10x1-in. baking pan. Brush with glaze. Bake, uncovered, 15-20 minutes or until lightly browned.
1 kabob: 144 cal., 3g fat (1g sat. fat), 39mg chol., 1109mg sod., 15g carb. (12g sugars, 1g fiber), 15g pro.

HAM & PINEAPPLE KABOBS

MINI
SAUSAGE PIES

CAST-IRON SAUSAGE PIZZA

This shortcut pizza starts with frozen dough in a cast-iron pan. Add your family's favorite toppings for variety.
—Taste of Home *Test Kitchen*

PREP: 30 min. • **BAKE:** 20 min.
MAKES: 6 slices

- 1 loaf (1 lb.) frozen bread dough, thawed
- 2 tsp. cornmeal
- 1½ cups pizza sauce
- ½ lb. bulk Italian sausage, cooked and drained
- 1½ cups shredded part-skim mozzarella cheese, divided
- 1 tsp. dried oregano
- 1 small green pepper, sliced into rings
  Crushed red pepper flakes, optional

1. Preheat the oven to 425°. On a lightly floured surface, roll and stretch dough into a 10-in. circle. Cover; let rest for 10 minutes. Roll and stretch dough into a 12-in. circle. Grease a 10-in. cast-iron or other ovenproof skillet; sprinkle with cornmeal. Press dough onto bottom and 1 in. up sides of prepared skillet.
2. Spread with pizza sauce; top with sausage, 1 cup cheese, oregano and green pepper. Sprinkle with remaining ½ cup cheese. Bake until crust is golden brown, 20-25 minutes. If desired, sprinkle with red pepper flakes.

1 slice: 424 cal., 18g fat (6g sat. fat), 39mg chol., 1092mg sod., 45g carb. (7g sugars, 4g fiber), 20g pro.

❄ MINI SAUSAGE PIES

The simple ingredients and family-friendly flavor of these little sausage cups make them a go-to dinner favorite. The fact that every person gets his or her own pie makes them even better!
—*Kerry Dingwall, Wilmington, NC*

PREP: 35 min. • **BAKE:** 30 min.
MAKES: 1 dozen

- 1 pkg. (17.3 oz.) frozen puff pastry, thawed
- 1 lb. bulk sage pork sausage
- 6 green onions, chopped
- ½ cup chopped dried apricots
- ¼ tsp. pepper
- ⅛ tsp. ground nutmeg
- 1 large egg, lightly beaten

1. Preheat oven to 375°. On a lightly floured surface, unfold pastry sheets; roll each into a 16x12-in. rectangle. Using a floured cutter, cut twelve 4-in. circles from 1 sheet; press onto bottoms and up sides of ungreased muffin cups. Using a floured cutter, cut twelve 3½-in. circles from remaining sheet.
2. Mix sausage, green onions, apricots and spices lightly but thoroughly. Place ¼ cup mixture into each pastry cup. Brush edges of smaller pastry circles with egg; place over pies, pressing edges to seal. Brush with egg. Cut slits in top.
3. Bake until pies are golden brown and a thermometer inserted in filling reads 160°, 30-35 minutes. Cool 5 minutes before removing from pan to a wire rack.
Freeze option: Cool baked pies and freeze in freezer containers. To use, partially thaw pies in refrigerator overnight. Reheat on a baking sheet in a preheated 350° oven until heated through, 14-17 minutes.
2 mini pies: 551 cal., 36g fat (10g sat. fat), 82mg chol., 784mg sod., 42g carb. (5g sugars, 5g fiber), 16g pro.

SHEET-PAN PORK SUPPER

I created this recipe to suit our family's needs. It is a delicious meal in one and so quick and easy to clean up since you use one pan for everything! Use any variety of small potatoes—fingerlings or other colored potatoes are a fun and delicious option.

—*Debbie Johnson, Centertown, MO*

PREP: 10 min. • **BAKE:** 35 min.
MAKES: 8 servings

- ¼ cup butter, softened
- 2 tsp. minced fresh chives or 1 tsp. dried minced chives
- 1 garlic clove, minced
- 1½ lbs. fresh green beans, trimmed
- 2 Tbsp. olive oil, divided
- ¾ tsp. salt, divided
- ½ tsp. pepper, divided
- 1½ lbs. baby red potatoes, halved
- 2 pork tenderloins (about 1 lb. each)
- ½ cup teriyaki glaze or hoisin sauce
  Optional: Toasted sesame seeds and additional fresh minced chives

1. Preheat oven to 450°. In a small bowl, combine butter, chives and garlic; set aside. In a second bowl, combine green beans with 1 Tbsp. olive oil, ¼ tsp. salt and ¼ tsp. pepper. Arrange green beans down 1 side of a 15x10x1-in. baking pan. In the same bowl, combine potatoes with the remaining olive oil, salt and pepper. Arrange potatoes on other side of pan.
2. Pat pork dry with paper towels; brush with teriyaki glaze. Place on top of beans.
3. Bake until a thermometer inserted in pork reads 145°, 25-30 minutes. Remove tenderloins to a cutting board and top with 2 Tbsp. seasoned butter. Tent pork with aluminum foil; let stand.
4. Stir green beans and potatoes; return to oven and cook until vegetables are tender and lightly browned, about 10 minutes longer. Stir remaining seasoned butter into vegetables.
5. Slice pork; serve with vegetables and pan drippings. If desired, top with sesame seeds and additional minced chives.
3 oz. cooked pork with 1¼ cups vegetables: 354 cal., 14g fat (6g sat. fat), 79mg chol., 1186mg sod., 30g carb. (9g sugars, 5g fiber), 28g pro.

HAM RAVIOLI BAKE

HAM RAVIOLI BAKE

I based this recipe on a dish my husband likes to order when we go out for Italian food. Not only does he love it, my young daughter does, too. She'll grab a whole ravioli and eat it!

—*Jennifer Berger, Eau Claire, WI*

PREP: 20 min. • **BAKE:** 20 min.
MAKES: 4 servings

- 1 pkg. (25 oz.) frozen cheese ravioli
- 1½ cups cubed fully cooked ham
- 1⅓ cups sliced fresh mushrooms
- ¼ cup chopped onion
- ¼ cup chopped green pepper
- 1 Tbsp. canola oil
- 1 jar (15 oz.) Alfredo sauce

1. Cook ravioli according to package directions. Meanwhile, in a large skillet, cook the ham, mushrooms, onion and green pepper in oil over medium heat 4-5 minutes or until vegetables are crisp-tender.
2. Spread 2 Tbsp. Alfredo sauce into a greased 8-in. square baking dish. Stir remaining sauce into ham mixture; cook 3-4 minutes or until heated through.
3. Drain ravioli; place half in prepared baking dish. Top with half the ham mixture. Repeat layers. Cover and bake at 375° for 20-25 minutes or until bubbly.
1 serving: 653 cal., 31g fat (16g sat. fat), 137mg chol., 1496mg sod., 61g carb. (5g sugars, 3g fiber), 35g pro.

MUSTARD PORK MEDALLIONS

These tasty pork medallions brushed with mustard and coated with seasoned dry bread crumbs before baking come out perfectly tender and juicy.
—Taste of Home *Test Kitchen*

TAKES: 25 min. • **MAKES:** 4 servings

- ½ cup seasoned dry bread crumbs
- ½ tsp. dried thyme
- ¼ tsp. garlic salt
- ¼ tsp. onion powder
- 1¼ lbs. pork tenderloin
- ¼ cup Dijon mustard
- 1 Tbsp. butter, melted

1. Preheat oven to 425°. In a shallow bowl, combine the crumbs, thyme, garlic salt and onion powder; set aside. Cut tenderloin widthwise into 12 pieces and pound each piece to ¼-in. thickness. Combine mustard and butter; brush on each side of pork, then roll in reserved crumb mixture.

2. Place in a greased shallow baking pan. Bake, uncovered, 10 minutes. Turn and bake until a thermometer reads 145°, about 5 minutes longer.

1 serving: 260cal.,8g fat (4g sat. fat), 87mg chol., 661mg sod., 10g carb. (1g sugars, 1g fiber), 25g pro. **Diabetic exchanges:** 3 lean meat, ½ starch, ½ fat.

LINGUINE WITH HAM & SWISS CHEESE

LINGUINE WITH HAM & SWISS CHEESE

My grandmother used to make this for parties and potlucks. It was loved by all back then, and it still is today. The classic combination of pasta, ham, cheese and a creamy sauce makes it irresistible.
—Mary Savor, Woodburn, IN

PREP: 15 min. • **BAKE:** 50 min.
MAKES: 8 servings

- 8 oz. uncooked linguine, broken in half
- 2 cups cubed fully cooked ham
- 1 can (10¾ oz.) condensed cream of mushroom soup, undiluted
- 2½ cups shredded Swiss cheese, divided
- 1 cup sour cream
- 1 medium onion, chopped
- ½ cup finely chopped green pepper
- 2 Tbsp. butter, melted

1. Cook linguine according to package directions; drain. Meanwhile, in a large bowl, combine the ham, soup, 2 cups cheese, sour cream, onion, green pepper and butter. Add the pasta; toss to coat.

2. Transfer to a greased 13x9-in. baking dish. Cover and bake casserole at 350° for 35 minutes. Uncover; sprinkle with remaining cheese. Bake until cheese is melted, 15-20 minutes longer.

1 cup: 402 cal., 23g fat (12g sat. fat), 68mg chol., 797mg sod., 27g carb. (3g sugars, 2g fiber), 22g pro.

CHILE TAMALE PIE

This crowd-pleasing potluck dish is easy to prepare. It packs a little heat, a little sweet and a big-time authentic southwestern flavor. There is no substitute for freshly ground chiles. A small food processor on high speed may be used to grind the chiles and cumin, or use a dedicated coffee grinder for fresh spices. It is a fantastic $15 investment for fresh spices anytime— and your palate will thank you!
—*Ralph Stamm, Dayton, OH*

PREP: 45 min. • **BAKE:** 50 min. + standing
MAKES: 12 servings

1 can (15¼ oz.) whole kernel corn
2 cups masa harina
1 can (14½ oz.) chicken broth
2 Tbsp. butter, melted
1 large egg, lightly beaten
2½ lbs. boneless pork loin roast, cut into ½-in. pieces
1 medium onion, chopped
1 can (16 oz.) refried beans
2 dried Anaheim chiles, chopped
2 dried ancho chiles, chopped
3 oz. Mexican or semisweet chocolate, grated
⅓ cup orange juice
2 Tbsp. lime juice
1 Tbsp. garlic powder
3 tsp. cumin seeds, toasted and crushed
¾ cup minced fresh cilantro, optional
1 jalapeno pepper, seeded and chopped, optional
2 cups shredded cheddar cheese

1. Drain corn, reserving liquid; set corn aside. Place masa harina in a large bowl. In a small bowl, combine broth, butter, egg and reserved corn liquid; stir into masa harina just until moistened. Set aside.
2. In a large skillet coated with cooking spray, cook pork and onion over medium heat until pork is no longer pink. Add the beans, chiles, chocolate, orange juice, lime juice, garlic powder, cumin, reserved corn, and cilantro and jalapeno if desired. Bring to a boil. Reduce heat; simmer, uncovered, 15 minutes. Meanwhile, preheat the oven to 325°.
3. Transfer to a greased 13x9-in. baking dish; sprinkle with cheese. Spread masa harina mixture over cheese.
4. Bake, uncovered, until golden brown, 50-60 minutes. Let stand for 10 minutes before serving.
1 cup: 371 cal., 15g fat (8g sat. fat), 93mg chol., 496mg sod., 32g carb. (7g sugars, 6g fiber), 28g pro.

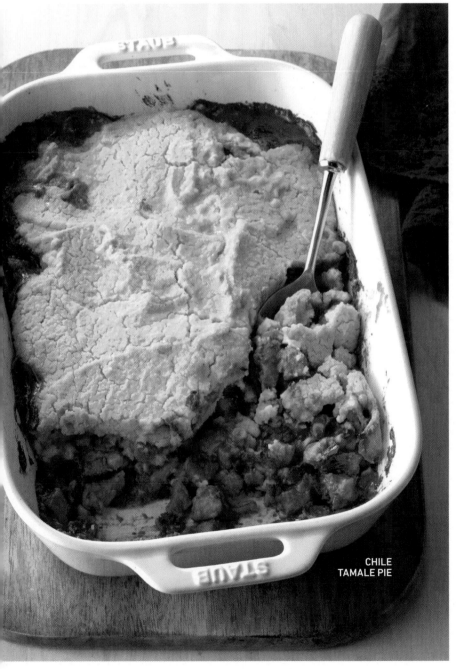

CHILE
TAMALE PIE

TEST KITCHEN TIP
Masa harina is a corn flour commonly used in Latin American cuisines. It's the base of corn tortillas and tamale fillings. Substitute cornmeal or corn tortillas finely ground in a food processor if you don't have masa harina.

DR SPICY
BBQ PORK

HAM & CHEESE POCKETS

These unique sandwich pockets are filled with ingredients most kids enjoy.
—*Callie Myers, Rockport, TX*

PREP: 15 min. + rising • BAKE: 15 min.
MAKES: 10 servings

- 1 loaf (1 lb.) frozen bread dough, thawed
- 2½ cups finely chopped fully cooked ham
- 1 cup shredded Swiss cheese
- 1 large egg yolk
- 1 Tbsp. water

1. Let dough rise according to package directions. Punch down; divide into 10 pieces. On a lightly floured surface, roll each piece into a 5-in. circle.
2. Preheat oven to 375°. Place 1 circle on a greased baking sheet; top with about ¼ cup ham and 2 Tbsp. cheese to within ½ in. of edge. Press filling to flatten. Combine egg yolk and water; brush edges of dough. Fold dough over filling and pinch edges to seal. Repeat with the remaining dough and filling. Brush tops with the remaining egg yolk mixture.
3. Bake pockets until golden brown, 15-20 minutes. Serve warm or cold.
1 pocket: 229 cal., 9g fat (3g sat. fat), 50mg chol., 729mg sod., 25g carb. (2g sugars, 1g fiber), 14g pro.

"If you don't have time to wait for the bread dough to thaw and rise, use refrigerated pizza crust. Tastes terrific, and uses a lot less time!"
—SOREN, TASTEOFHOME.COM

❄️
DR SPICY BBQ PORK

I served this at my son's graduation party and kept it warm in a slow cooker after roasting it in the oven. The pork is superb by itself or piled high on rolls. For a classic combination, serve it with warm biscuits and coleslaw.
—*Michelle Gauer, Spicer, MN*

PREP: 25 min. • BAKE: 4 hours
MAKES: 12 servings

- 1 boneless pork shoulder roast (5 to 7 lbs.)
- 1 tsp. garlic powder
- ½ tsp. salt
- ½ tsp. freshly ground pepper
- 6 chipotle peppers in adobo sauce, finely chopped (about ⅓ cup)
- 1 large sweet onion, halved and sliced
- 2 Tbsp. brown sugar
- 2 cans (12 oz. each) Dr Pepper
- 1 cup barbecue sauce
  Optional: French-fried onions, biscuits and deli coleslaw

1. Preheat oven to 325°. Sprinkle roast with garlic powder, salt and pepper; rub with chipotle peppers. Place in a Dutch oven. Top with sweet onion; sprinkle with brown sugar. Pour Dr Pepper around roast. Bake, covered, until meat is tender, 4-4½ hours.
2. Remove roast; cool slightly. Strain cooking juices, reserving onion; skim fat from juices.
3. Shred pork with 2 forks. Return juices, onion and pork to Dutch oven. Stir in barbecue sauce; heat through over medium heat, stirring occasionally. If desired, sprinkle with french-fried onions and serve with biscuits and coleslaw.
Freeze option: Freeze cooled meat mixture in freezer containers. To use, partially thaw in refrigerator overnight. Heat through in a saucepan, stirring occasionally; add a little water if necessary.
⅔ cup pork mixture: 372 cal., 20g fat (7g sat. fat), 112mg chol., 466mg sod., 15g carb. (14g sugars, 1g fiber), 33g pro.

HAM & CHEESE
POCKETS

Fish & Seafood

BROILED
LOBSTER TAIL

BROILED LOBSTER TAIL

No matter where you live, these succulent, buttery lobster tails are just a few minutes away. Here in Iowa, we use frozen lobster with delicious results, but if you're near the ocean, by all means use fresh. Serve the lobster with melted butter, or whip up one of the flavored butters below.
—*Lauren McAnelly, Des Moines, IA*

PREP: 30 min. • **COOK:** 5 min.
MAKES: 4 servings

 4 **lobster tails (5 to 6 oz. each), thawed**
 ¼ **cup cold butter, cut into thin slices**
     Salt and pepper to taste
     Lemon wedges

1. Preheat broiler. Using kitchen scissors, cut a 2-in.-wide rectangle from the top shell of each lobster tail; loosen from lobster meat and remove.
2. Pull away edges of remaining shell to release lobster meat from sides; pry meat loose from bottom shell, keeping tail end attached. Place in a foil-lined 15x10x1-in. pan. Arrange the butter slices over the lobster meat.
3. Broil 5-6 in. from heat until the meat is opaque, 5-8 minutes. Season with salt and pepper to taste; serve with lemon wedges.
1 lobster tail: 211 cal., 13g fat (8g sat. fat), 211mg chol., 691mg sod., 0 carb. (0 sugars, 0 fiber), 24g pro.
Lemon-Chive Butter: Add 2 Tbsp. chopped fresh chives, 2 Tbsp. chopped fresh parsley, 1 Tbsp. minced shallot, 1 minced garlic clove, ½ tsp. grated lemon zest and ¼ tsp. salt to ¼ cup softened butter.
Chimichurri Butter: Add 2 Tbsp. chopped fresh cilantro, 2 Tbsp. chopped fresh parsley, 1 Tbsp. minced shallot, 1 tsp. grated lemon zest, 1 tsp. minced fresh oregano, 1 minced garlic clove, ¼ tsp. salt and ⅛ tsp. crushed red pepper flakes to ¼ cup softened butter.

This thick, gooey tuna-spinach bake has been one of our family's favorites for years.
—*Karla Hamrick, Wapakoneta, OH*

- -

PREP: 25 min. • **BAKE:** 50 min.
MAKES: 8 servings

   5   cups uncooked egg noodles
   2   cups sour cream
1½   cups mayonnaise
   2   to 3 tsp. lemon juice
   2   to 3 tsp. 2% milk
   ¼   tsp. salt
   1   pkg. (10 oz.) frozen chopped spinach, thawed and squeezed dry
   1   pkg. (6 oz.) chicken stuffing mix
   ⅓   cup seasoned bread crumbs
   1   can (6 oz.) tuna, drained and flaked
   3   Tbsp. grated Parmesan cheese

1. Cook noodles according to package directions. Meanwhile, in a large bowl, combine the sour cream, mayonnaise, lemon juice, milk and salt. Stir in the spinach, stuffing mix, bread crumbs and tuna until well combined. Preheat oven to 350°.
2. Drain noodles and place in a greased 13x9-in. baking dish. Top with the tuna mixture; sprinkle with cheese. Cover and bake 45 minutes. Uncover; bake until lightly browned and heated through, 5-10 minutes longer.
Freeze option: Cool unbaked casserole; cover and freeze. To use, partially thaw in refrigerator overnight. Remove from refrigerator 30 minutes before baking. Preheat oven to 350°. Bake casserole as directed, increasing time as necessary to heat through and for a thermometer inserted in center to read 165°.
1 serving: 673 cal., 46g fat (12g sat. fat), 90mg chol., 927mg sod., 42g carb. (5g sugars, 2g fiber), 17g pro.

**APRICOT CRAB
STUFFED ACORN SQUASH**

This light squash recipe is quick, simple and bursting with rich flavors. It looks so elegant when served on a lovely platter.
—*Judy Armstrong, Prairieville, LA*

- -

PREP: 20 min. • **BAKE:** 35 min.
MAKES: 8 servings

   2   large acorn squash, quartered and seeds removed
   ½   cup apricot nectar, divided
   1   tsp. salt, divided
   1   tsp. white pepper, divided
   1   tsp. butter
   1   tsp. olive oil
   4   green onions, thinly sliced, plus additional for garnish
   ⅓   cup dried apricots, chopped
   1   garlic clove, minced
   ½   cup half-and-half cream
   4   cans (6 oz. each) lump crabmeat, drained

1. Preheat oven to 375°. Place squash in a greased 13x9-in. baking pan; drizzle with ¼ cup apricot nectar. Sprinkle with ½ tsp. each salt and white pepper. Bake, covered, until fork-tender, 35-40 minutes.
2. Meanwhile, in a large skillet, heat butter and oil over medium-high heat. Add green onions; cook and stir 3-5 minutes or until tender. Add the apricots and garlic; cook 1 minute longer. Stir in half-and-half and the remaining apricot nectar, salt and white pepper. Bring to a boil; reduce the heat. Simmer for 5 minutes. Gently stir in crab; heat through.
3. Arrange squash on a serving dish; spoon crab mixture over top. Sprinkle with additional green onions.
1 serving: 217 cal., 3g fat (2g sat. fat), 91mg chol., 794mg sod., 31g carb. (11g sugars, 4g fiber), 18g pro. **Diabetic exchanges:** 2 starch, 2 lean meat, ½ fat.

**APRICOT CRAB
STUFFED ACORN SQUASH**

PUFF PASTRY SALMON BUNDLES

SPEEDY SHRIMP FLATBREADS

My husband and I are hooked on flatbread pizzas. I make at least one a week just to have something tasty around as a snack. This one came together easily because I had all the ingredients on hand.
—*Cheryl Woodson, Liberty, MO*

TAKES: 15 min. • **MAKES:** 2 servings

- 2 naan flatbreads or whole pita breads
- 1 pkg. (5.2 oz.) garlic-herb spreadable cheese
- ½ lb. peeled and deveined cooked shrimp (31-40 per pound)
- ½ cup chopped oil-packed sun-dried tomatoes
- ¼ cup fresh basil leaves Lemon wedges, optional

Preheat oven to 400°. Place flatbreads on a baking sheet. Spread with cheese; top with shrimp and tomatoes. Bake until heated through, 4-6 minutes. Cut flatbreads in half; sprinkle with basil. If desired, serve with lemon wedges.

1 flatbread: 634 cal., 41g fat (24g sat. fat), 263mg chol., 1163mg sod., 38g carb. (3g sugars, 3g fiber), 33g pro.

PUFF PASTRY SALMON BUNDLES

The combination of tender salmon, fresh cucumber sauce and a crisp, flaky crust makes this impressive dish perfect for special occasions. Mom likes to decorate the pastry with a star or leaf design for the holidays.
—*Kimberly Laabs, Hartford, WI*

PREP: 20 min. • **BAKE:** 25 min.
MAKES: 8 servings

- 2 pkg. (17.3 oz. each) frozen puff pastry, thawed
- 8 salmon fillets (6 oz. each), skin removed
- 1 large egg
- 1 Tbsp. water
- 2 cups shredded cucumber
- 1 cup sour cream
- 1 cup mayonnaise
- 1 tsp. dill weed
- ½ tsp. salt

1. Preheat oven to 400°. On a lightly floured surface, roll each pastry sheet into a 12x10-in. rectangle. Cut each into two 10x6-in. rectangles. Place a salmon fillet in the center of each rectangle.
2. Beat egg and water; lightly brush over pastry edges. Bring opposite corners of pastry over each fillet; pinch seams to seal tightly. Place seam side down in a greased 15x10x1-in. baking pan; brush with remaining egg mixture.
3. Bake until the pastry is golden brown, 25-30 minutes. In a small bowl, combine the cucumber, sour cream, mayonnaise, dill and salt. Serve with bundles.
1 serving: 611 cal., 46g fat (11g sat. fat), 69mg chol., 536mg sod., 36g carb. (2g sugars, 5g fiber), 11g pro.

SPEEDY SHRIMP
FLATBREADS

CRISPY ALMOND
TILAPIA

CRISPY ALMOND TILAPIA

Since changing to a healthier style of cooking, I've come up with new coatings for baked fish. I use almonds, panko bread crumbs and a smidge of hot sauce to add crunchy texture with nice heat.
—*Amanda Flinner, Beaver, PA*

- -

TAKES: 30 min. • **MAKES:** 4 servings

- 1 large egg
- ¼ cup Louisiana-style hot sauce
- ¾ cup slivered almonds, chopped and toasted
- ⅓ cup panko bread crumbs
- 1 tsp. grated lemon zest
- 1 tsp. seafood seasoning
- ¼ tsp. garlic powder
- 4 tilapia fillets (4 oz. each)
- ½ tsp. salt
- ¼ tsp. pepper

1. Preheat oven to 400°. Whisk together egg and hot sauce in a shallow bowl. In a separate shallow bowl, toss together the next 5 ingredients.

2. Halve fillets lengthwise; sprinkle with salt and pepper. Dip in egg mixture, then in almond mixture, patting to adhere; place on a greased or parchment-lined baking sheet. Bake until lightly browned and fish just begins to flake easily with a fork, 12-15 minutes.

2 fillet pieces: 251 cal., 13g fat (2g sat. fat), 102mg chol., 537mg sod., 9g carb. (1g sugars, 3g fiber), 28g pro. **Diabetic exchanges:** 4 lean meat, 2 fat.

MISO SALMON

MISO SALMON

I love miso salmon! It was the obvious choice for developing a healthy weeknight meal. This dish is full of Asian flavors and fresh, colorful veggies. It is so beautiful and doesn't feel as if the meal was thrown together quickly.
—*Ann Piscitelli, Nokomis, FL*

- -

PREP: 15 min. • **BAKE:** 15 min.
MAKES: 4 servings

- ¼ cup rice vinegar
- 4½ tsp. honey
- 3 Tbsp. white miso paste, divided
- ⅓ cup plus 1 Tbsp. canola oil, divided
- ½ tsp. sesame oil
- 4 salmon fillets (4 oz. each)
- 2 cups fresh snow peas
- 1 medium sweet red pepper, julienned
- 1 small onion, halved and thinly sliced
- 1 pkg. (8½ oz.) ready-to-serve whole grain brown and wild rice medley
- 6 oz. fresh baby spinach (about 7 cups) Black sesame seeds

1. In a small bowl, whisk vinegar, honey and 4½ tsp. miso until smooth. Gradually whisk in ⅓ cup canola oil and the sesame oil; set aside.

2. Spread remaining 4½ tsp. miso over salmon. Bake at 400° for 12-15 minutes, or until fish just begins to flake easily with a fork.

3. Meanwhile, in a large skillet, heat remaining canola oil over medium heat. Add snow peas, pepper and onion; cook and stir until crisp-tender, 8-10 minutes. Add rice. Cook and stir until heated through. Remove from the heat. Stir in spinach until wilted. Serve with salmon; drizzle with reserved vinaigrette and sprinkle with sesame seeds.

1 salmon fillet with 1 cup rice mixture and 3 Tbsp. vinaigrette: 591 cal., 36g fat (4g sat. fat), 57mg chol., 1255mg sod., 42g carb. (16g sugars, 4g fiber), 26g pro.

SALSA CATFISH

Give your fish a southwestern kick with this change-of-pace idea. My sister doesn't like seafood, so I figured I'd disguise it with a mix of interesting tastes and textures. Everyone was surprised by the slightly crunchy tortilla chip coating.
—*Teresa Hubbard, Russellville, AL*

TAKES: 20 min. • **MAKES:** 4 servings

- 1 cup finely crushed baked tortilla chip scoops
- ½ to 1 tsp. chili powder
- 3 Tbsp. lemon juice
- 1 Tbsp. canola oil
- 4 catfish fillets (4 oz. each)
- 1 cup salsa, warmed

1. Preheat oven to 450°. In a shallow bowl, combine the tortilla chip crumbs and chili powder. In another bowl, combine lemon juice and oil. Dip fish in lemon mixture, then coat with crumb mixture.

2. Place in a 13x9-in. baking dish coated with cooking spray. Sprinkle with any remaining crumbs.

3. Bake until fish just begins to flake easily with a fork, 8-10 minutes. Serve with the salsa.

1 serving: 278 cal., 16g fat (3g sat. fat), 53mg chol., 429mg sod., 12g carb. (3g sugars, 3g fiber), 19g pro. **Diabetic exchanges:** 3 lean meat, 1½ starch, ½ fat.

CRAB-STUFFED FLOUNDER WITH HERBED AIOLI

If you enjoy seafood, you'll love this scrumptious flounder. The light and creamy aioli sauce tops it off with fresh tones of chives and garlic.
—*Beverly O'Ferrall, Linkwood, MD*

PREP: 20 min. • **BAKE:** 20 min.
MAKES: 6 servings

- ¼ cup egg substitute
- 2 Tbsp. fat-free milk
- 1 Tbsp. minced chives
- 1 Tbsp. reduced-fat mayonnaise
- 1 Tbsp. Dijon mustard
  Dash hot pepper sauce
- 1 lb. lump crabmeat
- 6 flounder fillets (6 oz. each)
  Paprika

AIOLI
- ⅓ cup reduced-fat mayonnaise
- 2 tsp. minced chives
- 2 tsp. minced fresh parsley
- 2 tsp. lemon juice
- 1 garlic clove, minced

1. In a small bowl, combine the first 6 ingredients; gently fold in crab. Cut fillets in half widthwise; place 6 halves in a 15x10x1-in. baking pan coated with cooking spray. Spoon crab mixture over fillets; top with remaining fish. Sprinkle with paprika.

2. Bake at 400° for 20-24 minutes or until fish flakes easily with a fork. Meanwhile, in a small bowl, combine aioli ingredients. Serve with fish.

1 stuffed fillet with 2½ tsp. aioli: 276 cal., 8g fat (1g sat. fat), 153mg chol., 585mg sod., 3g carb. (1g sugars, 0 fiber), 45g pro. **Diabetic exchanges:** 5 lean meat, 1 fat.

CRAB-STUFFED FLOUNDER WITH HERBED AIOLI

OVEN-ROASTED SALMON

ALFREDO SHRIMP SHELLS

Premade Alfredo sauce streamlines the preparation of these tasty stuffed shells. They're filled with shrimp, mushrooms and green onion. I like to serve them with sauteed zucchini followed by cubed cantaloupe and watermelon for dessert.
—*Gertrude Peischl, Allentown, PA*

PREP: 15 min. • **BAKE:** 20 min.
MAKES: 2 servings

- ½ cup chopped fresh mushrooms
- 1 tsp. butter
- 1 green onion, sliced
- 1 pkg. (5 oz.) frozen cooked salad shrimp, thawed
- 2 Tbsp. plus ½ cup Alfredo sauce, divided
- 6 jumbo pasta shells, cooked and drained
    Lemon wedges and fresh parsley

1. In a small skillet, saute mushrooms in butter until almost tender. Add onion; cook until tender. Stir in the shrimp and 2 Tbsp. Alfredo sauce. Pour ¼ cup remaining sauce into a greased 8-in. square baking dish.
2. Fill each pasta shell with 2 Tbsp. shrimp mixture; place in baking dish. Top with the remaining Alfredo sauce.
3. Cover and bake at 350° until bubbly, 20-25 minutes. Serve with lemon wedges and parsley.
3 stuffed shells: 322 cal., 12g fat (7g sat. fat), 177mg chol., 1002mg sod., 29g carb. (2g sugars, 2g fiber), 24g pro.

OVEN-ROASTED SALMON

After work, I want a fast meal. Roasted salmon is super tender and has a delicate sweetness. It's also an easy wowza for weekend company. Try it with one of the toppings that follow the recipe.
—*Jeanne Ambrose, Milwaukee, WI*

TAKES: 20 min. • **MAKES:** 4 servings

- 1 center-cut salmon fillet (1½ lbs.)
- 1 Tbsp. olive oil
- ½ tsp. salt
- ¼ tsp. pepper

1. Place a large cast-iron or other ovenproof skillet in a cold oven. Preheat oven to 450°. Meanwhile, brush salmon with oil and sprinkle with salt and pepper.
2. Carefully remove skillet from oven. Place the fish, skin side down, in skillet.
Return to oven; bake uncovered, until salmon flakes easily and a thermometer reads 125°, 14-18 minutes. Cut salmon into 4 equal portions.
1 piece: 295 cal., 19g fat (4g sat. fat), 85mg chol., 380mg sod., 0 carb. (0 sugars, 0 fiber), 29g pro. **Diabetic exchanges:** 4 lean meat, ½ fat.
For Gremolata: In a small bowl, mix ¼ cup minced fresh parsley, 2 Tbsp. olive oil, 1 Tbsp. lemon juice, 1 minced garlic clove, 1 tsp. grated lemon zest, ½ tsp. salt and ¼ tsp. pepper.
For Dill and Caper Butter: In a small bowl, mix ¼ cup softened butter, 1 Tbsp. minced shallot, 1 Tbsp. minced fresh dill, 1 tsp. Dijon mustard and 1 tsp. chopped capers.
For Maple Soy Glaze: In a small bowl, mix ¼ cup maple syrup, 2 Tbsp. soy sauce, 1 minced green onion, ½ tsp. grated fresh ginger and ¼ tsp. red pepper flakes.

CRUNCHY CHILE
CILANTRO LIME
ROASTED SHRIMP

CRUNCHY CHILE CILANTRO LIME ROASTED SHRIMP

Easy, quick and family friendly, this shrimp recipe is dairy free and comes together in about 30 minutes. The secret is the bright, flavor-packed sauce. Serve over greens, store-bought slaw or cauliflower rice.
—*Julie Peterson, Crofton, MD*

TAKES: 30 min. • **MAKES:** 8 servings

- 2 lbs. uncooked shrimp (26-30 per lb.), peeled and deveined
- 4 garlic cloves, minced
- 1 tsp. paprika
- 1 tsp. ground ancho chile pepper
- 1 tsp. ground cumin
- ½ tsp. salt
- ¼ tsp. pepper
- 1 medium lime
- 1 cup crushed tortilla chips
- ¼ cup chopped fresh cilantro
- ¼ cup olive oil
- 1 cup cherry tomatoes, halved
- 1 medium ripe avocado, peeled and cubed
  Optional: Additional lime wedges and cilantro

1. Preheat oven to 425°. Place the first 7 ingredients in a greased 15x10x1-in. pan. Finely grate zest from lime. Cut lime crosswise in half; squeeze juice. Add zest and juice to shrimp mixture; toss to coat.
2. In a small bowl, combine crushed chips, cilantro and oil; sprinkle over shrimp mixture. Bake until shrimp turn pink, 12-15 minutes. Top with tomatoes and avocado. If desired, serve with additional lime wedges and cilantro.
1 serving: 230 cal., 13g fat (2g sat. fat), 138mg chol., 315mg sod., 10g carb. (1g sugars, 2g fiber), 20g pro. **Diabetic exchanges:** 3 lean meat, 1½ fat, ½ starch.

OVEN-FRIED FISH & CHIPS

OVEN-FRIED FISH & CHIPS

My baked fish is a shoo-in when you want fish and chips without the frying mess. Dare I say, they're a little upgrade from the English pub classic.
—*Reeni Pisano, Wappingers Falls, NY*

PREP: 15 min. • **BAKE:** 55 min.
MAKES: 4 servings

- ⅓ cup mayonnaise
- 2 Tbsp. dill pickle relish or chopped dill pickle
- 2 tsp. grated lemon zest

FISH AND POTATOES

- 1½ lbs. baking potatoes (about 3 medium)
- 2 tsp. olive oil
- ¾ tsp. kosher salt, divided
- ½ tsp. coarsely ground pepper, divided
- ½ cup panko bread crumbs
- ¼ cup seasoned bread crumbs
- 4 cod fillets (4 oz. each)
- 2 Tbsp. mayonnaise
- 2 Tbsp. grated Parmesan cheese
- 2 tsp. chopped fresh parsley
  Malt vinegar, optional

1. For tartar sauce, in a small bowl, mix mayonnaise, relish and lemon zest. Refrigerate until serving.
2. Preheat oven to 400°. Cut potatoes lengthwise into 1-in.-thick wedges; toss with oil, ½ tsp. salt and ¼ tsp. pepper. Spread evenly in a greased 15x10x1-in. baking pan. Roast until golden brown, stirring occasionally, 40-45 minutes.
3. Meanwhile, in a small skillet, toast panko bread crumbs over medium-low heat until lightly browned, stirring occasionally, 5-7 minutes. Transfer to a shallow bowl; stir in seasoned bread crumbs.
4. Sprinkle cod with the remaining salt and pepper; spread top and sides of fish with mayonnaise. Dip in crumb mixture to cover mayonnaise, pressing firmly to help adhere. Place in a greased 15x10x1-in. baking pan, crumb side up. Sprinkle with any remaining crumb mixture. Bake until fish just begins to flake easily with a fork, 12-15 minutes.
5. Toss potatoes with cheese and parsley. Serve fish and potatoes with tartar sauce and, if desired, vinegar.
1 serving: 475 cal., 24g fat (4g sat. fat), 54mg chol., 789mg sod., 40g carb. (2g sugars, 5g fiber), 23g pro.

BEST SEAFOOD ENCHILADAS

When you want a change from the usual beef and chicken enchiladas, try these tortillas stuffed with crab, shrimp and scallops. They're cheesy, creamy and absolutely delicious!
—*Mary Halpin, King George, VA*

PREP: 25 min. • BAKE: 20 min.
MAKES: 8 enchiladas

- ½ lb. crabmeat, flaked and cartilage removed
- ½ lb. uncooked medium shrimp, peeled and deveined
- ½ lb. bay scallops
- 1   medium onion, chopped
- 2   Tbsp. butter

SAUCE

- ½ cup butter, cubed
- 1   tsp. grated onion
- ¼ cup chicken broth
- 3   large egg yolks, lightly beaten
- 1   cup heavy whipping cream
- 1   Tbsp. tomato paste
- 8   flour tortillas (6 in.)
- 2   cups shredded Monterey Jack or Colby cheese

1. In a large skillet, cook the seafood and onion in butter over medium heat 4-5 minutes or until onion is tender and shrimp turn pink. Remove from the heat; set aside.

2. In a small saucepan, melt butter. Add onion and broth. Combine egg yolks and cream; stir into broth mixture. Cook and stir until a thermometer reads 160° and sauce is thick enough to coat the back of a metal spoon. Stir in tomato paste. Remove from the heat.

3. Spoon ⅓ cup seafood mixture down center of each tortilla. Top with 1 Tbsp. sauce and 2 Tbsp. cheese; roll up.

4. Spread ½ cup sauce into a greased 13x9-in. baking dish. Place enchiladas seam side down in dish. Top with the remaining sauce and cheese.

5. Bake, uncovered, at 350° until heated through, 20-25 minutes.

1 serving: 531 cal., 40g fat (22g sat. fat), 264mg chol., 738mg sod., 17g carb. (3g sugars, 1g fiber), 27g pro.

ARTICHOKE COD WITH SUN-DRIED TOMATOES

I think cod is a fabulous break from really rich dishes that take so long to prepare. I like to serve this dish over a bed of greens, pasta or even quinoa. A little squeeze of lemon gives it another layer of freshness.
—*Hiroko Miles, El Dorado Hills, CA*

TAKES: 30 min. • MAKES: 6 servings

- 1   can (14 oz.) quartered water-packed artichoke hearts, drained
- ½ cup julienned soft sun-dried tomatoes (not packed in oil)
- 2   green onions, chopped
- 3   Tbsp. olive oil
- 1   garlic clove, minced
- 6   cod fillets (6 oz. each)
- 1   tsp. salt
- ½ tsp. pepper
     Optional: Salad greens and lemon wedges

1. Preheat oven to 400°. In a small bowl, combine the first 5 ingredients; toss to combine.

2. Sprinkle both sides of cod with salt and pepper; place in a 13x9-in. baking dish coated with cooking spray. Top with the artichoke mixture.

3. Bake, uncovered, 15-20 minutes or until fish just begins to flake easily with a fork. If desired, serve over salad greens with lemon wedges.

Note: This recipe was tested with sun-dried tomatoes that can be used without soaking. When using other sun-dried tomatoes that are not oil-packed, cover with boiling water and let stand until soft. Drain before using.

1 fillet with ⅓ cup artichoke mixture: 231 cal., 8g fat (1g sat. fat), 65mg chol., 665mg sod., 9g carb. (3g sugars, 2g fiber), 29g pro. **Diabetic exchanges:** 4 lean meat, 1½ fat, 1 vegetable.

ARTICHOKE COD WITH
SUN-DRIED TOMATOES

RED PEPPER & PARMESAN TILAPIA

MINI TUNA LOAVES

Our Test Kitchen has packed all the comfort of Mom's mouthwatering tuna casserole into six cute, individual serving-sized loaves drizzled with melted cheese. Try this quick and easy recipe on your family and reel in the raves!
—Taste of Home *Test Kitchen*

- -

PREP: 15 min. • **BAKE:** 25 min.
MAKES: 6 servings

½	cup chopped celery
⅓	cup chopped onion
2	tsp. canola oil
3	cans (5 oz. each) white water-packed solid tuna, chopped
2	cups soft bread crumbs
½	cup toasted wheat germ
2	large eggs, lightly beaten
¼	cup 2% milk
2	Tbsp. minced fresh parsley
½	tsp. dried thyme
¼	tsp. salt
¼	tsp. pepper
⅓	cup shredded cheddar cheese

1. Preheat oven to 350°. In a small skillet, saute celery and onion in oil for 5 minutes or until tender. In a large bowl, combine the tuna, bread crumbs, wheat germ, eggs, milk, parsley, thyme, salt and pepper. Stir in celery mixture. Shape into 6 oval loaves.
2. Place in a 15x10x1-in. baking pan coated with cooking spray. Bake until lightly browned, 20-25 minutes. Sprinkle with cheese. Bake until cheese is melted, 5 minutes longer.
Freeze option: Securely wrap cooled loaf in foil, then freeze. To use, partially thaw in refrigerator overnight. Unwrap loaf; reheat on a greased 15x10x1-in. baking pan in a preheated 350° oven until heated through and a thermometer inserted in center reads 165°.
1 serving: 257 cal., 10g fat (3g sat. fat), 116mg chol., 578mg sod., 14g carb. (2g sugars, 2g fiber), 28g pro. **Diabetic exchanges:** 3 lean meat, 2 fat, 1 starch.

RED PEPPER & PARMESAN TILAPIA

My husband and I are always looking for light fish recipes because of their health benefits. This one is a hit with him, and we've served it at our dinner parties, too. It's a staple!
—*Michelle Martin, Durham, NC*

- -

TAKES: 20 min. • **MAKES:** 4 servings

1	large egg, lightly beaten
½	cup grated Parmesan cheese
1	tsp. Italian seasoning
½	to 1 tsp. crushed red pepper flakes
½	tsp. pepper
4	tilapia fillets (6 oz. each)

1. Preheat oven to 425°. Place egg in a shallow bowl. In another shallow bowl, combine the cheese, Italian seasoning, pepper flakes and pepper. Dip fillets in egg and then in cheese mixture.
2. Place fillets in a 15x10x1-in. baking pan coated with cooking spray. Bake until fish just begins to flake easily with a fork, 10-15 minutes.
1 fillet: 179 cal., 4g fat (2g sat. fat), 89mg chol., 191mg sod., 1g carb. (0 sugars, 0 fiber), 35g pro. **Diabetic exchanges:** 5 very lean meat, ½ fat.

LEMON PARSLEY SWORDFISH

FAST BAKED FISH

We always have a good supply of fresh fish, so I make this dish often. It's moist, tender and flavorful.
—Judie Anglen, Riverton, WY

TAKES: 25 min. • **MAKES:** 4 servings

1¼	**lbs. fish fillets**
1	**tsp. seasoned salt**
	Pepper to taste
	Paprika, optional
3	**Tbsp. butter, melted**

1. Preheat oven to 400°. Place fish in a greased 11x7-in. baking dish. Sprinkle with seasoned salt, pepper and paprika if desired. Drizzle with butter.
2. Cover and bake until fish just begins to flake easily with a fork, 15-20 minutes.
Note: Haddock, trout or walleye may be used in this recipe.
1 serving: 270 cal., 17g fat (7g sat. fat), 110mg chol., 540mg sod., 0 carb. (0 sugars, 0 fiber), 28g pro.

TUNA-STUFFED TOMATOES FOR TWO

I created these broiled tomato halves one afternoon when I wanted a warm lunch. The addition of chopped celery gives the tuna mixture a nice crunch.
—Renee McGowen, Aurora, CO

TAKES: 10 min. • **MAKES:** 2 servings

1	**large tomato**
1	**can (6 oz.) tuna, drained and flaked**
4	**tsp. mayonnaise**
1	**Tbsp. chopped celery**
½	**tsp. Dijon mustard**
¼	**tsp. seasoned salt**

1. Cut tomato in half through the stem. Scoop out pulp, leaving a ½-in. shell. Invert onto paper towels to drain.
2. In a small bowl, combine the remaining ingredients. Fill tomato shells with tuna mixture; place on a baking sheet. Broil 3-4 in. from the heat 4-5 minutes or until heated through.
1 serving: 187 cal., 8g fat (1g sat. fat), 29mg chol., 570mg sod., 4g carb. (3g sugars, 1g fiber), 23g pro.

LEMON PARSLEY SWORDFISH

This dish looks impressive and is easy to prepare—a winner in my book! I like that it comes together fast enough for a family weeknight meal but is special enough to serve guests for Sunday dinner.
—Nathan Leopold, Mechanicsburg, PA

TAKES: 25 min. • **MAKES:** 4 servings

4	**swordfish steaks (7 oz. each)**
½	**tsp. salt**
½	**cup minced fresh parsley, divided**
⅓	**cup olive oil**
1	**Tbsp. lemon juice**
2	**tsp. minced garlic**
¼	**tsp. crushed red pepper flakes**

1. Preheat oven to 425°. Place fish in a greased 13x9-in. baking dish; sprinkle with salt. In a small bowl, combine ¼ cup parsley, oil, lemon juice, garlic and pepper flakes; spoon over fish.
2. Bake, uncovered, until the fish just begins to flake easily with a fork, basting occasionally, 15-20 minutes. Sprinkle with remaining parsley.
1 swordfish steak: 390 cal., 26g fat (5g sat. fat), 72mg chol., 171mg sod., 1g carb. (0 sugars, 0 fiber), 37g pro.
Artichoke-Tomato Swordfish: Omit last 6 ingredients. Place the fish in prepared dish. Mix 2 jars (7½ oz. each) chopped, drained artichoke hearts; ½ cup chopped, drained, oil-packed sun-dried tomatoes; and 4 chopped shallots. Spread mixture over fish. Drizzle with 2 Tbsp. melted butter and 1 tsp. lemon juice. Bake, covered, 15 minutes. Uncover; bake an additional 6-8 minutes.

FAST BAKED FISH

SCRUMPTIOUS
CALIFORNIA
SALMON

CREOLE SHRIMP PIZZA

Pizza and the flavors of Creole cuisine blend amazingly well in this hearty dish with a crispy crust. Add more hot sauce to boost the heat if you like things spicy.
—*Robin Haas, Cranston, RI*

PREP: 15 min. • **BAKE:** 25 min.
MAKES: 6 servings

- 1 prebaked 12-in. pizza crust
- 1 Tbsp. olive oil, divided
- 1½ cups shredded part-skim mozzarella cheese, divided
- 1 Tbsp. lemon juice
- 1½ tsp. reduced-sodium Creole seasoning, divided
- 1 lb. uncooked shrimp (31-40 per lb.), peeled and deveined
- 1 large onion, chopped
- ½ tsp. coarsely ground pepper
- ¼ tsp. celery seed
- 2 garlic cloves, minced
- 1 cup pizza sauce
- ¼ tsp. Louisiana-style hot sauce
- 1 large green pepper, thinly sliced

1. Preheat oven to 425°. Place crust on an ungreased baking sheet. Brush with 1½ tsp. oil; sprinkle with ½ cup mozzarella cheese. Set aside. Combine lemon juice and ½ tsp. Creole seasoning. Add shrimp; toss to coat.
2. In a skillet, heat remaining oil over medium heat. Add onion, pepper, celery seed and remaining Creole seasoning; saute until onion is tender. Add garlic; cook 1 minute longer. Stir in pizza sauce and hot sauce. Remove from heat.
3. Drain shrimp. Spread sauce mixture over crust. Top with shrimp and green pepper; sprinkle with remaining cheese.
4. Bake until shrimp turn pink and cheese is melted, 25-30 minutes.
1 slice: 378 cal., 13g fat (4g sat. fat), 110mg chol., 969mg sod., 39g carb. (6g sugars, 3g fiber), 27g pro.

SCRUMPTIOUS CALIFORNIA SALMON

To me, California cuisine is all about balancing flavors. This recipe brings out the sweetness in orange juice and honey and balances it with the kick of ancho chili pepper and balsamic vinegar.
—*Dustin Anderson, Camarillo, CA*

PREP: 35 min. • **BAKE:** 10 min.
MAKES: 4 servings

- 3 garlic cloves, minced
- 1 tsp. minced shallot
- 1 cup orange juice
- 1 Tbsp. balsamic vinegar
- 3 Tbsp. honey
- 1 Tbsp. ground ancho chili pepper
- ¼ tsp. salt
- ⅛ tsp. pepper
- 1 salmon fillet (1 lb.)
- 2 tsp. canola oil
- 2 Tbsp. minced fresh cilantro

1. In a small saucepan coated with cooking spray, saute garlic and shallot until tender. Add the orange juice and vinegar. Bring to a boil. Reduce heat; simmer, uncovered, until reduced to ¼ cup, 20-25 minutes. Stir in the honey, chili pepper, salt and pepper.
2. In a large cast-iron or other ovenproof skillet, brown the salmon in oil, about 3 minutes on each side. Brush with sauce. Bake, uncovered, at 400° until fish just begins to flake easily with a fork, 8-10 minutes.
3. Brush with any remaining sauce and sprinkle with cilantro.
3 oz. cooked salmon: 317 cal., 15g fat (3g sat. fat), 67mg chol., 217mg sod., 21g carb. (19g sugars, 0 fiber), 23g pro.

CREOLE
SHRIMP PIZZA

Bonus: 5-Ingredient Main Dishes

PESTO
HAMBURGERS

PESTO HAMBURGERS

Give an Italian twist to basic burgers by topping them with pesto, roasted red peppers strips and mozzarella cheese.
—Taste of Home *Test Kitchen*

- -

TAKES: 20 min. • **MAKES:** 4 servings

  1½ lbs. ground beef
  ⅛ tsp. salt
  ⅛ tsp. pepper
  4 slices part-skim mozzarella cheese
  ½ cup prepared pesto
  ⅓ cup roasted sweet red pepper strips
  4 hamburger buns, split and toasted

1. Shape beef into four ¾-in.-thick patties. Season with salt and pepper. In a large skillet, cook patties over medium heat until the meat is no longer pink, about 5 minutes on each side.
2. Top each burger with a slice of cheese, 2 Tbsp. pesto and pepper strips. Reduce heat; cover and simmer until cheese is melted, about 2 minutes. Serve on buns.
Note: This recipe was tested with Vlasic roasted red pepper strips.
1 serving: 716 cal., 45g fat (17g sat. fat), 161mg chol., 779mg sod., 25g carb. (3g sugars, 2g fiber), 51g pro.

"Love these burgers! I have made them several times. Very quick, easy and yummy!"
—SULYNN051467, TASTEOFHOME.COM

CHEESY CHICKEN
WAFFLEWICHES

HEARTY CANNELLINI & SAUSAGE SOUP

Is there anything better than a soup full of smoked sausage, creamy cannellini beans and hearty cabbage? I don't think so!
—*Pauline White, El Cajon, CA*

TAKES: 30 min. • **MAKES:** 6 servings

- 12 oz. beef summer or smoked sausage, cut into ½-in. pieces
- 4½ cups vegetable broth
- 2 cans (15 oz. each) cannellini beans, rinsed and drained
- 4 cups coarsely chopped Chinese or napa cabbage
- 3 green onions, chopped
- ¼ tsp. salt
- ¼ tsp. pepper

In a large saucepan, cook and stir sausage over medium heat until lightly browned; drain. Add the remaining ingredients; bring to a boil. Reduce heat; simmer for 5-10 minutes or until cabbage is tender and flavors are blended.
1⅓ cups: 283 cal., 14g fat (5g sat. fat), 35mg chol., 1672mg sod., 24g carb. (3g sugars, 6g fiber), 15g pro.

CORN DOG TWISTS

Kids will have as much fun making as they will eating these cute twists on hot dogs and buns! Set out bowls of relish, mustard and ketchup for dunkable fun.
—*Melissa Tatum, Greensboro, NC*

TAKES: 25 min. • **MAKES:** 8 servings

- 1 tube (11½ oz.) refrigerated cornbread or plain twists
- 8 hot dogs
- 1 Tbsp. butter, melted
- 1 Tbsp. grated Parmesan cheese

1. Separate cornbread twists; wrap 1 strip around each hot dog. Brush with butter; sprinkle with cheese. Place on a lightly greased baking sheet.
2. Bake at 375° for 11-13 minutes or until golden brown.
1 serving: 302 cal., 21g fat (8g sat. fat), 30mg chol., 815mg sod., 19g carb. (5g sugars, 0 fiber), 8g pro.

CHEESY CHICKEN WAFFLEWICHES

I've had lots of fun experimenting with my waffle maker. I decided to use shredded meat, cheese and vegetables for a savory twist. Make sure the griddle is hot before adding the sandwiches.
—*Marietta Slater, Justin, TX*

PREP: 25 min. • **COOK:** 5 min./batch
MAKES: 8 servings

- 1 Tbsp. olive oil
- ½ cup chopped onion
- ½ cup chopped fresh mushrooms
- 1 cup shredded rotisserie chicken
- 1 cup shredded Swiss cheese
- 1 pkg. (17.3 oz.) frozen puff pastry, thawed

1. In a large skillet, heat oil over medium heat; saute the onion until softened, 3-4 minutes. Reduce heat to medium-low; cook onion until caramelized, 6-8 minutes, stirring occasionally. Add mushrooms; cook and stir until tender, 2-3 minutes. Cool slightly. Stir in chicken and cheese.
2. Preheat a 4-square waffle maker. Unfold 1 puff pastry sheet onto a lightly floured surface; cut into 4 squares. Top each square with ¼ cup filling; bring up corners over filling and pinch firmly to seal. Refrigerate until ready to cook. Repeat with remaining pastry and filling.
3. In batches, place each pastry bundle in a separate section of waffle maker. Bake until golden brown and crisp, 5-7 minutes.
1 wafflewich: 405 cal., 24g fat (7g sat. fat), 28mg chol., 243mg sod., 36g carb. (1g sugars, 5g fiber), 13g pro.

**CHEESEBURGER
OMELET SLIDERS**

BEST EVER LAMB CHOPS

My mom just loved a good lamb chop, and this easy recipe was her favorite way to prepare them. I've also grilled these chops with amazing results.
—Kim Mundy, Visalia, CA

- -

PREP: 10 min. + chilling • **BROIL:** 10 min.
MAKES: 4 servings

1	tsp. each dried basil, marjoram and thyme
½	tsp. salt
8	lamb loin chops (3 oz. each)
	Mint jelly, optional

1. Combine herbs and salt; rub over lamb chops. Cover and refrigerate for 1 hour.
2. Broil 4-6 in. from heat for 5-8 minutes on each side or until the meat reaches desired doneness (for medium-rare, a thermometer should read 135°; medium, 140°; medium-well, 145°). Serve with mint jelly if desired.

2 lamb chops: 157 cal., 7g fat (2g sat. fat), 68mg chol., 355mg sod., 0 carb. (0 sugars, 0 fiber), 22g pro. **Diabetic exchanges:** 3 lean meat.

Honey-Glazed Lamb Chops: Omit step 1, herbs and salt. In a saucepan, heat ⅓ cup each honey and prepared mustard and ⅛ tsp. each onion salt and pepper over medium-low heat 2-3 minutes or until honey is melted. Brush sauce over both sides of lamb chops. Proceed as directed in step 2.

CHEESEBURGER OMELET SLIDERS

A cheeseburger inside an omelet? Yes, please! This fun twist on two breakfast and dinner faves is easy to assemble and delicious any time of day.
—Denise LaRoche, Hudson, NH

- -

PREP: 25 min. • **COOK:** 25 min.
MAKES: 6 servings

1	lb. lean ground beef (90% lean)
1	tsp. salt, divided
½	tsp. pepper, divided
8	large eggs
½	cup water
1	cup shredded Havarti cheese
12	dinner rolls, split
12	tomato slices
	Optional: Ketchup, sliced onion and pickle slices

1. Combine beef, ½ tsp. salt and ¼ tsp. pepper; mix lightly but thoroughly. Shape into twelve 2-in. patties. In a large skillet, cook burgers over medium heat until cooked through, 2-3 minutes per side. Remove from heat; keep warm.
2. Whisk together eggs, water and the remaining salt and pepper. Place a small nonstick skillet, lightly oiled, over medium-high heat; pour in ½ cup egg mixture. Mixture should set immediately at edges. As eggs set, push cooked edges toward the center, letting uncooked eggs flow underneath. When eggs are thickened and no liquid egg remains, sprinkle ⅓ cup cheese on 1 half. Top cheese with 3 burgers, spacing them evenly; fold omelet in half. Slide onto a cutting board; tent with foil to keep warm. Repeat to make 3 more omelets.
3. To serve, cut each omelet into 3 wedges; place each wedge on a roll. Add tomatoes and, if desired, ketchup, onion and pickles.

2 sliders: 507 cal., 23g fat (9g sat. fat), 348mg chol., 1032mg sod., 39g carb. (5g sugars, 3g fiber), 34g pro.

BEST EVER
LAMB CHOPS

BUTTERMILK BISCUIT SAUSAGE PINWHEELS

Serve these delicious biscuits with scrambled eggs and fruit for a quick but filling breakfast or brunch. Use a lean pork sausage for best results.
—*Gladys Ferguson, Rossville, GA*

PREP: 15 min. + chilling • **BAKE:** 25 min.
MAKES: about 9 servings

- ¼ cup shortening
- 2 cups unsifted self-rising flour
- 1 cup buttermilk
- 1 lb. raw bulk pork sausage, room temperature

With a pastry blender, cut shortening into flour. Add buttermilk; mix. On a lightly floured surface, knead for a few seconds, adding additional flour if necessary. Roll out on a lightly floured surface into a 12x9-in. rectangle. Spread sausage over dough. Roll up, jelly roll-style, starting from the short side Chill. Cut into ½-in. slices. Place, cut side down, on a lightly greased baking sheet. Bake at 425° for 25 minutes or until lightly browned.

2 biscuits: 312 cal., 20g fat (6g sat. fat), 35mg chol., 768mg sod., 23g carb. (1g sugars, 1g fiber), 10g pro.

EASY ASIAN-STYLE CHICKEN SLAW

The first time I made this chicken dish, I knew it was a winner because the bowl came back to the kitchen scraped clean.
—*Bess Blanco, Vail, AZ*

TAKES: 15 min. • **MAKES:** 8 servings

- 1 pkg. (3 oz.) ramen noodles
- 1 rotisserie chicken, skin removed, shredded
- 1 pkg. (16 oz.) coleslaw mix
- 6 green onions, finely chopped
- 1 cup reduced-fat Asian toasted sesame salad dressing

Discard seasoning packet from noodles or save for another use. Break noodles into small pieces; place in a large bowl. Add chicken, coleslaw mix and green onions. Drizzle with salad dressing; toss to coat.

1½ cups: 267 cal., 10g fat (3g sat. fat), 70mg chol., 405mg sod., 18g carb. (8g sugars, 2g fiber), 26g pro. **Diabetic exchanges:** 3 lean meat, 1 starch, ½ fat.

BUTTERMILK BISCUIT
SAUSAGE PINWHEELS

O'BRIEN
SAUSAGE SKILLET

SUPER QUICK CHICKEN FRIED RICE

After my first child was born, I needed meals that were satisfying and fast. This fried rice is now part of our routine dinners.
—Alicia Gower, Auburn, NY

TAKES: 30 min. • **MAKES:** 6 servings

- 1 pkg. (12 oz.) frozen mixed vegetables
- 2 Tbsp. olive oil, divided
- 2 large eggs, lightly beaten
- 4 Tbsp. sesame oil, divided
- 3 pkg. (8.8 oz. each) ready-to-serve garden vegetable rice
- 1 rotisserie chicken, skin removed, shredded
- ¼ tsp. salt
- ¼ tsp. pepper

1. Prepare frozen vegetables according to package directions. Meanwhile, in a large skillet, heat 1 Tbsp. olive oil over medium-high heat. Pour in eggs; cook and stir until eggs are thickened and no liquid egg remains. Remove from pan.
2. In same skillet, heat 2 Tbsp. sesame oil and remaining olive oil over medium-high heat. Add rice; cook and stir until rice begins to brown, 10-12 minutes.
3. Stir in the chicken, salt and pepper. Add eggs and vegetables; heat through, breaking eggs into small pieces and stirring to combine. Drizzle with the remaining sesame oil.
1½ cups: 548 cal., 25g fat (5g sat. fat), 163mg chol., 934mg sod., 43g carb. (3g sugars, 3g fiber), 38g pro.

O'BRIEN SAUSAGE SKILLET

Inspiration hit me one night when I was in a time crunch. This was so satisfying and easy to make, many friends now serve it as well.
—Linda Harris, Wichita, KS

TAKES: 20 min. • **MAKES:** 6 servings

- 1 pkg. (28 oz.) frozen O'Brien potatoes
- ¼ cup plus 2 tsp. canola oil, divided
- 1 pkg. (14 oz.) smoked turkey kielbasa, sliced
- 2 medium tart apples, peeled and chopped
- 1 medium onion, chopped
- 1 cup shredded cheddar cheese

1. In a large nonstick skillet, prepare potatoes according to package directions, using ¼ cup oil. Meanwhile, in another skillet, heat remaining oil over medium-high heat. Add kielbasa, apples and onion; cook and stir 8-10 minutes or until onion is tender.
2. Spoon sausage mixture over the potatoes; sprinkle with cheese. Cook, covered, 3-4 minutes longer or until cheese is melted.
1 serving: 377 cal., 21g fat (6g sat. fat), 61mg chol., 803mg sod., 29g carb. (8g sugars, 4g fiber), 17g pro.

MINI CHICKEN &
BISCUIT SANDWICHES

MINI CHICKEN & BISCUIT SANDWICHES

My 11-year-old son invented these sliders at dinner one night when he set his chicken on a biscuit. The rest of us tried it his way, and now we enjoy these sandwiches all the time.
—*Jodie Kolsan, Palm Coast, FL*

- -

TAKES: 30 min. • **MAKES:** 5 servings

- 1 tube (12 oz.) refrigerated buttermilk biscuits
- 5 boneless skinless chicken breasts (4 oz. each)
- ½ tsp. salt
- ½ tsp. dried thyme
- ¼ tsp. pepper
- 1 Tbsp. canola oil
- 1 Tbsp. butter
  Optional: Cranberry chutney, lettuce leaves, sliced tomato and red onion

1. Bake biscuits according to package directions. Meanwhile, cut the chicken crosswise in half. Pound with a meat mallet to ¼-in. thickness. Sprinkle with salt, thyme and pepper.

2. In a large skillet, heat oil and butter over medium-high heat. Add chicken in batches; cook until a thermometer reads 165°, 2-3 minutes on each side. Split biscuits in half; top with chicken and toppings as desired. Replace tops.

2 mini sandwiches: 367 cal., 16g fat (4g sat. fat), 69mg chol., 1029mg sod., 28g carb. (4g sugars, 0 fiber), 27g pro.

Athenian Chicken Grilled Cheese: Prepare chicken as directed. Mix 6 oz. diced fresh mozzarella cheese, ½ cup crumbled feta, ½ cup grated Parmesan, ⅓ cup chopped fresh mint, 2 Tbsp. minced fresh oregano and 2 Tbsp. capers. Divide half the mixture among 4 slices Italian bread; layer each with the chicken breast, remaining mixture and a bread slice. Toast sandwiches in a large skillet in olive oil.

SHRIMP & FETA SKILLET

SHRIMP & FETA SKILLET

My friend's feisty Italian grandmother, Gemma, makes a dish similar to my shrimp with tomatoes. When I make this recipe, I think of Gemma and smile while stirring.
—*Celeste Ehrenberg, Topeka, KS*

- -

TAKES: 25 min. • **MAKES:** 4 servings

- 2 cans (14½ oz. each) diced tomatoes with basil, oregano and garlic, undrained
- 2 tsp. garlic powder
- 2 tsp. dried basil
- 1¼ lbs. uncooked shrimp (31-40 per lb.), peeled and deveined
- 1 cup crumbled feta cheese
  Crusty whole grain bread, optional

1. In a large skillet, combine tomatoes, garlic powder and basil; bring to a boil. Reduce heat; simmer, uncovered, 4-6 minutes or until slightly thickened.

2. Add shrimp; cook and stir 3-4 minutes or until shrimp turn pink. Sprinkle feta over shrimp; serve with bread if desired.

1¼ cups: 261 cal., 6g fat (3g sat. fat), 187mg chol., 1092mg sod., 15g carb. (7g sugars, 5g fiber), 30g pro.

BRISKET WITH GINGERSNAP GRAVY

This is the first and only recipe I've ever used to prepare a fresh beef brisket. We even use it for sandwiches.
—*Teri Lindquist, Gurnee, IL*

- -

PREP: 2½ hours + chilling • **BAKE:** 30 min.
MAKES: 18 servings

- 1 beef brisket (about 5 lbs.)
- 1 cup water
- ¾ cup chili sauce
- 1 envelope onion soup mix
- 5 to 6 gingersnaps, crushed

1. Preheat oven to 325°. Place brisket in a roasting pan. In a bowl, combine the water, chili sauce and soup mix; pour over meat. Cover and bake until meat is tender, 2½-3 hours. Cool; cover. Chill overnight.

2. Preheat oven to 350°. Remove meat and cut into ¼-in.-thick slices; return to the pan. Sprinkle with gingersnap crumbs. Cover and bake until heated through, 30-45 minutes.

1 slice: 181 cal., 6g fat (2g sat. fat), 53mg chol., 345mg sod., 5g carb. (2g sugars, 0 fiber), 26g pro.

BROILED CHICKEN & ARTICHOKES

My wife and I first made this chicken entree as newlyweds, and we've been hooked on it ever since. We make it almost weekly now. It's so simple and affordable, yet delicious and healthy. Can't beat that!

—*Chris Koon, Midlothian, VA*

TAKES: 15 min. • **MAKES:** 8 servings

- 8 boneless skinless chicken thighs (about 2 lbs.)
- 2 jars (7½ oz. each) marinated quartered artichoke hearts, drained
- 2 Tbsp. olive oil
- 1 tsp. salt
- ½ tsp. pepper
- ¼ cup shredded Parmesan cheese
- 2 Tbsp. minced fresh parsley

1. Preheat boiler. In a large bowl, toss chicken and artichokes with oil, salt and pepper. Transfer to a broiler pan.
2. Broil 3 in. from heat 8-10 minutes or until a thermometer inserted in chicken reads 170°, turning the chicken and artichokes halfway through cooking. Sprinkle with cheese. Broil 1-2 minutes longer or until cheese is melted. Sprinkle with parsley.
1 serving: 288 cal., 21g fat (5g sat. fat), 77mg chol., 584mg sod., 4g carb. (0 sugars, 0 fiber), 22g pro.

PRESSURE-COOKER PINEAPPLE CHICKEN

We love Hawaiian-style chicken in a slow cooker, but sometimes we need something that comes together fast! We tweaked our favorite recipe to work in a pressure cooker for a quick and easy weeknight dinner. Add a side salad for a complete meal.

—*Courtney Stultz, Weir, KS*

PREP: 10 min. • **COOK:** 20 min. + releasing
MAKES: 6 servings

- 1½ lbs. boneless skinless chicken breasts
- 1 can (20 oz.) unsweetened pineapple chunks, undrained
- ¼ cup barbecue sauce
- 1 cup chicken broth
- 1 cup uncooked long grain brown rice
- ½ tsp. salt
  Optional: Minced fresh cilantro and sliced green onions

1. Combine the first 6 ingredients in a 6-qt. electric pressure cooker. Lock lid; close pressure-release valve. Adjust to pressure-cook on high for 20 minutes.
2. Let pressure release naturally. Remove chicken to a cutting board and shred with 2 forks. Add shredded chicken back to pot and stir until combined. If desired, sprinkle with cilantro and green onions.
1 cup: 313 cal., 4g fat (1g sat. fat), 63mg chol., 536mg sod., 41g carb. (16g sugars, 3g fiber), 27g pro. **Diabetic exchanges:** 3 lean meat, 2½ starch.

PRESSURE-COOKER
PINEAPPLE CHICKEN

MUSHROOM PEAR MELTS

I really like mushrooms with cheese. Add pears, broil away and you've got a scrumptious open-faced sandwich. Serve with a salad and fruity tea.
—*Marla Hyatt, St. Paul, MN*

TAKES: 25 min. • MAKES: 4 servings

- 2   Tbsp. butter
- 4   cups sliced fresh shiitake or baby portobello mushrooms (about 10 oz.)
- ½   tsp. salt
- ¼   tsp. pepper
- 8   slices whole wheat bread, toasted
- 2   large ripe Bosc pears, thinly sliced
- 8   slices provolone cheese

1. Preheat broiler. In a large cast-iron or other heavy skillet, heat butter over medium-high heat. Add mushrooms; cook and stir until tender, 5-7 minutes. Stir in salt and pepper.

2. Place toast slices on a rack of a broiler pan. Top with mushrooms; layer with pears and cheese. Broil 3-4 in. from heat until cheese is lightly browned, 2-3 minutes.

2 open-faced sandwiches: 421 cal., 20g fat (11g sat. fat), 45mg chol., 883mg sod., 46g carb. (15g sugars, 9g fiber), 19g pro.

MUSHROOM
PEAR MELTS

CHEESY
BLACK BEAN NACHOS

CHEESY BLACK BEAN NACHOS

We're trying to go meatless once a week, and this dish helps make those meals fun, quick and super delicious. It's also a smart way to use up beans and canned tomatoes from your pantry.
—*Cynthia Nelson, Saskatoon, SK*

TAKES: 20 min. • **MAKES:** 4 servings

- 1 can (15 oz.) black beans, rinsed and drained
- 1 can (14½ oz.) diced tomatoes, well drained
- 3 to 4 jalapeno peppers, seeded and sliced
- 4 cups multigrain tortilla chips
- 1 cup shredded cheddar cheese
  Optional: Sour cream, chopped fresh cilantro and additional jalapeno slices

1. Preheat oven to 350°. Mix black beans, tomatoes and jalapenos. Arrange chips in an even layer in a 15x10x1-in. pan. Top with bean mixture and cheese.
2. Bake, uncovered, until cheese is melted, 10-12 minutes. Serve immediately with toppings as desired.
Note: Wear disposable gloves when cutting hot peppers; the oils can burn skin. Avoid touching your face.
1 serving: 371 cal., 17g fat (6g sat. fat), 28mg chol., 672mg sod., 42g carb. (6g sugars, 7g fiber), 15g pro.

TEST KITCHEN TIP

A little naughty gets a little nice with multigrain chips and black beans. Regular tortilla chips can be used if you want to go all out. Spreading the ingredients in a large pan helps the chips stay crunchy and evenly coated with the toppings.

SAUSAGE MANICOTTI

❄ SAUSAGE MANICOTTI

This classic Italian entree comes together in a snap but tastes as if it took hours. It's so tasty and easy to fix. My family always enjoys it.
—*Carolyn Henderson, Maple Plain, MN*

PREP: 15 min. • **BAKE:** 65 min.
MAKES: 7 servings

- 1 lb. uncooked bulk pork sausage
- 2 cups 4% cottage cheese
- 1 pkg. (8 oz.) manicotti shells
- 1 jar (24 oz.) marinara sauce
- 1 cup shredded part-skim mozzarella cheese

1. In a large bowl, combine the sausage and cottage cheese. Stuff into uncooked manicotti shells. Place in a greased 13x9-in. baking dish. Top with the marinara sauce.
2. Cover and bake at 350° until a thermometer inserted into the center of a shell reads 160°, 55-60 minutes.
3. Uncover; sprinkle with mozzarella cheese. Bake 8-10 minutes longer or until cheese is melted. Let stand for 5 minutes before serving.
Freeze option: Transfer individual portions of cooled manicotti to freezer containers; freeze. To use, partially thaw in refrigerator overnight. Transfer to a microwave-safe dish and microwave on high, stirring occasionally; add a little spaghetti sauce if necessary.
2 pieces: 489 cal., 24g fat (10g sat. fat), 59mg chol., 1232mg sod., 41g carb. (12g sugars, 3g fiber), 27g pro.

PRESSURE-COOKER
SMOKED SALMON &
DILL PENNE

AIR-FRYER CRISPY CURRY DRUMSTICKS

These air-fryer chicken drumsticks are flavorful, crispy on the outside and juicy on the inside. Sometimes I'll add some red pepper flakes in addition to the curry powder if I want to spice them up a bit. I like to serve them with chicken-seasoned rice and boiled broccoli.
—Zena Furgason, Norman, OK

PREP: 35 min. • **COOK:** 15 min./batch
MAKES: 4 servings

- 1   lb. chicken drumsticks
- ¾   tsp. salt, divided
- 2   Tbsp. olive oil
- 2   tsp. curry powder
- ½   tsp. onion salt
- ½   tsp. garlic powder
  Minced fresh cilantro, optional

1. In a large bowl, place chicken and enough water to cover. Add ½ tsp. salt; let stand 15 minutes at room temperature. Drain and pat dry.
2. Preheat air fryer to 375°. In a another bowl, mix oil, curry powder, onion salt, garlic powder and remaining ¼ tsp. salt; add chicken and toss to coat. In batches, place chicken in a single layer on tray in air-fryer basket. Cook until a thermometer inserted in chicken reads 170°-175°, 15-17 minutes, turning halfway through. If desired, sprinkle with cilantro.
2 oz. cooked chicken: 180 cal., 13g fat (3g sat. fat), 47mg chol., 711mg sod., 1g carb. (0 sugars, 1g fiber), 15g pro.

TEST KITCHEN TIP

Air-fried chicken has fewer calories and fat than deep-fried or even pan-fried chicken. It is nutritionally similar to oven-baked chicken but can have the crispy texture of fried chicken.

PRESSURE-COOKER SMOKED SALMON & DILL PENNE

I love making one-pot pastas in my pressure cooker. Every noodle soaks up the flavors of the delicious ingredients you throw in. I tried pasta with some leftover smoked fish and fresh dill, and boom—this was born. It's now a staple in our house because it's on the table in a half hour and the kids love it!
—Shannon Dobos, Calgary, AB

TAKES: 20 min. • **MAKES:** 6 servings

- 2¼ cups chicken broth
- ½   lb. smoked salmon fillets, flaked
- ½   cup heavy whipping cream
- 2   Tbsp. snipped fresh dill
- ½   tsp. pepper
- 12 oz. uncooked penne pasta
  Optional: Additional dill and lemon slices

Place broth, salmon, cream, dill and pepper in a 6-qt. electric pressure cooker; top with penne (do not stir). Lock lid; close pressure-release valve. Adjust to pressure-cook on high for 8 minutes. Quick-release pressure. Gently stir before serving. If desired, top with additional dill and lemon slices.
1¼ cups: 322 cal., 10g fat (5g sat. fat), 33mg chol., 672mg sod., 42g carb. (3g sugars, 2g fiber), 15g pro.

**AIR-FRYER CRISPY
CURRY DRUMSTICKS**

BEAN & CHEESE QUESADILLAS

My son doesn't eat meat, so I created this recipe as a way for me to cook one meal for the family instead of two. It's so easy, even my toddler grandson helps me make it!
—*Tina McMullen, Salina, KS*

TAKES: 30 min. • **MAKES:** 6 servings

1   can (16 oz.) refried beans
½   cup canned petite diced tomatoes
2   green onions, chopped
12   flour tortillas (8 in.)
2   cups shredded cheddar cheese
     Optional: Sour cream and salsa

1. In a small bowl, mix beans, tomatoes and green onions. Spread half the tortillas with bean mixture. Sprinkle with cheese; top with remaining tortillas.
2. Heat a griddle over medium heat. Place tortillas on griddle in batches. Cook until golden brown and cheese is melted, 2-3 minutes on each side. If desired, serve with sour cream and salsa.

1 quesadilla: 544 cal., 21g fat (9g sat. fat), 37mg chol., 1028mg sod., 67g carb. (1g sugars, 6g fiber), 21g pro.
Bacon-Tomato Quesadillas: Substitute 10 medium tomatoes, seeded and finely chopped; 8 bacon strips, cooked and crumbled; and 3 cups (12 oz.) shredded Mexican cheese blend for the first 3 ingredients. Omit cheddar cheese. Assemble and cook as directed.

❄ PULLED PORK PARFAIT

I tried a version of this meaty parfait at Miller Park, the then-home of my favorite baseball team, the Milwaukee Brewers. I take it up a notch by adding layers of corn and creamy mac and cheese. It truly is a full barbecue meal you can take on the go.
—*Rachel Bernhard Seis, Milwaukee, WI*

TAKES: 15 min. • **MAKES:** 4 servings

1   pkg. (16 oz.) refrigerated fully cooked barbecued shredded pork
1   cup frozen corn
2   cups refrigerated mashed potatoes
2   cups prepared macaroni and cheese

In each of four 1-pint wide-mouth canning jars, divide and layer ingredients in the following order: pulled pork, corn, mashed potatoes, and macaroni and cheese. Cover and freeze or refrigerate until ready to serve. When ready to serve, remove jar lids and microwave until heated through.
Freeze option: To serve from the freezer, partially thaw in the refrigerator overnight before microwaving.
1 serving: 349 cal., 8g fat (4g sat. fat), 45mg chol., 1116mg sod., 41g carb. (20g sugars, 1g fiber), 17g pro.

BEAN & CHEESE QUESADILLAS

FAVORITE LASAGNA ROLL-UPS

This crowd-pleasing take on lasagna offers a new way to enjoy a classic dish in individual portions. And it requires only a few ingredients.
—*Susan Sabia, Windsor, CA*

PREP: 25 min. • **BAKE:** 30 min.
MAKES: 10 servings

10 uncooked lasagna noodles
1 pkg. (19½ oz.) Italian turkey
   sausage links, casings removed
1 pkg. (8 oz.) cream cheese, softened
1 jar (26 oz.) pasta sauce
1¾ cups shredded cheddar cheese,
   divided
   Minced fresh parsley, optional

1. Preheat oven to 350°. Cook noodles according to the package directions. Meanwhile, in a large skillet, cook sausage over medium heat until no longer pink, breaking into crumbles; drain. Stir in cream cheese and ⅓ cup pasta sauce.
2. Drain noodles; spread ¼ cup meat mixture on each noodle. Sprinkle each with 2 Tbsp. cheese; carefully roll up.
3. Spread ⅔ cup pasta sauce into an ungreased 13x9-in. baking dish. Place roll-ups seam side down over sauce. Top with remaining sauce and cheese. Cover and bake for 20 minutes. Uncover; bake until sauce is bubbly, 10-15 minutes longer. If desired, sprinkle with parsley.
1 roll-up: 372 cal., 22g fat (11g sat. fat), 81mg chol., 885mg sod., 25g carb. (6g sugars, 2g fiber), 19g pro.

FAVORITE LASAGNA
ROLL-UPS

WAFFLE-IRON PIZZAS

These little pizza pockets are a fun mashup using a waffle iron. Try adding your most-loved toppings or even a few breakfast fillings such as ham and eggs.

—*Amy Lents, Grand Forks, ND*

- -

TAKES: 30 min. • **MAKES:** 4 servings

1 **pkg. (16.3 oz.) large refrigerated buttermilk biscuits**
1 **cup shredded part-skim mozzarella cheese**
24 **slices turkey pepperoni (about 1½ oz.)**
2 **ready-to-serve fully cooked bacon strips, chopped**
    Pizza sauce, warmed

1. Roll or press biscuits to fit waffle iron. On 1 biscuit, place ¼ cup cheese, 6 slices pepperoni and 1 scant Tbsp. chopped bacon to within ½ in. of edges. Top with a second biscuit, folding bottom edge over top edge and pressing to seal completely.

2. Bake in a preheated waffle iron according to manufacturer's directions until golden brown, 4-5 minutes. Repeat with remaining ingredients. Serve with pizza sauce.

1 pizza: 461 cal., 21g fat (8g sat. fat), 28mg chol., 1650mg sod., 50g carb. (5g sugars, 2g fiber), 19g pro.

"My son had a blast helping me put these little pizza pockets together. So much fun for our pizza-themed Friday. We will definitely make these again!"
—ANGEL182009, TASTEOFHOME.COM

TOMATO-BASIL BAKED FISH

This recipe can be made with different kinds of fish as desired, and I usually have the rest of the ingredients on hand. Baked fish is wonderful, and I fix this healthy dish often.
—*Annie Hicks, Zephyrhills, FL*

- -

TAKES: 15 min. • **MAKES:** 2 servings

1	Tbsp. lemon juice
1	tsp. olive oil
8	oz. red snapper, cod or haddock fillets
¼	tsp. dried basil
⅛	tsp. salt
⅛	tsp. pepper
2	plum tomatoes, thinly sliced
2	tsp. grated Parmesan cheese

1. In a shallow bowl, combine lemon juice and oil. Add fish fillets; turn to coat. Place in a greased 9-in. pie plate. Sprinkle with half each of the basil, salt and pepper. Arrange tomatoes over top; sprinkle with cheese and remaining seasonings.
2. Cover and bake at 400° until the fish flakes easily with a fork, 10-12 minutes.
1 serving: 121 cal., 4g fat (1g sat. fat), 24mg chol., 256mg sod., 4g carb. (2g sugars, 1g fiber), 18g pro. **Diabetic exchanges:** 3 lean meat, 1 vegetable, ½ fat.

"Quick, easy and delicious. I made it with cod fillets and my family loved it!"
—JEAN89, TASTEOFHOME.COM

TACO BISCUIT BAKE

Your whole gang will enjoy this fresh Mexican bake. I think that it's a tasty new take on taco night.
—*Sara Martin, Whitefish, MT*

- -

PREP: 20 min. • **BAKE:** 25 min.
MAKES: 8 servings

1	lb. lean ground beef (90% lean)
⅔	cup water
1	envelope taco seasoning
2	tubes (12 oz. each) refrigerated buttermilk biscuits
1	can (15 oz.) chili con carne
1	cup shredded reduced-fat cheddar cheese
	Salsa and sour cream, optional

1. In a large skillet, cook beef over medium heat until no longer pink, breaking into crumbles; drain. Stir in water and taco seasoning. Bring to a boil; cook and stir for 2 minutes or until mixture is thickened.
2. Meanwhile, quarter the biscuits; place in a greased 13x9-in. baking dish. Layer with beef mixture, chili and cheese.
3. Bake, uncovered, at 375° 25-30 minutes or until cheese is melted and biscuits are golden brown. Serve with salsa and sour cream if desired.
1 serving: 481 cal., 23g fat (10g sat. fat), 64mg chol., 1487mg sod., 46g carb. (5g sugars, 1g fiber), 24g pro.

TOMATO-BASIL BAKED FISH

Recipe Index